21/.-

STUDIES IN
SOCIAL HISTORY

GEORGE MACAULAY TREVELYAN, O.M.

STUDIES IN
SOCIAL HISTORY

A Tribute to G. M. Trevelyan

Edited by
J. H. PLUMB

LONGMANS, GREEN AND CO
LONDON · NEW YORK · TORONTO

LONGMANS, GREEN AND CO LTD
6 & 7 CLIFFORD STREET LONDON W I
BOSTON HOUSE STRAND STREET CAPE TOWN
531 LITTLE COLLINS STREET MELBOURNE

LONGMANS, GREEN AND CO LTD
55 FIFTH AVENUE NEW YORK 3

LONGMANS, GREEN AND CO
20 CRANFIELD ROAD TORONTO 16

ORIENT LONGMANS LTD
CALCUTTA BOMBAY MADRAS
DELHI VIJAYAWADA DACCA

First published 1955

PRINTED IN GREAT BRITAIN BY
SPOTTISWOODE, BALLANTYNE AND CO. LIMITED
LONDON AND COLCHESTER

TO

GEORGE MACAULAY TREVELYAN, O.M.

who for more than fifty years has maintained
the tradition that history is literature

CONTENTS

I

Nicholas Roscarrock and His Lives of the Saints
A. L. ROWSE

Roscarrock, near Padstow—Exeter College, Oxford—Inner Temple—
Life at Roscarrock—Cuthbert Mayne's Trial—The Catholic Associa-
tion—Roscarrock in the Tower—The Tregian Circle—Recusant
Fines—Naworth Castle—Lord William Howard—Antiquarian In-
terests—Books—Life at Naworth—Correspondence with Camden—
Richard Carew—Roscarrock's Portrait—Description of MS. Lives
of the Saints—Roscarrock's Preface, an Apology—His Authorities—
St. Endellion—St. Minver—Roscarrock on Miracles—An Elizabethan
Mind—St. Modwen—St. Nona—St. Perran—Saints' Day Observances
in Cornwall in Mary's Reign—Memories of Childhood—St. Austell

II

An Elizabethan Provincial Town: Leicester
W. G. HOSKINS

London and the Regional Capitals—Leicester and its Suburban
Development—The Distribution of Wealth in Sixteenth-Century
Leicester—The Occupations of Elizabethan Leicester—Borough
Government and Finances—Purchase of the Fee-Farm—Refounding
of the Free Grammar School—Houses in Elizabethan Leicester—
Costs of Building and Rents—Disposition of Rooms—Introduction
of Glazing for Windows—Furnishing of Houses—Rise of the Butchers
and Tanners—Decline of Textile Trades—Longevity of Leicester

III

The English Woman, 1580 to 1650
WALLACE NOTESTEIN

Sources—The Praise and Criticism of Women—Their Handicrafts—
Lack of Education—Subordination—Effects of Childbearing—
Gentlewomen—Merchants' Wives—Tradesmen's and Yeomen's
Wives—The Dramatists' Views of Women—The Spirited Heroine—
The Importance of Courtship—Improvement in the Position of
Women—Husbands more Considerate—Reasons for the Change—
Elizabeth I—Growth of Literacy and Wealth—The Influence of

IV
Comedy in the Reign of Charles I
C. V. WEDGWOOD

V
Daniel Finch, 2nd Earl of Nottingham: His House and Estate
H. J. HABAKKUK

VI
The Walpoles: Father and Son
J. H. PLUMB

VII

The Romantic Element, 1830 to 1850

G. S. R. KITSON CLARK

VIII

The Intellectual Aristocracy

N. G. ANNAN

ILLUSTRATIONS

frontispiece
George Macaulay Trevelyan, O.M.
(*Photograph by Ramsay and Muspratt*)

facing page 16
Naworth Castle
(*Photograph by the Mustograph Agency*)

facing page 17
Nicholas Roscarrock
(*Reproduced by kind permission of Mrs. H. Levin*)

facing page 48
The Blue Boar Inn in Highcross Street, Leicester
(*Reproduced from John Flower, 'Views of Ancient Buildings in the Town and County of Leicester'*)

facing page 49
The Courtyard of the Mitre and Keys in Applegate Street
(*Reproduced from John Flower, 'Views of Ancient Buildings in the Town and County of Leicester'*)

facing page 96
Mary, Lady Verney, by Vandyck
(*Reproduced by kind permission of Major R. B. Verney, D.S.O.*)

facing page 97
Mary, Lady Clitherow, wife of a Lord Mayor of London
(*Reproduced by courtesy of the Director of the Guildhall Art Gallery*)

facing page 128
The Piazza at Covent Garden, from the etching by Wenceslaus Hollar
(*In the Department of Prints and Drawings, British Museum*)

xi

facing page 129
Two Ladies of Fashion, from etchings by Wenceslaus Hollar
(*In the Department of Prints and Drawings, British Museum*)

facing page 160
Daniel Finch, second Earl of Nottingham
(*Reproduced from the engraving by Houbraken, in the Department of Prints and Drawings, British Museum*)

facing page 161
Burley-on-the-Hill from the north
(*Photograph by 'The Leicester Evening Mail'*)

facing page 192
Colonel Robert Walpole by Mary Beale
(*Reproduced by kind permission of the Marquess of Cholmondeley*)

facing page 193
Sir Robert Walpole by John Wootton
(*Reproduced by kind permission of the Marquess of Cholmondeley*)

facing page 224
Romantic Politics: the title page of the volume of national ballads produced by Young Ireland
(*Reproduced by kind permission of the National Library of Ireland*)

facing page 225
Romantic Acting: Charles Kean as Sir Giles Overreach
(*Reproduced by kind permission of the Committee of the Garrick Club*)

facing page 254
William Wilberforce with the Thornton Family
(*Reproduced by kind permission of E. M. Forster, Esq., C.H., L.L.D.*)

facing page 255
Josiah Wedgwood and his Family by George Stubbs
(*Reproduced by kind permission of Messrs. Josiah Wedgwood & Sons, Ltd.*)

Introduction

MEN write history for many reasons; to try and understand the forces which impel mankind along its strange course; to justify a religion, a nation, or a class; to make money; to fulfil ambition; to assuage obsession; and a few, the true creators, to ease the ache within. But hundreds of thousands of men and women read history for a simpler, and perhaps more worthy reason—curiosity mixed with the desire to escape into another world. Some return to their own time with relief; others with nostalgic regret; yet most with a sense of man's tragedy and endurance, of time and timelessness. And here the creative historians and the common reader are linked in purpose and understanding.

> 'The poetry of history', George Macaulay Trevelyan writes, 'lies in the quasi-miraculous fact that once, on this earth, once, on this familiar plot of ground, walked other men and women, as actual as we are today, thinking their own thoughts, swayed by their own passions, but now all gone, one generation vanishing after another, gone as utterly as we ourselves shall shortly be gone like ghosts at cock-crow.'

And there lies the secret of his success, the reason why his books have been more widely read than those of any other historian of his day. His compassion grows from the realization of the tragedy of man caught inexorably in the temporal world of the flesh, and that compassion leads to curiosity, curiosity not merely about great and heroic events but about the simple lives of ordinary men and women whose sole memorials are the fading letters and account books of the lumber room.

Although the mainspring of Trevelyan's interest in social history may be poetic, the result is more than poetry, and the impetus which he has given to the study of this branch of history has deepened our understanding of the historical process as a whole. The rôle of the aristocracy, the place of the yeoman, the catharsis of capitalism or the effects of technology

xiii

cannot be investigated without the help of those ordinary men and women and their fading letters and account books. So much of the reality of human existence lies therein as well as its poetry; or perhaps the poetry springs from that very reality. But social history, in the fullest and deepest sense of the term, is now a field of study of incomparable richness and the one in which the greatest discoveries will be made in this generation. Its purpose has long ceased to be merely evocative.

> Each one, gentle and simple, in his commonest goings and comings was ruled by a complicated and ever-shifting fabric of custom and law, society and politics, events at home and abroad, some of them little known by him and less understood. Our effort is not only to get what glimpses we can of his intimate personality, but to reconstruct the whole fabric of each passing age, and see how it affected him; to get to know more in some respects than the dweller in the past himself knew about the conditions that enveloped and controlled his life.
>
> There is nothing that more divides civilized from semi-civilized man than to be conscious of our forefathers as they really were, and bit by bit to reconstruct the mosaic of the long forgotten past.

These words from the introduction to Trevelyan's *Social History* are an admirable definition of the aim and worth of such studies as we now offer to him.

*   *   *

G. M. Trevelyan is more than a social historian—the great Garibaldi series, the history of Queen Anne, the remarkable book on the Stuarts, the nineteenth-century biographies; these contributions to history will long endure. But they created an impossible problem for an editor. If this tribute to his genius had contained an essay, dealing with all the subjects upon which he has written, it would have run to volumes. It is a pity that there is nothing here on the Italian *risorgimento*, nothing on the age of Wycliffe, nothing on the nature and purpose of history. The loss is great. There was an even more difficult choice. Trevelyan has many pupils; there are few historians who are not indebted to him; none who would not have wished to salute him in this way. But *Festschriften* have an unhappy knack of quickly becoming formless and unreadable, and to have presented our most readable historian with a massive monument of unreadability would have been indeed graceless. So a limited theme was chosen, English social history of the last four centuries, for in my opinion at least, this subject lies nearest to the heart of Trevelyan's work, nearest to that fund of poetic understanding which is the key to his creative endeavour. And the number of contributors was likewise limited to keep the book a reasonable size, even though that meant leaving out many distinguished historians whose contributions would have made this a worthier tribute to a great writer who for more than fifty years has maintained the noble tradition established by Clarendon, Gibbon and Macaulay.

J. H. PLUMB

I

Nicholas Roscarrock
and
His Lives of the Saints

———

A. L. ROWSE

I

Nicholas Roscarrock's Lives of the Saints,[1] though known to hagiographers, have never been studied or at any rate much commented on.[2] My interest in the manuscript, needless to say, is not hagiographical but historical: in the personality of Roscarrock, in the light he throws upon the observances of saints' days and the survival of medieval customs in the Cornwall of his youth, in the mind and attitude of a Catholic antiquary, who had suffered for his faith, caught in the conflict of Counter-Reformation with Protestantism, in the critical blast of scoffing Protestants at his beloved subject. He had an uncomfortable time of it, though he came into haven at last; he was in an awkward situation: it makes him interesting.

I

Roscarrock was a Domesday manor, the chief holding in the parish of St. Endellion.[3] It is situated on the north coast of Cornwall near Port Isaac, on the east side of the Camel estuary, which can be seen from the old mullioned windows at the back of the house, the pleasant Georgian front looking south over the gull-speckled fields. The family had been there since at least the end of the twelfth century: one of those families of small gentry of Cornish stock going back a long way—not grand like Norman Arundells or Grenvilles, but with their own pride, armigerous and autocthonous. Roscarrock's father, Richard, married Isabella Trevennor, heiress of a similar family and had a large number of children, of whom Nicholas and Trevennor were the youngest sons. The father provided for them during his life-time, settling Penhale, Carbura and Newton in St. Cleer and St. Germans on Nicholas, and Trentinny near St. Endellion on Trevennor. Richard died in 1575, leaving his eldest son Thomas to succeed him: he had been sheriff in 1550 and in 1562, so that under both Edward VI and Elizabeth he had had no difficulties of conscience. The family, closely related to the aggressive, the Protestant Grenvilles, conformed. The eldest son followed in his father's steps and became sheriff in 1586, when his brother Nicholas was in the Tower.

What accounts for the convinced—it is not too much to say— the passionate, undeviating Catholicism of the two youngest sons, Nicholas and Trevennor?

It would seem that the atmosphere of Exeter College, from which Nicholas supplicated for his B.A. at Oxford in 1568, is the answer.[4] Exeter was, along with St. John's, the most strongly Catholic in its sympathies of all Oxford colleges at this time. Its Rector, John Neale, was deprived by Elizabeth's Visitors in 1570 and went to Douai.[5] His successor, Robert Newton, resigned in 1578 to be received as a Catholic.[6] A list of the members of the College in 1572 brings home the situation.[7] Of the Fellows, Richard Bristowe—who, like Campion, had shone at Elizabeth's visit in 1566—went into exile in 1570, became President of Douai College and one of the translators of the Bible. Ralph Sherwin was martyred with Campion in 1581. Edmund Lewkenor resigned in 1577 and went to Douai; John Curry became a priest and was for some time chaplain to the Arundells with John Cornelius, a student a little later, who was martyred in 1594. Among the students we find, along with the two Roscarrocks, members of known Catholic families, Fitzherberts, Habingtons, Coningsbys, a Throgmorton, a Fulford, a Bawden.

We shall come across one or other of these in association with the Roscarrocks. They formed a conscious group, devout and loyal to each other: tribute to the strength of the early influences they received in that atmosphere at Oxford.

In November 1572 we find Nicholas Roscarrock admitted as a student to the Inner Temple, at the same time as Tichborne, of that ardent Catholic family, and Edward Coke who was no less ardently the other way.[8] The year before, William Camden and Giles Risdon were admitted: whose antiquarian interests Roscarrock shared to the full.[9] Camden and he remained always friends. There is no indication that Roscarrock intended to follow the law; indeed one of the two dominant interests of his mind, antiquities and heraldry, is revealed at this time in the long verses he wrote—pedestrian enough, but no worse than many such Elizabethan exercises—to preface to John Bossewell's *The Workes of Armorie*.[10] These verses are entitled 'Cyllenius censure of the Author in his high Court of Herhaultrie', and are a long and tedious conceit about the court resplendent which no man may enter unless he has the herald's art:

> Within these sundry rooms, through walls ybuilt of crystal clear
> Each thing that longs to herald's art doth perfectly appear.

And so on, with a reference to Pegasus, the patron of the young men of the Temple,[11] to cite the names of these friends-in-heraldry—Gerard Leigh, Alan Sutton and Upton—and to a final complimentary flourish in honour of Bossewell.

Four years later, we find a better set of verses prefaced to a better-known book, George Gascoigne's *The Steele Glas*, by N. R.: these initials have always been taken for Roscarrock's, and his verses stand next to those of a very different spirit indeed, though a fellow West Countryman—'Walter Raweley of the Middle Temple, in commendation of *The Steele Glasse*'.[12]

Meanwhile, at home at Roscarrock the kindly, familiar, hospitable life continued, with friends and relations always in and out of the house, dining together, playing at bowls or at cards, business of the county or the family. It is lucky that the Diary of William Carnsew, their neighbour of the next parish, St. Kew, should cover just this year: it provides some helpful touches where so much is dark and there are so few facts to go upon.[13] On 2 February 1576, Carnsew rode over to Roscarrock and lay there that night, for there was a great storm: 'won at play, lost health'. Early next month, he sent for the Roscarrocks to dine with him: Thomas came over to dinner, and John at night; they stayed and played at saint, at which Carnsew won. Ten days later he went over to his friends and there met Richard Grenville and Mr. Arundell of Trerice—of the Protestant and sea-going branch of the Arundells: 'lay there at Roscarrock all day playing and trifling the time away'. And so on throughout the year these agreeable visits continued, just as Carew charmingly describes them; Carnsew meets Grenville once again with the Roscarrocks.

But at the end of March, a more urgent note in relation to Nicholas Roscarrock, who does not otherwise appear in the laconic Diary, slips in. 'March 24: Sent letters to N. Rosca: and received answer. 25: Wrote to him again. 26: Wrote to Nicholas Roscarrock, but he was gone before my letters came to him. 27: W. Penkivell rode into Devonshire. Sent my letters to N. R. to be carried to him by young Nance to Oxford.' (The Penkivells were Catholics and were ultimately squeezed out, and down, by it.) In September Thomas Roscarrock was with Carnsew at Bokelly on his way home from assizes at Launceston. Could they have known that in time for next year's assizes, their friend Grenville would have struck with all his vigour and harshness at the important circle of Cornish Catholics, bringing the first of the seminary priests, Cuthbert Mayne, to execution, involving the life-long imprisonment of his patron, Francis Tregian, exposing the young Roscarrocks as recusants, condemning them to an unending opposition to the whole course of the nation, uprooting them for ever from their home?

For that was what was involved by Grenville's campaign. No need to go into it here, still less to defend it.[14] At a time of increasing danger, with the declared policy of the Papacy to absolve the Queen's subjects from their allegiance and drive her from her throne, with Allen's first seminary priests arriving in the country—and Mayne had the full Counter-Reformation position, the duty to support an invader and the rest of it—here was a fifth column. The government was being openly defied by an important group: what exacerbated feeling was that they were a section of the governing class. Grenville was determined to bring this more or less open defiance of the law to an end in his sheriffwick; he was encouraged and supported by the Privy Council, may even have been made sheriff in order to round up the group. Among the haul of prisoners at assizes at Launceston in September 1577, we find Nicholas Roscarrock indicted for recusancy, his estate rated at £20 p.a. in lands, his goods and chattels at £40, for the payment of Recusancy fines.[15] For the young Roscarrocks it was the end of the old pleasant life: henceforth it was opposition, defiance, danger, imprisonment, torture, expropriation—and what consolations the inner life of devotion, the outer interests in antiquities and scholarship, could give them.

With the 1580's the crisis heightened, the danger of invasion grew near; the infiltration of the Jesuits and the considerable success of Campion and Parsons' mission in 1580 gave acute alarm to the government. In London an association of young Catholic gentlemen of good family was formed to aid and conduct the incoming seminary priests, to provide them with money and supplies; they took an oath to restrict themselves to bare necessities and bestow all they had on the Catholic cause.[16] They were fanatics and they were dangerous. Their association was blessed by the Pope in April 1580. Among their members we find the names of Babington and Gunpowder Plot conspirators, some later exiles, others from the old circle of students at Exeter in Oxford days: Anthony Babington, Chideock Tichborne, William Tresham, Edward and Francis Throgmorton, Charles Arundel, Charles Basset, Edward Habington, Thomas Fitzherbert, George Gilbert. Nicholas Roscarrock was one of them. In September we find him journeying to Rome in the company of Cresswell, who became a Jesuit there and succeeded Parsons as Rector of the English College: the two of them spent twelve days at Douai on the way.[17]

These activities did not escape the attention of the authorities. Shortly after Roscarrock's return to England, Ralph Sherwin— who had been at Exeter with him and was now a seminary priest—was taken in the act of preaching after mass in Roscarrock's chamber.[18] They were apprehended by Hunsdon, the Lord Chamberlain; and the Privy Council ordered their examination, 'forasmuch as the said Roscarrock, by certain examinations heretofore taken of certain persons as evilaffected towards her Majesty and the present state, hath been detected to have been a practiser with foreign states and a conveyor of letters both abroad and into this realm'.[19] This was a most dangerous charge, and upon the result of their examination they were both consigned to the Tower. On 15 and 16 December Sherwin was racked—it is said, in a cell near

Roscarrock, *pour encourager l'autre*, no doubt. On 14 January Roscarrock was put to the rack. In December Sherwin, Campion and Bryant were hanged, drawn and quartered at Tyburn. Roscarrock remained in the Tower, unwavering, unyielding, obdurate. In April 1581 we find his servant Greene passing through Douai, evidently on some mission.[20] A priest, writing to Allen in November 1582, says that 'Pound, Brinkley and Roscarrock, laymen, have—I am ashamed to say—shown themselves braver than many priests'.[21]

Roscarrock did not desist from his tricks, or from taking risks. In 1584 the Scottish Jesuit, Crichton, captured at sea, was imprisoned in the Tower; he was a political, who had been a chief agent in the Duke of Lennox's schemes for capturing the young James VI for Catholicism and was now engaged in furthering plans for Mary Stuart's liberation and the invasion of England. (Because Crichton had declared to a Catholic conspirator that it was unlawful to kill the Queen, the government handsomely released him.) While in the Tower Crichton was lodged over Roscarrock, who contrived to open two doors between them and to converse with Crichton at leisure; and then to smuggle his letters out of the Tower for him, through his own window near the ground, by the hand of a girl who took them to one of the faithful Catholic companionship in the city.[22] A government note of prisoners in the Tower, 27 May 1585, states: 'Thomas Pound, Nicholas Roscarrock: for religion only committed and for intelligence with Jesuits and priests, two dangerous men and apt for any practice; fit they should be banished'.[23] Roscarrock, as a gentleman of means, was in the Tower at his own charges; and on 6 March 1586, we find the Lieutenant of the Tower, Sir Owen Hopton, renewing his old suit that Roscarrock might be released upon bond, upon condition he were forthcoming at all times when called for; since he had been a prisoner for over five years and was now £140 in debt to the Lieutenant for his diet and charges.[24] (Multiply by twenty or so for a contemporary valuation.) Roscarrock had taken part in no political conspiracy, and about this time he seems to have been released as well as Crichton.

Meanwhile, his brother Trevennor was in Newgate prison in 1583 and 1584 for hearing mass and refusing to come to church.[25] Both the brothers remained obstinate recusants. Nicholas was in trouble again in the 1590's, when we find him in the Fleet with Francis Tregian—their movements spied on and reported to the government by a Catholic spy, Benjamin Tichborne alias Beard, whom they entertained, perhaps not wholly unawares, as a host its parasite. In December 1593 Beard was writing to Sir Robert Cecil, 'I was with Roscarrock continually private in his study, and might have effected something ere this'.[26] At least Roscarrock was now living in conditions of some comfort. It was an agreeable, cultivated Catholic circle that lived together in the Fleet in those years, with plenty of opportunity for entertaining friends, and much coming and going; music, antiquities, versifying, conversation. Nor were they deprived of the consolations of religion: plenty of opportunity for secret masses in the Fleet, and there were always priests in and out. But the spy complains that Tregian and Roscarrock do not wholly confide in him. In May 1594, a man known as the Green Man was taken, who had lately been sent over from abroad; Mrs. Tregian let out to Beard that he was a seminary priest. The spy reports to the government that 'there is one now in the Fleet who is greatly suspected about his taking [he means himself], but not one word is spoken of him by Tregian or Roscarrock', which makes Beard think the man the more dangerous.[27] Later on, in 1599—it must have been a regular thing—a Middlesex jury found a true bill against Roscarrock for not coming to church. But, indeed, neither of the brothers ever did attend church—and they paid for it with their inheritance.

From the 1590's we can watch the process in the Recusants' Rolls. Two-thirds of a recusant's lands were taken over by the Crown and leased out to pay the Recusancy fines. Year after year in the Recusants' Roll for Cornwall we find two-thirds of Trevennor Roscarrock's remaining possessions returning their small sum: 31*s.* p.a. for the farm of half of four messuages in Tregonan, two messuages in Tregarrick and four messuages in Gear, parcel of the manor of Lamoran.[28] In Devon we find a still smaller return (10*s.* 8*d.* p.a.) for the farm of two parts of the half of two messuages in Smith's hill and Ashwater, in the hands of the Queen by Nicholas Roscarrock's recusancy.[29] But what had happened to his property in Cornwall? It was evidently no longer in his hands; most probably he had had to sell it in order to exist. He may have turned it into cash, or into an annuity, as a precautionary measure. Recusants were driven to all sorts of expedients—as with modern income-tax—in order to protect themselves from the full harshness of the law; and we have to admit that, in the one case as in the other, we do not know often how it all worked out. With the younger Roscarrocks, as with many lesser Catholic families, it was a case of the liquidation of the kulaks.

II

With the accession of James and the end of the war with Spain, there was—in spite of the idiocy of Gunpowder Plot—a *détente*, a real relaxation of the severity for Catholics. Nicholas Roscarrock came into port at last, and a very pleasant port it was.

In his last year in the Tower two very important Catholic persons came to join the select company there: two of the dead Norfolk's sons, Philip, Earl of Arundel who had designed to leave the country—to lend himself to what dangerous purposes his godfather, Philip II, intended—and his brother, Lord William Howard. Imprisonment provided a regular way of making friends in Tudor times: after all, had not companionship in the Tower in Mary's reign made Elizabeth and Robert Dudley something more than friends? It must have been then that Roscarrock became friendly with the Howard brothers; Lord William was released about the same time as Roscarrock, Arundel remained there till he died in 1595.

Now, with James' move south, Lord William was free to move north and consolidate his—or rather, his wife's—splendid inheritance on the Border. She was one of the two Dacre coheiresses whom the Duke had providently married to these two of his sons. (It was the only provident thing he ever did.) From about 1604 Lord William was engaged in making Naworth, the chief Dacre castle in Cumberland, ready to live there: rebuilding and repairing, for it was in a state of complete disrepair, planting, making orchards and gardens round about, bringing stained glass for the windows, timbers and carved roofs for the rooms, restoring the chapel. For he, too, was a

Catholic: brought up by Gregory Martin, another of the
Oxford men of the 1570's who had gone to Douai. And when
Lord William settled at Naworth, he brought Roscarrock to
live there as his companion. Here, on the Scottish Border,
within those rose and grey walls looking up to the high fells, the
Waste of Bewcastle, the pleasant pastures of the Irthing beneath
the walls, the sound of the river mounting up to the windows—
so different a scene from his native Cornwall—Roscarrock
passed the rest of his life.

He and Lord William had the two chief interests of their
lives in common: religion and a love of antiquities, books,
scholarship. If it is true that odium archæologicum is even
worse than odium theologicum, it is also true that nothing
binds friends faster than archæology. These two "archæologis-
ing buddies"—freed from their worries and from persecution in
middle age—set to work to form a collection of Roman antiquities from the Wall near by. They had a wonderful opportunity
and they made the most of it: the sheltered garden was full of
Roman altars and gravestones and inscribed slabs. When
Stukeley visited it in the eighteenth century, he found it in a
state of great neglect, the stones being cut up for gate-posts;
later, it was completely dispersed.[30] Lord William also gathered
a fine collection of manuscripts; here too with the cartularies of
Northern monasteries, he had a grand opportunity. They have
all been dispersed, mostly disappeared. In this field Roscarrock
would be specially helpful: he was a collector himself. We know
from his Lives of the Saints that he possessed a few manuscript
Vitae of Cornish saints. But only two of his manuscripts have
been identified. The Bodleian possesses a fifteenth-century
illuminated MS., John Dade's *De Arte Heraldica*; this seems to
have belonged first to George, Lord Bergavenny, and then to
Henry Ferrers, one of the group of Catholic antiquaries, like
Erdeswicke and Habington: Ferrers intended to write a
Perambulation of Warwickshire, which Dugdale later accom-
plished: he was a friend of Roscarrock's and may have given
him the MS.[31] Later, it came into the possession of Sir William
Waad, Lieutenant of the Tower, by the good offices of King
James: 'Wy. Waad lieutenant of the Tower to our Sovereain
Lord King Jaymes owethe this booke'. In the Cambridge

University Library is another MS. that belonged to Roscarrock, Hoccleve's *De Regimine Principum*, with Roscarrock's signature on the first and last pages, and on f. 68b. the arms of the family, a chevron between two roses in chief and a fish in base (actually, according to Carew, a sea-tench nageant proper).[32]

Lastly, Lord William brought together a library, chief solace of the two old friends: it was strong in works of Catholic devotion and apologetics, mainly in Latin, and in medieval chronicles; nothing Anglican: just what one would expect.[33] Lord William's study, in the solitude at the top of his tower, with the stream sounding pleasantly as it tumbles through its gully under the green foliage far below, survived unchanged up to our own time: it remained for us to disperse that.

From the *Household Books of Lord William Howard* we derive a charming impression of the very full life of that friendly, hospitable great house, the cautious, unostentatious Catholicism, the ordered days. There are the payments to men bringing salmons from the rivers round about, oysters from the coast, larks and moorcocks from the fells, the fat capons and geese, occasionally a swan or a fawn; to the maids bringing cherries, plums, pears, cowslips; cakes are brought from Penrith, sugar candy for the children. The tailor is paid for shapening my lady's waistcoat. Strolling players perform within the castle, or there is a play acted at Brampton; there are dancers, minstrels, pipers at the gate, sometimes a blind harper, singing no doubt the ballads of the Border. A picture of St. Francis is purchased; painted glass for the chapel. Books are frequently bought: the *History of the Queen of Scots* (Con's Latin life published at Rome) —of acute, inextinguishable interest in such a circle, which had shared the experience of persecution, and the secrets; Bellarmine's *Works*; Attorney Doddridge's book on the Duchy of Cornwall, of particular appeal to Roscarrock. There are payments for stringing and binding the books, skins for parchment; and with increasing frequency in this so bookish, so studious, a house, money laid out for spectacles, horn for spectacles and silver frames. Along with this went the careful, prudent management of the estates; Lord William was able to bring not only order into his wife's neglected and much challenged inheritance, but greatly to increase its revenues and in the end to purchase further estates in the country round him. Underneath it all were the everlasting arms of the faith: there was always, unobtrusively, a priest in the house.

In this busy household, with its wide spaces for silence, prayer and study, Roscarrock made an important, an independent, figure. Earlier, he may have given a hand with the tuition of the sons; we find him making some small payments for the expenses of the house; four gallons of sack in a rundlet[34] are bought for him. In 1622 his brother Trevennor pays Naworth a visit; for he is given 10*s.* to bestow in Cornish diamonds—I suppose, quartz stones.[35] What is obvious from the accounts, and rather surprising, is that Nicholas was quite well off. Perhaps he had sold his lands well, after all, and salted away the proceeds in an annuity. He seems to have received an annuity of £200 from Lord Arundel, presumably Lord William's nephew, the great connoisseur and patron of the arts. I do not fully understand the financial arrangements, but we find entries like the following in 1620: 'Received of Mr. Dix for Mr. Roscarrock, part of the money due by my Lord Arundel £100, ultra £100, before charged'. Again, the same year: 'Received of Mr. Dix by my Lord's appointment, 26 Nov., £100 in payment of Mr. Roscarrock's debt, taken into my Lord's hands, and another £100 which my Lord doth allow, which my Lord borrowed of Mr. Dix and my Lord hath taken to pay Mr. Roscarrock £100'.[36] And then, in November 1633, shortly before his death, 'Received of Nicholas Roscarrock, being part of £400 paid in to him by Mr. Henry Lawson, £100'.[37]

At any rate, the upshot of it was that so far from being a dependent of the house, Roscarrock had an independent status as a friend of the family, a room of his own, sack of his own, and was a convenient source of ready money when anybody— usually my Lady—was short. Among the steward's accounts we read: 'Delivered my lady, borrowed of Mr. Roscarrock, £5'.[38] Or, 'Borrowed of Mr. Roscarrock and delivered my lady, £5'. Or, 'To Mr. Howard, by my lady's commandment, going to Malton, which was borrowed of Mr. Roscarrock and paid by me, £3'. Upon his death it is not surprising, therefore, to find: 'More to Sir Francis Howard which he laid out for buying a ring for Mr. William Howard [Sir William's son], more than the legacy Mr. Roscarrock gave, 20*s*'. Then, 'Given as legacies to several servants at Naworth from Nicholas Roscarrock, which my lady was owing him, £20'. [39] Lastly, 'To Sir Francis Howard, money owing to Nicholas Roscarrock esquire, late deceased, by my Lord and to be disposed by Sir Francis Howard according to Mr. Roscarrock's appointment, £300'. (Multiply by twenty or twenty-five.)

It is nice to think that virtue and kindness were rewarded; but it would be nicer still to have Roscarrock's will.

One relic of Lord William and Roscarrock's friendship remains to us, something unique: a gold rosary: no other medieval English rosary has survived.[40] It consists of fifty small oval beads, six lozenges and a large knop at the bottom. But two of the beads are not originals: they are late sixteenth-century additions. On one of these Roscarrock's patron saint, Endelient, is represented with her ox, a palm and a cauldron; at the back, St. William of Norwich. On another bead, there are two more St. Williams. It looks like having been Lord William's rosary, with him sharing Roscarrock's cult of St. Endelient. Or perhaps it was Roscarrock's?—for the arrangement of two saints on each head is dictated by the occurrence of their festivals in the Calendar, which was a primary interest of Roscarrock's. Perhaps it belonged to them both and they shared the rosary, as they did the faith: at any rate a touching memento of their friendship.

Such was the background to the last quarter of a century of Roscarrock's long life. (If he supplicated for his B.A. in 1568 he would have been born about 1550; he died towards the end of 1633.) Naworth gave him the security and the peace for what was, next religion, nearest his heart: his antiquarian studies; the Lives of the Saints brought these two together. But it was getting late to bring them to a point.

Roscarrock was settled at Naworth by August 1607, and probably had been for some time before, to judge from a letter he wrote to Camden in that month: it gives us a pleasant insight into the kindly relations subsisting among those antiquaries and friends.[41]

Understanding (good Mr. Clarenceulx) that your *Britain* is at this present in printing and ready to come forth, I thought fit (in a small show of our ancient love) to give you notice of two escapes in the last edition. The one in Cornwall (f. 156), where you make St. Columbanus, a man, to give name unto St. Columb: whereas, in truth, it taketh name of Columba, a woman-saint, who was a virgin and martyr, whose Life I have in my hands translated out of Cornish; besides, the day of her Feast differeth from the Feast of St.Columbanus, or St. Columba, the Scottish or Irish.

In his next edition Camden duly made the correction. Roscarrock went on to correct Camden's description of an inscribed stone which he had seen at Thoresby:

My Lord William, who hath it now with a great many more in his garden-wall at Naworth, where he would be glad to see you to read them, hath made it shorter [i.e. in measurement]; as also for the lines and letters which I have sent you here enclosed, drawn out by our good lord's own hands; and would have sent you some more, but that we think it too late, and that you mean not to over-charge your book with too many of that kind. I also send you here an inscription which my lord found out in a cross in a green before the abbey-church of Lanercost; which, though it be since the Conquest, yet it is (for the rareness) not to be contemned ... And now if you would give me leave from crosses to fall across you, I beseech consider whether you in Staffordshire (p. 519), or Capgrave in the Life of St. Bertelm, be more extreme: you in terming him *minorum gentium Divum*, and he in making a king's son so great a saint and miracle-worker. In this kind, I could be longer, but it needeth not for that you out of your love and friend-ship will, I hope, pardon me and make use of it. Commend me, I beseech, most heartily to your good self, and remember my service to the good knight Sir Robert Cotton, when you chance to see him; and request him to conceive no unkindness of my boldness, upon his own offer, to take his Capgrave, Jocelyn, and other of his written books of that argument with me unto Naworth. If he would have them, I will most willingly send them whensoever he pleaseth. If you chance to see our old friend, Mr. Henry Ferrers, I beseech you tell him that I live, remember and love him.

Meanwhile, at home in Cornwall, another of the antiquarian circle, Richard Carew, friend of Camden and Cotton, in describing Roscarrock in his *Survey of Cornwall*, had paid a compliment to Nicholas.

Roscarrock in Cornish meaneth a flower and a rock in English. Roses are his arms and the north rocky cliffs, which bound his desmesnes, perhaps added the rest. The heir hath issue by the daughter of Trevanion. His father married the sole inheritrix to Pentire, whose dwelling, Pentewan, is seated on the south sea, so as he might make use of either climate for his residence. The family is populous; but of them two brothers, Hugh for his civil carriage and kind hospitality, and Nicholas for his industrious delight in matters of history and antiquity, do merit a commending remembrance.[42]

Nothing of all the past: it is pleasant that the love of antiquities should sometimes transcend silly religious differences.

Fourteen years after Roscarrock's letter to Camden, Lord William writes to Sir Robert Cotton in August 1621:

Brother, your old friend and mine, Mr. Roscarrock, understanding that you have a manuscript of Johannes Anglicus, is very desirous to borrow the same; that, though he cannot take a view thereof, yet he much longeth to lend his ear to hearken to the reading of the same; and if it please you to send it down by this bearer it shall be safely, by God's blessing, returned to you again with all convenient speed, after he hath satisfied himself therewith.[43]

There we have the explanation of Roscarrock's uncompleted work; it was now too late: he was blind.

There is no sign of this in the portrait that exists of him at Corby Castle: out of which he looks at us with dark, lively eyes undimmed.[44] This portrait of him would have been painted in the early years of his residence at Naworth: it is of a man in his late fifties, already bald and with a careful, brushed white beard. Nothing to show what he had been through—except perhaps the questioning lines on the forehead, the quizzically sad expression about the eyes. For the rest, a long, slightly bulbous nose, the high domed forehead of the scholar: it is the honest, sober face of a countryman, with something of that indefinable air of a lived inner life and of inner discipline that submission to the Catholic faith gives. It is the face of a celibate, who has seen the other side of life.

All the same, with his experiences—the early days in Cornwall, the good friends there and at Exeter, the exciting underground life of militant Catholics in London, the visits to Douai

Naworth Castle

Nicholas Roscarrock

and Rome, the private communications with Jesuits, Cresswell, Robert Parsons, Crichton, imprisonment and the rack, spies, the secrets he kept, the confidences never divulged, the friends he knew, so many of them torn limb from limb, traitors in a time of extreme danger—if only, one feels, he had written an Autobiography, instead of Lives of the Saints!

However, his Lives of the Saints are not without an autobiographical interest.

III

From the careful form of Roscarrock's book it seems clear that he meant it for publication. As the MS. now stands it numbers some 402 leaves; a previous deleted numbering gives 479 leaves. There are small fragments of a considerable number of missing leaves at the end: the MS. is now incomplete, breaking off in the middle of an account of Simon of Sudbury—what followed on alphabetically from that point being now wanting. A letter from one Ff. Webbe, inserted at f. 313, gives us some information. It refers to Trevennor Roscarrock's having come across in an Oxford library the story of the 'children of Brechan'— the group of some twenty-odd saints who came from Brechan's country in S.E. Wales to found churches in North and East Cornwall: 'the story at large Mr. Roscarrock wrote and, keeping no copy of it, sent it to his brother Mr. Nicholas Roscarrock, who lived and died at my Lord William Howard's house in the North. Now some worthy Catholics of Cornwall being desirous to understand the full story, to the end they may the better honour these saints of their country, besought me to write into the North about this and to get out of Mr. Nicholas Roscarrock's writings this story, they knowing that he was wont to compile together such monuments for future memory.' Mr. Webbe had heard that Sir William Howard, Lord William's son, 'had Mr. Nicholas Roscarrock's book and papers, and that he could give me some light of it'. One sees that the group of Cornish Catholics, which was quite strong in the early seventeenth century, knew of Roscarrock's work; but knowledge of it faded as they petered out later in that century, to become practically extinct in the eighteenth century.

The MS. is almost wholly in Roscarrock's hand; but there

are later interpolations in one or, at most, two other hands—of which we now know the explanation.

Roscarrock's title-page describes his work as 'A Brief Register: or Alphabetical Catalogue of such saints [and saint-like persons—has been added] as the Collector hath taken notice of to have graced our island of Great Britain, Ireland and other British islands bordering about it, with their births, deaths, presence, preachings or relics'.[45] This is followed by 'A Sonnet. To the Courteous and well-minded reader, showing the Collector's resolution', which I give as a specimen of Roscarrock's original spelling:

> If this my labour serve but for a foyle
> to lend a luster to som learned quill
> to perfect this my undertaken toyle
> I have my wishe although I want my will
> depriv'de of helps and destitute of skill.
> whoe wholy in this work applied my penn
> to honnor God and not to humor men.
>
> If he be pleas'd I have my harts desyre
> wishing good mynds in doubts to deame the best
> and for my paines I seek noe better hyre
> of such as are with scorne and spleene possest
> but base contempt wth w[ch] content I rest
> Beleive well, and live well, and hope well for Bliss
> farewell, and wish well, to him that wrote this.

On the next page there follow more verses—'A friendly warning to the reader, wishing him to have due respect and reverence of saints and not to reject the true writers of their lives, many of them being also saints'. We thus early come upon the defensive note which is heard again and again in the course of the fabulous stories Roscarrock has to relate, and is not the least interesting feature of his book as a revelation of an Elizabethan mind.

> As for the rest which sensuall drown'd in sense
> so sensles are as nothing will beleive
> but self conceipt, and self wills false pretence
> It recks not much what Censure they do give
> for sunn and starrs they scarsely will esteeme
> of greater circuitt then there sense dothe deeme.

There follows a short preface on the moral utility of saints'
lives, assuring himself that those who 'take a just view of them
cannot but find all the commendable parts of an history in
them, in which they may see how infidelity hath been sup-
planted and true religion advanced', etc.[46]

Before the title-page there are some twenty-three leaves of
preliminary matter, beginning with 'A Brief Discourse. How
saints may be esteemed so. Secondly of their canonisation and
the truest, infalliblest manner of discerning them, and what
course the Collector of this Alphabet of Saints hath observed
in this his Collection.' [47] He cites Scripture to show that it is the
will of God that we should honour saints—'their miracles
deserving it and our necessities requiring it, we are to receive
benefits by praying unto them, which we could not do safely
were we not in a sort warranted by the Church's canonisation
of them to pray unto them or to adore them'. This consideration has moved not only Catholics, but the very heretics themselves, 'imitating therein, saith St. Augustine, (like apes) the
Catholics, have reverenced their false and counterfeit martyrs
and professors as saints: yea, Luther himself was not afraid to
canonise in a sort John Huss the heretic by the name of a saint
and a prophet, whom he maketh a goose to prove himself to
be a swan'. And so with the veneration of Luther himself.

> But what need I go into Germany for examples when we may find
> so many of this sort in John Foxe's huge heap of saints and
> martyrs of his own making, whereof some were long after living, as
> How and Marbecke, who played long after merrily on the organs
> at Windsor, some that were never in being, as Sir Roger only;
> some never put to death, nor as much as imprisoned, as Wyclif,
> a condemned heretic; others justly imprisoned as Cowbridge,
> likewise condemned and burned in Oxford for heresy, who could
> not endure the name of Christ in the Bible; Acton executed for
> treason; Joan-of-the-eye for witchcraft; Trudgeover for felony;
> Debnam and others for sacrilege and thievery, and others for
> other like villainies.

All the same we may point out, as Protestants did not cease
to point out at the time, that Mary did burn upwards of 260
people for heresy in the course of three years. This was the
greatest propaganda-point of Elizabeth's new deal: the

burnings unspeakably shocked the English people; and Foxe's Book of Martyrs proved a most effective propaganda-weapon for Elizabeth's government. No wonder Catholics were so raw on the subject: they could not get round him; Roscarrock abuses once and again 'that huge and vain volume of his Monuments, which in truth doth rather serve the title of Miniments'.[48] We note with wry amusement the mutual exclusiveness of men's idiotic opinions, for which they kill or for which they die.

Roscarrock quotes Bellarmine's statement, *De Sanctis*, that there are many saints not canonized by the Pope who are venerated by the Church: saints in ancient time were not so much reverenced by any law or order, as by custom. He does not scruple therefore to include in his Catalogue many ancient saints, especially of the Britons, who were not canonized, but have altars, churches, dedications and feasts observed, without contradiction of prelates or Pope: 'which connivency seemeth to be a privy consent . . . though of many such I cannot find their feast days, hoping others will effect what is not thoroughly performed'. It is indeed this heavy list in the direction of the Celtic saints that gives Roscarrock's book its special interest; for the rest, he relies on the known authorities, but for these he has some sources of his own: manuscript lives of such saints as Petrock, Nectan, Brechan, Perran and Samson, which he had collected; and, for their observances and festivals, his memories of Cornwall.

Roscarrock's basic authority throughout his book is the work that goes under the name of Capgrave, *Nova Legenda Anglie*, but is essentially the work of John of Tynemouth or Johannes Anglicus—we have seen Lord William Howard asking Cotton to lend his MS. of this for Roscarrock's use as late as 1621, when he was blind. But, indeed, we are struck by the immense range of reading that has gone into Roscarrock's Lives: not only Capgrave, but almost the whole of medieval English chronicles—Bede, Ordericus Vitalis, William of Malmesbury, Giraldus Cambrensis, Matthew Paris, Matthew of Westminster, Thomas Walsingham, John Rouse. He is equally well-read in recent chroniclers and antiquaries—Polydore Vergil, Leland, Bale, Dr. Caius, Camden, Speed, Carew. He has the advantage of a Catholic's more cosmopolitan reading over these last nationally-minded writers: Roscarrock has not only read Bellarmine but Baronius. And he has read widely for his purpose in continental chronicles of the Middle Ages: Ado and Aimoin's *Historica Francorum*, Molinet and the voluminous works of Sigebert. When writing of the foundation of Mont-St.-Michel, he refers to the pamphlet of Dr. Francis Feuardent, printed at Constance [Coutances] in 1610.[49] He was on the look-out for whatever was grist to his mill. There were the works of his co-religionists, Nicholas Harpsfield, J. W.'s *English Martyrologe*, published in 1608, and others in MS. to which he refers, like the MSS. collected by a Welsh priest, Edward Powell alias Hughes, or by Father John Whitford. Then there were his Cornish sources. Indeed it looks as if Roscarrock suffered, in addition to everything else, from a plethora of authorities, a certain scholarly constipation, not unknown in our own time. But when we consider the immensity of the task, its encyclopædic character—something comparable to Camden in his sphere, or Holinshed, or Stow—we may say that it was, in the spirit of the endeavour, if not in the subject it tackled, a true expression of the age.

For the Cornish interest of his book, we cannot do better than to begin with the charming legend of St. Endelient, the patron saint of his native parish.[50]

She lived in a place in Cornwall called Trentinny: [This was, we recall, where Trevennor Roscarrock's property lay], where I remember there stood a chapel dedicated (as I take it to her), which at this day is decayed, and the place in which it stood is yet called the chapel-close and lieth on the south-west of the parish church. Here she lived a very austere course of life. That with the milk of a cow only, which cow the lord of Trentinny killed as she strayed into his grounds, as old people speaking by tradition do report. She had a great man to her godfather, which they also say was King Arthur, who took the killing of the cow in such sort as he killed or caused the man to be slain, whom she miraculously revived. And when she perceived the day of her death draw near, she entreated her friends after her death to lay her dead body on a sled and to bury her there where certain young stots, bullocks or calves of a year old should of their own accord draw her. Which being done, they brought her to a place which at that time was a miry waste ground and a great quagmire at the top of an hill; where in time after there was a church builded on her and dedicated to her, which since proved a fine firm and fruitful plot of ground, where her feast was accustomed to be yearly remembered the 29 of April. And I have heard it credibly reported that the chapel in Lundy was likewise dedicated unto her and bare her name. Yet my good friend, Mr. Camden, saith the chapel was dedicated unto St. Helen; but under correction, except he have better warrant than bare conjecture, I still hold the former report more likely, because her brother St. Nectan had a church dedicated at Hartland point over against it, but fourteen miles from it ... whereof it is not improbable that she did also sometimes dwell in that island.[51] For many of St. Brechan's children planted themselves near one another. As this St. Endelient, St. Memfry or St. Minver, St. Mabyn, St. Tudy, etc.

Roscarrock follows this with verses in honour of his patroness, the fourth stanza of which runs:

> For in that church a Christian I became
> And of Christ's church a member first to be
> And also was confirmed in the same
> For which I thank my God and pray to thee
> This work to further in thy church begun
> With prayers that I my race may rightly run.

There were in the parish two holy wells bearing her name, but the tradition was that the one farther away from the church was that frequented by her in her lifetime. 'Her tomb was defaced in King Henry VIII's time and afterwards placed upon one Mr. Batten in Chenduit's aisle, where it standeth at this present ... the table whereof is of polished stone like black marble.' In our time it has been re-erected as an altar in that same aisle.

Within the parish was a chapel and a holy well dedicated to St. Illick, whose feast was solemnly held on the Saturday after Epiphany.

And the inhabitants used to say by tradition that she came miraculously out of Ireland on a harrow or hurdle, and that she lived there in the time of St. Endelient, which by guess we may think to be about the year 550. And the path whereon they used to walk or pass one to the other is noted by the inhabitants to be greener than any other part, especially after tillage. There was a tree over her well, which those that attempted to cut down had ever harm, so as they gave over to cut it. Till one more bold than the rest did cut it down, who hurting himself was noted to die shortly after. This happened in our time.

Old conservatives have often consoled themselves with this sort of futile reflection, never more than over the losses from the Dissolution and Reformation.

A neighbouring parish bears the name of St. Mabyn, 'the church of which being new builded about the year 1500, there was, as I have heard from the report of such as lived there at that time, a song or hymn sung of her signifying that she had twenty-three brothers and sisters'. [52] Roscarrock finds this confirmed in the Life of St. Nectan and St. Brechan, yet her name is not in the Book of Llandaff nor in Edward Powell's Welsh pedigree. There is no difficulty in accepting the twenty-four children of Brechan: they formed an obvious missionary group from the country which took its name from Brechan and they founded churches, probably in the sixth century as Roscarrock says, along the north coast of Cornwall and Devon and particularly in the district he knew best. [53]

St. Minver, the eponymous saint of the next parish, was another of them: a fair church was builded over her half a mile from the place where she was said to live, today called Tredrizzick, 'where in my time there stood a chapel also dedicated to her, less than two miles from where St. Endelient lived'. [54] All memory of this chapel, like that of St. Illick in St. Endellion, seems to have gone. How thick with chapels and holy wells pre-Reformation Cornwall must have been, and how fascinating to the antiquary their cults and observances! No wonder Roscarrock had such a nostalgia for the irrecoverable past; his book gives us a sense of it and lets us, as few things do, into the mind of the medieval Cornish. He tells us the pretty legend of St. Minver's well, 'where the ghostly Adversary coming to molest her as she was combing her hair by the well, she flinging her comb at him enforced him to fly, who left a note behind him at a place called at this day Topalundy; where, at the top of a round high hill, there is a strange deep hole then made by the Devil in avoiding St. Minver'.

There follows a revealing defensive comment:

In report of which I shall, I fear me, as in many other parts of this my collection, be thought as simple as I may have just cause to think others irreverent in writing of this and other saints. For I do sincerely, in the testimony of my conscience, write that which I find, not daring to correct that which I know not how to control. Assuring myself with the prophet that God is wonderful in his saints; not caring to be scorned with him by any the followers of Micholl in the service of God, how basely soever men conceive of me for it. I wish to God we had some more intelligence than we have of our British saints; and particularly such as have churches dedicated unto them in Cornwall; for I am persuaded there are as many churches builded in honour of such saints as lived there (whereof most were British and Irish) as there is in any one shire in England. And could wish that Mr. Carew (if he do again set forth his Cornish Survey) would be a little more large, as he would not be irreverent in discoursing of them. In which, in respect of my love to his person and parts, that he would rather imitate our good friend Mr. Camden in his *Britain*, than Mr. Lambarde in his *Kent*. For the first, being better advised in his later editions, hath discreetly retracted some faults, as I would he had done in all which he had formerly written. As namely of St. Nectan, whom he resembled to Neptune; St. Bartholin, whose pattens he played with, as Mr. Carew doth of St. Meneg and St. Issey; and as Mr. Lambarde doth generally, where occasion is offered, to show himself a censurer of saints. . . . Of which good meaning of mine, if Mr. Carew consider well, he will omit his poem on St. Keyne's well in his irreligious scorning, and that also at St. Nun's well.[55] For, in truth, otherwise his work will be disgraced in the judgment of many that are no fools. For in these matters of saints, when we can say nothing that is good, we should in reason forbear to write that which is ill; being bound in all doubtful things to think the best.

That gives us Roscarrock's point of view. But he is sometimes hard put to it, as in the account he has to give of the miracles of St. Perran, patron of tin-miners, whose friend, St. Brendan, 'turned water into milk by blessing it, showing thereby he had no use of a cow, when St. Perran by blessing the said milk turned it again into water'.[56] After these useful operations, St. Perran performed many strange miracles, raising from death his mother's handmaid Brunetta and seven musicians, making a stork to sing, causing a snow, going on the water dry-footed, procuring fire, turning water into wine and cold water into warm. He lived to be two hundred.

> I doubt not but the curious will think many things incredible in this Life of St. Perran and other Britain saints, and censure me of simplicity and too too much credulousness. But I had rather be censured without cause than presume with some to censure such as report it, except I were justly able to control them, finding that which I relate here in Capgrave, a man neither childish nor vain, but grave and learned. The length of his life, besides his miracles is, I confess, not easily to be believed, and so the age of Johannes de Temporibus, and the long living of one in our time in the Indies, to wit, three hundred years, as Mapheus and Torquemada report, may seem as incredible. Yea, of many other saints, as of St. Patrick who lived 122 years and St. David 146, St. Kentigern 185, and St. Modwen whose life must be very long, if that which is written of her be true; which, whether it be God knows, no man's salvation dependeth upon the believing or not believing of it.

This shows how acutely conscious Roscarrock was of the difficulties made for him by his chosen subject in the full consciousness of the Jacobean age. To the medievals these legends presented no such difficulties: they lived within the cocoon of faith, so certain that they could afford to take them even humorously: these legends were *contes*, they were their fireside tales told on long winter nights in the remote parishes where they belong, attaching to the familiar places where, ages before —we need not doubt—the eponymous characters had lived by well or stream, in frequented spots or by the sea-shore, or journeying round that southern Celtic world from Wales or Ireland to Cornwall and on to Brittany. Humour was not a part of Roscarrock's composition: it was not humorous to have been racked for one's faith. But the Protestants who scoffed at the nonsense he believed had no idea that the things they believed were no less so. Roscarrock's mind is not uncharacteristic of the age he lived in, in its combination of credulity and criticality. We find him always scrupulous, and even delicate, in regard to his sources; but once his source is accepted as to be believed, it is beyond criticism. Is that so very different from the position of those today who are 'born to believe'? Protestantism was, of course, a step towards rationality: impossible to arrest it there. It was a challenge: the medievals could be poetic and humorous, but with the Protestant challenge to the cocoon of faith, these things had to be taken seriously. They had either to be believed or not believed. Roscarrock was uncomfortable: one sees it in his temper.

His life of St. Modwen is a long one full of incident and impossible stories, collected mostly out of Capgrave.[57] But he had seen two other manuscripts, 'one of which I had of my learned friend, Mr. Thomas Allen of Oxford'. Allen, we recall, was one of a group of Catholics who lurked in Gloucester Hall: a mathematician and astrologer, who had the reputation with the vulgar of being a conjurer. Aubrey tells us that his servitor used to impose on them by telling them that sometimes he would meet the spirits coming up Allen's stairs like bees.[58] Here is Roscarrock's dilemma.

> In this and many other lives I look to be freely censured by such as use to measure the wonderful works of God with the silly and shallow capacity of man, though I write nothing but what I find written before me by such as I have cited. But I resolve to bear it, choosing rather in the honour of God and his faith to subdue human reason to divine grace. But whereas I find some difficulties in the time in which St. Modwen lived, I thought needful to note to others, though I can hardly reform it, for I cannot see how she could live in the time of St. Patrick the Apostle of Ireland sent thither by Pope Celestinus about the year 431.

He concludes that there must have been another Patrick with whom she lived, *c.* 870. Dates are not a matter of belief; the miraculous events are. We see Roscarrock, the miraculous accepted, struggling scrupulously to get the historical framework accurate.

St. Nona, mother of St. David, was a religious woman, 'but not as Bale, the vowed enemy of virgins, babbleth a Vestal virgin, but a Christian nun'.[59] She was ravished and got with child, who became a virtuous bishop, St. David. She afterwards lived a life of penance and was reputed a saint, 'no way to be scorned at by Bale, who had been much more happy had he made the like satisfaction for his apostasy and vow-breach'.

(Bale was, of course, a former monk.) St. Nona's ravisher was a king of Cardigan, 'which Capgrave maketh N. Wales, Leland S. Wales and Camden W. Wales, which by a favourable interpretation must be made good and that perhaps in respect of divers situations; for that which is north in respect of one place may be south in respect of another'. (One is reminded of Newman's famous piece of obscurantism, about the Bible telling us that the sun moves round the earth, science that the earth moves round the sun, and never shall we know which is right until we know what motion is.) In fact the Protestants were geographically right about Cardigan.

Roscarrock continues with the practice of 'bowsening' the demented at St. Nun's pool in Altarnun parish, of which Carew gives an amused, sceptical account: how the patients were thrown into the water and afterwards brought to the altar, where prayers were offered and masses said for them, 'by which it was thought that some have been dispossessed and others cured of their frenzy, howsoever it pleaseth some to make themselves merry with it. It is likely that this saint, which giveth name to this church, well and pool, lived there, but I dare not assure myself of it, till I find more warrant than a bare conjecture.' Meticulous Roscarrock, straining at a gnat: there is no reason to doubt that she once lived there.

So, too, with St. Perran's miracle of carrying a live coal in his bare hands to warm St. Rodanus, 'by which I gather the stone was coal such as they call sea-coal, for had it been a flint it had been no marvel, much less a miracle, to get fire out of it or to carry it in his naked hands without hurt'.[60] (It must have been best South Wales steam-anthracite.) Poor Roscarrock, what a time he had, struggling to make sense of these medieval stories in a post-Reformation world which had shattered the Middle Ages for ever!

He is happier remembering for us, centuries later, the familiar places and the old observances attaching to them. Roscarrock criticizes his co-religionist, J. W. of *The English Martyrologe*, for making St. Perran's relics to have been reserved at Padstow:

Methinks the records of Padstow should hardly err so grossly in a thing so apparent, as every fisherboy in the town knoweth that St. Perran and Padstow are two distinct places and are twelve or thirteen miles asunder . . . I, who was born within three miles of Padstow and not far from St. Perran, remember his relics were wont to be carried up and down in the country upon occasion and have seen them so carried in the time of Queen Mary . . . There was a chapel not far from Padstow bearing his name but his relics were (I take it) always reserved in St. Perran's . . . where he was buried, being called St. Perran's-in-the-Sand; which chapel hath been overblown with the sands, though there standeth one at this day near that place.

At St. Breward, 'there was a tree growing in our memory in the place of his martyrdom, which was much regarded and reverenced, and thought to have continued there ever since his death'. At the feast of St. Petrock on 4 June, the priests of Padstow, Bodmin and Little Petherick used to meet at St. Breoke's beacon with their crosses and banners at a sermon and collation.[61] In the parish of Newlyn there was a chapel dedicated to St. Nighton with a yard belonging; within was a little mount with four stones where the crosses and relics of St. Perran, Crantock, Cubert and Newlyn were wont to be placed in Rogation week, at which time a sermon was made to the people.[62] 'And the last was preached by parson Crane in Queen Mary's time, as I have been credibly informed by a priest who had been an eye-witness.' One of these four stones was taken and turned into a cheese-press by Mistress Borlace about the year 1580; but later one night it was 'carried back by one, willed so by her after her death or by something assuming her personage, and remaineth still where it did. And this I have from report of such as were of her kinsfolks and friends, who have cause to know it.' It has the makings of a Cornish ghost-story.

It is clear how much alive for the ageing man so far away at Naworth were the memories of the religion of his childhood in Cornwall: some part of his heart—as with most Cornishmen living away from home—was anchored there. We note how narrow and restricted his experience of the county naturally was: he only knew well the parishes in the immediate neighbourhood of his home. He had once made the pilgrimage to St. Michael's Mount, 'sometime a religious house, now a place of strength'; for in the main rock of that Mount there was a seat which I have seen, neither easy to climb unto nor to sit in, which is called St. Michael's Chair, where they say he hath made his apparition, which caused it to be frequented as a great pilgrimage. The true story of his apparition not fully known to me, I forbear to write more of it, referring you if your fortune be to see it, to Mr. Johnson's Ecclesiastical History, lib. 5, cap. 20.

When Roscarrock did not know, he took trouble to inform himself, as we can see from the case of the patron saint of my native parish, St. Austell.[63] Roscarrock writes, 'there was usually a feast kept in memory of that saint the Thursday in Whitsun week'. Feast-week at St. Austell is still that week; and when Bishop Bronescombe re-dedicated the church in the thirteenth century, by a title known to the Roman Calendar, he chose the Holy Trinity as falling nearest the feast-day of the Celtic saint, so as not to disturb the age-long custom. Roscarrock continues: 'I should be apt to think that this St. Austell and the Doctor of the Church or our Apostle should be one, but that their feasts do differ; which perhaps may grow of that the one is the day of his death, the other of the dedication of the church. The reason moving me to think so is the statue of a bishop or abbot, which standeth in the wall of the said church. More I cannot say, but wish others would inquire, both of that and many other saints in these parts and in Wales whereof by the injury of time we are ignorant.'

A different hand has added: 'And yet they hold by tradition there that this St. Austell and St. Mewan were great friends, whose parishes join. And enjoy some privileges together, and that they lived there together.' A third hand adds further: 'The feast of which St. Mewan is November 19'. This information is correct: in his blindness, Roscarrock's inquiries had been answered and the problem solved. St. Austell was the inseparable companion of St. Mewan, who—as St. Méen—is one of the best known and most widely venerated of the Breton saints.[64]

The folk-lore of a people has a creative vitality continuing beyond the ages of faith. Perhaps it would not greatly surprise Roscarrock to know that many of these observances—rogations, processions, pilgrimages to holy wells, masses in the churches of his beloved saints—have come back, after long sleep, in our time; for what is founded on the rock of the irrational in human beings has undying strength.

NOTES

[1] Cambridge University Library, Add MSS. 3041. I am much indebted to Mr. H. R. Creswick, the University Librarian, for arranging—and to the University Senate for granting permission—for this MS. to be deposited at the Bodleian for me to study it at leisure, and to the Bodleian authorities for their co-operation.

[2] Carl Horstman described the MS. as 'very valuable' and recommended it to workers in this department (*v.* his edition of *Nova Legenda Anglie*, I. x.) He printed in App. 1 Roscarrock's Life of St. Christina. Curiously enough, the scholarly hagiographer Canon G. H. Doble does not seem to have consulted the MS.; but he uses Charles Henderson's notes from it in his admirable *Cornish Saints Series*. Canon T. Taylor excerpted the entry relating to St. Endelient in his brochure *St. Endellion Prebendal Church*.

[3] Sir John Maclean, *History of Trigg Minor*, I. pp. 556–64.

[4] J. Foster, *Alumni Oxonienses*, 1500–1714, p. 1280.

[5] C. W. Boase, *Registrum Collegii Exon.*, p. 68.

[6] *Ibid.*, p. 65.

[7] Boase, *op. cit.*, pp. xcvi–xcvii.

[8] W. H. Cooke, *Students admitted to Inner Temple*, p. 71.

[9] *Ibid.*, p. 68.

[10] Published by R. Tottel in 1572; reprinted by H. Ballard in 1597.

[11] Cf. 'Grand Christmas at the Temple, 1562' in J. Nichols, *Progresses of Queen Elizabeth*, I.

[12] Cf. George Gascoigne, *The Glasse of Government*, ed. J. W. Cunliffe (Cambridge, 1910), 138–9.

[13] S.P. 46/16.

[14] Cf. my *Sir Richard Grenville of the Revenge*, C. VII.

[15] S.P. 12/177, 25. In a subsequent list (S.P. 12/118, 46) appear the names of Humphrey Trevilian and his wife as 'suspected only'. But this remaining branch of the family in Cornwall—the spelling reveals the proper pronunciation of the name—became recusants and in time were squeezed out of their estate at Lower Basil in the parish of St. Clether. Their pleasant old hall remains there not much changed. *v.* my *Tudor Cornwall*, p. 370.

[16] Dodd's *Church History*, ed. Tierney, III. p. 223.

[17] T. F. Knox, ed. *First and Second Douai Diaries*, p. 169.

[18] Dodd, *ed. cit.*, III. pp. 151–3, 258.

[19] *Acts of the Privy Council*, 1580–1, ed. J. R. Dasent, pp. 264–5.

[20] Knox, *op. cit.*, p. 178.

[21] Catholic Record Society, *Miscellanea*, IV. pp. 74–5.

[22] S.P. 12/178, 11.

[23] *Ibid.*, 12/178, 74.

[24] *Ibid.*, 12/187, 19.

[25] S.P., 12/170, 8.

[26] *Hist. MSS. Com. Salisbury MSS.*, IV. p. 432.

[27] *Cal. S.P. Dom. 1591–4*, p. 499.

[28] *Catholic Record Society. Recusants' Roll, 1592–3*, p. 17; and for subsequent years the Roll itself, E. 377.

[29] *Ibid.*, p. 35.

[30] *The Household Books of Lord William Howard*, Surtees Soc., pp. lix–lx.

[31] Laud MSS., 733.

[32] Cambridge Univ. Lib. Hh. IV. 11.

[33] There is a delightful description of it by Dr. David Mathew, 'The Library at Naworth', in *For Hilaire Belloc*, ed. Douglas Woodruff.

[34] *The Household Books of Lord William Howard*, p. 95.

[35] *Ibid.*, p. 189.

[36] *Ibid.*, pp. 121, 143.

[37] *Ibid.*, p. 302.

[38] *Ibid.*, pp. 198, 187, 139.

[39] *Ibid.*, pp. 302–3.

[40] Now in the Victoria and Albert Museum; cf. Sir Eric Maclagan and C. C. Oman, 'An English Gold Rosary of about 1500', *Archæologia*, LXXXV.

[41] *Household Books*, pp. 506–7.

[42] R. Carew, *Survey of Cornwall* (ed. 1769), 127b.

[43] *Household Books*, pp. 451–2.

[44] I am indebted to Mr. C. C. Oman for drawing my attention to this portrait, and to Lt.-Col. Hugh Levin of Corby Castle for kindly sending me a photograph of it.

[45] f. 24.

[46] f. 25.

[47] f. 1 foll.

[48] f. 5.

[49] f. 65b.

[50] f. 202b.

[51] The tower of St. Endellion is built of Lundy Island granite—appropriately for her association with the island.

[52] f. 290b.

[53] Cf. G. H. Doble, *St. Nectan, St. Keyne and the Children of Brychan in Cornwall. Cornish Saints Series*, no. 25.

[54] Roscarrock, Lives, f. 312b. foll.

[55] Cf. Carew, *ed. cit.*, pp. 123, 130.

[56] Roscarrock, Lives, f. 359b.

[57] f. 314.

[58] *Aubrey's Brief Lives*, ed. A. Clark, I. p. 27.

[59] Roscarrock, Lives, f. 327b.

[60] *Ibid.*, f. 384b.

[61] f. 357b.

[62] f. 323b.

[63] f. 78b.

[64] Cf. G. H. Doble, *St. Mewan and St. Austol, Cornish Saints Series*, no. 8.

II

An Elizabethan Provincial Town:
Leicester

W. G. HOSKINS

II

THE city of London—'a large, excellent and mighty city of business', as Frederick duke of Würtemberg saw it in 1592—towered over all other English cities during the sixteenth century. In the great subsidy of 1543–4, the last comprehensive assessment before the lay subsidies became something of a farce, London paid fully thirty times as much tax as Norwich, the wealthiest city in the provinces, and well over forty times as much as Bristol, the third city of the kingdom. Even the suburb of Southwark, across the river, paid more tax than Bristol. London contributed as much on that occasion as all the other towns of England put together, from Norwich down to the smallest place that functioned as a local market-centre for its own countryside. Relatively speaking, Elizabethan London took a larger place in the economy of the nation than the London of the twentieth century.

And yet the provinces of England, too, were incomparably more individual and distinctive than they are today. The landed gentry still spoke, not the standardized speech of a social class, but with all the rich variety of their native parts. And though writers, like Shakespeare, may have been drawn to London and some country merchants may have sought their fortunes in it, the provincial towns in general kept their ablest men and hence a lively culture of their own, not a pale reflection of the metropolis. In each province of England, above all in the peripheral regions, certain towns played the part of capital cities to their regions—Norwich and York, Exeter and Salisbury, Newcastle and Bristol, for example. Most of them were cathedral cities, and hence centres of ecclesiastical administration. They were also local centres of government and public administration, where the justices of the peace met in Quarter Sessions and wrestled with the increasing burden of duties laid upon them by

Though drawn specifically to show the topography of Leicester in the early sixteenth century, the map on the opposite page shows the town as it still appeared in Elizabethan days. The only notable changes in the intervening period had been the disappearance of the Black Friars, the White Friars, and the Grey Friars; the conversion of the dissolved hospital of St. John into a Wool Hall about 1592; and the building of the Free Grammar School at the N. corner of High Street and Dead Lane in 1573–4 out of the materials of St. Peter's church, the crumbling fabric of which was pulled down for the purpose.

BOUNDARIES

----	Borough Boundary	--·--·	Ward Boundaries (conjectural)
········	Ward Boundaries	———	Religious Houses
	▦▦▦	Town Wall and Ditch	

KEY

1. Shirehall
2. Gaol
3. St. John's Hospital
4. Old Guildhall (Mayor's Hall)
5. Common Oven & Shambles
6. High Cross
7. Berehill Cross or Roundel
8. Guildhall
9. Wigston's Hospital
10. Castle View
11. Castle Buildings

12. Newark Hospital
13. Wigston's Chantry Houses
14. Newark Gateway
15. North Gate
16. East Gate
17. South Gate
18. West Gate
19. Castle House
20. Red Cross
21. Gun Dyke

(The map is reproduced from the *Transactions of the Leicestershire Archæological Society* 1951, by permission of Mr. Derek Charman and the Society)

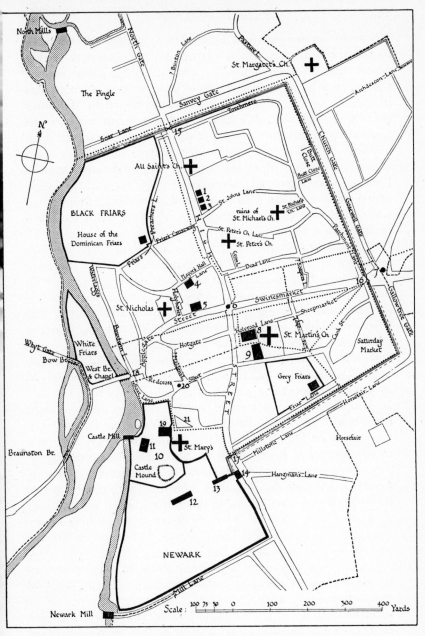

Leicester in the Sixteenth Century

the Tudor monarchs. And they were in process of becoming social capitals also, in which a growing proportion of the larger gentry had a 'town house' to which they migrated for the winter months. It is curious how little is known about this interesting social change. It was well developed by the latter part of the seventeenth century, and one seems to detect its beginnings in the closing years of the sixteenth. It was to these provincial capitals that the larger gentry, those who could afford to keep up two establishments, migrated rather than to London, which generally attracted the peerage and the larger gentry of the Home Counties. Such provincial capitals had eight to twelve thousand people by the year 1600, Norwich possibly some 17,000.

Beneath the regional capitals of Elizabethan England lay a considerable group of towns—"county towns" for the most part—which had no cathedral churches and no social pretentions, but were either the seat of county government or markets for an unusually wide area, or both. Such were Derby and Leicester, which numbered five hundred and six hundred households respectively at the beginning of Elizabeth's reign, and Manchester with rather more than four hundred households. Towns which had no administrative functions but served as market-centres for a wider radius than the average ran to a fairly uniform size, somewhere between two and three hundred households. Such were Bridgwater or Crewkerne in Somerset, Cranbrook or Maidstone in Kent, Walsall or Wolverhampton in Staffordshire, Bridgenorth in Shropshire, Stratford-upon-Avon in Warwickshire, or Stamford in Lincolnshire.[1] Roughly speaking, we may say that they numbered a thousand to two thousand people each. Some of them, if not most, were smaller than they had been in the early fourteenth century, before successive epidemics of bubonic plague and economic change had diminished their people and their prosperity.

Below this group again lay a great number of places accustomed to regard themselves without question as towns. Bideford had rather fewer than a thousand people at the time of its incorporation in 1573. Burford, in Oxfordshire, is described in a chantry certificate of 1545 as 'a great market town replenished with much people', but the same record elsewhere gives the

number of 'houselyng people' (communicants) as 544, which
suggests a total population of about eight hundred. Chipping
Norton is described in the same terms and had an almost
identical number of people.[2]

In speaking of the Elizabethan provincial towns, then, we
are dealing with very small communities by modern standards,
generally from one to three thousand people in all, a few
larger and some smaller. But the historian must not share the
modern obsession with large (and often meaningless) numbers:
he is concerned with a quality of life when he reflects upon the
Elizabethan town, a quality which—to take the extreme case—
could produce a William Shakespeare out of a town of a dozen
streets and perhaps twelve hundred people. Everything is on a
miniature scale: all except the quality of the people. It is against
this scale of measurement that we turn to study in detail the
economy and everyday working of an Elizabethan town of the
middling sort, neither a regional capital nor yet an insignificant
market-town for a backwoods area, nor even a minor textile
town. The special interest of Leicester to the economic and
social historian is indeed that it had no industry worth speaking
of. Here was a community of some three thousand people, the
largest and wealthiest town between the Trent and the Thames,
which had no obvious means of livelihood. The economic
historian has his clichés no less than the political historian: his
easy reference to the "cloth trade" is hardly more helpful than
the "fire and sword" of the other. Towns which had no marked
industrial character (such as Leicester) greatly outnumbered
those which had (such as Coventry), and it will be salutary to
study such a one in sixteenth-century England. The picture that
emerges may be of some interest also to the sociologist.

The town of Leicester, situated upon the insignificant river
Soar, lay in the centre of one of the richest farming counties in
England, and one which had been amongst the most densely
populated since the fourteenth century. It was a town of Roman
foundation (possibly a little older even than that) and the
medieval walled area, which followed the original Roman lines,
included rather more than one hundred acres. Within this area
there were, as in most English towns in the sixteenth century,

considerable stretches of open ground, some belonging to the castle and to sundry former religious foundations, but much the result of the diminution of population since 1349. Estimates of the town population before the Black Death are difficult to make with certainty, but there is good reason to believe that it may have been between four and five thousand. Even in 1377 it was somewhat larger than it was in 1563, and it was not until towards the end of the seventeenth century that the town again attained the size it had reached in the late thirteenth. Both economically and politically, the town was far less important at the beginning of Elizabeth's reign than it had been in medieval times. Much of this decline is attributable to the decay in the importance of Leicester Castle, and to the disappearance of the rich and powerful household that had dwelt there. The merging of the duchy of Lancaster with the Crown in 1399 meant that the Castle ceased to be a ducal residence; and in a small town this was a heavy blow to the local economy.

Much of the intra-mural area had never been available for building and a suburb had therefore developed on the level ground outside the east gate at an early date. In 1269–71 the suburban dwellers numbered some seventeen per cent of the total population paying tallage.[3] At a somewhat later date, other suburbs had taken root outside the south and north gates, so that by the early sixteenth century the suburban population amounted to no less than forty-five per cent of the total. The east suburb alone housed one-quarter of the tax-paying population in 1524–5, and the north and south suburbs roughly ten per cent each.[4] Only on the western side of the town, which was flanked by the wandering channels of the Soar, did no suburb develop until the nineteenth century.

Beyond the built-up area lay the three open fields of the borough. Over the river lay the West Field, some eight hundred acres in extent; the East Field covered nearly twelve hundred acres in all (arable and pasture); and the South Field with its meadows some six hundred acres. The arable, meadow, and pasture around Leicester thus amounted altogether to about 2,600 acres. Many of the burgesses had holdings in the open fields in the sixteenth century, besides the general right of all burgesses to common their beasts over part of this area; the inhabitants were still obliged to grind their corn at the town mills and to bake their bread in the common ovens. A plan drawn in the late sixteenth century[5] shows five water-mills along the Soar (St. Mary's mills, Newark mills, Castle mills, North mills, and Abbey mills), and we know from this and other records that a considerable number of windmills were also at work, above all on the high ground of the South Field. Elizabethan Leicester kept a country air about it. Orchards, barns and stables, and large gardens lay among the streets; windmills stood silhouetted as one looked up against the southern skyline; the streets petered out in ten minutes' walk into lanes redolent of cowdung and hay.

So far as the distribution of wealth in the town is concerned, we are dependent on the lay subsidies levied some years before the beginning of Elizabeth's reign, for after 1546 they decrease rapidly in comprehensiveness, and even such assessments as were made were largely conventional. Thus the subsidy levied in 1590 contains only ninety-three assessments for Leicester (as compared with 403 in 1524, or about 350 in 1543), although it is one of the more comprehensive assessments of the Elizabethan period. In the 1524 assessment, more than two out of three were roped in; in 1590 only one in seven. Again, the highest assessment in 1590 is only £14 14s. od., whereas in 1544 it was £70 and in 1524 £600. To reconstruct the social pyramid of Elizabethan Leicester we must therefore have recourse to the subsidy of 1543–4,[6] of which one instalment was paid in each year, and for certain basic facts we must look even farther back to the larger assessment of 1524–5.

Leicester paid altogether in 1543–4 the sum of £99 16s. 7d., the first instalment yielding almost exactly twice as much as the second. In the provinces, five cities paid more than £400 each to this subsidy (Norwich, Bristol, Exeter, York, and Salisbury), and twelve other towns paid more than £150 each. Leicester ranked about twenty-fifth among the provincial towns, in order of wealth, in the second quarter of the sixteenth century; and a ranking in 1576 suggests that the town had then sunk to about thirtieth place.[7]

The Leicester assessment for 1543 survives in an incomplete form, but sufficient to show that the highest assessments were those of Nicholas Reynolds, merchant (£70) and William Olyff, fishmonger (£67), both reduced to £40 in the assessment of the following year. Incomplete as this record is, it shows us, too, that the economic domination of the town by one family (the Wigstons) had dissolved since William Wigston's death in 1535, and that wealth was now somewhat more evenly spread throughout the "upper class" of the town. In 1524, six families (eight assessments) between them had owned one-third of the taxable wealth of the town. In 1544 the top twenty-four payers owned one-third of the wealth. It is to be regretted that we do not possess the complete assessment for 1543 in which the wealthier taxpayers are generally more highly assessed; but an analysis of the complete 1544 assessment gives the following results:

TABLE I: *Analysis of the 1544 subsidy for Leicester*

Assessment	No. in group	Total taxable wealth
£40	5	£200
£20 to under £40	19	£415
£10 to under £20	36	£443
£5 to under £10	67	£438
£2 to under £5	101	£269
£1 to under £2	83	£ 85½
	311	£1,850½

To the above table we have to add those below the exemption limit of £1. The size of this group may be safely estimated at about one-third of the population at this date. We know that at Coventry in 1522 no fewer than 37 per cent of the population had a *nil* assessment. Coventry was an industrialized town, twice the size of Leicester, and undoubtedly had a higher proportion of "poor"; but Mr. Charman rightly concluded from a close analysis of the records around the 1520's that at Leicester there was 'something like a submerged third of the population'.[8] Now the town contained 591 families in 1563 and possibly about 540 twenty years earlier. There is reason to suppose that the complete 1543 assessment had about 350 names, so that some 190 names appear to be excluded as being below the exemption limit. It is safe to say that a good third of the population escaped the subsidy in 1543 (as in 1524), and in 1544 the exempted class rose to some 42 per cent of the total population. Theoretically the size of the exempted class should have been no greater in 1544 than in the preceding year. The assessors must have been lighter in their touch in the second year; and the rate in the pound was also halved on assessments up to £20.

The suburbs were the most thickly populated area and also the poorest. That outside the South Gate was the poorest in 1524 and again in 1544, when nearly forty per cent of the taxable population were assessed at the minimum level of £1. The suburb that extended north-eastwards along Belgrave Gate also contained a large number of the labouring poor once one got past the dozen or so houses nearest the town. The suburb that extended south-eastwards, on the other hand, contained few poor, and showed a high average assessment— possibly because it lay along the London road and was the busiest line of movement into and out of the town. As in 1524 the most wealthy streets were the Swinesmarket (the present High Street) from the High Cross to the east gate, and the High Street (the present Highcross Street) which ran from the north gate to the south gate. In this pattern of a wealthy central area, and of suburbs largely composed of the labouring class, Leicester conformed to a general pattern (so far as it is known) among English towns. As the size of the labouring class grew in the towns, the tendency was to house them, not within the walled area where there was in fact plenty of space for building, but outside the walls where land was cheaper. The more well-to-do retained their ample gardens, orchards, and courtyards[9]; the poor were housed elsewhere, though in some streets there was a certain intermingling of the classes if one can assume (as is often apparent from the record) that the assessors were proceeding systematically from house to house. Not all the poor property was suburban; there were patches of it in some old streets that must have dated from very early times. But the greater part of the working-class in English towns seem to have been housed outside the walled area, or outside the traditional central area if there were no walls.

The assessments to the lay subsidies are clearly to a high degree conventional, if we compare them with the valuation of a man's personal estate at the time of his death. This is true even of the 1524-5 subsidy, where we can test the assessment against the valuation for probate purposes; and the disparity between the two values becomes farcically great in the later subsidies. Thus Robert Newcombe, the Leicester bellfounder, was among the five most highly assessed men (all at £40 each) in 1544, but at his death in 1561 his personal estate was valued at £261 16s. 8d. Henry Halfpenny, chandler, was assessed at £5 5s. od. in 1590, but his estate was valued at £148 3s. 2d. when he died nine years later. William Hobby, wheelwright, was assessed at £3 3s. od. in the same subsidy and his personal estate at £120 8s. 2d. seven years later. For Richard Overend, fishmonger, the respective valuations are £3 3s. od. in 1590 and £107 15s. od. in 1595. A commissioner of taxes in the 1590's declared that no one had been assessed at above a tenth of his true wealth, and some at only a twentieth or thirtieth or even less. The Leicester figures show this view to be correct. Direct taxation had become almost nonsensical and after the 1540's we cannot use the tax assessments to arrive at any notion of the distribution of wealth. 'The Englishman', declared Francis Bacon, 'is most master of his own valuation and the least bitten in purse of any nation in Europe.'

Harking back to the economic structure of the town in 1524, about thirty per cent of the total population were too poor to pay any direct taxation, and another thirty per cent only just came within the net, being assessed on wages or goods to the value of £1. The first group we may legitimately regard as "the poor"; and the second group, though not poor, as living dangerously near the margin, precariously dependent on fairly full employment whether as wage-earners, small craftsmen, or shopkeepers. The class assessed at between £2 and £10 we could loosely call a lower middle class, to use modern terms, and they constituted another thirty per cent of the town population. Those assessed at £10 to £40 constituted about seven per cent of the population and formed the solid core of the middle class. At £40 and above we enter a group who may be rightly regarded as comfortably well-off—as the government recognized when it made them pay their tax in advance (the "Anticipation" of 1523) or taxed them on other occasions as a separate group. At Leicester there were only fifteen families in this class in 1524—representing about three per cent of the total population. Such was the social pyramid in 1524, and it cannot have been noticeably different at the beginning of Elizabeth's reign. By the end of her reign the base of the pyramid was perceptibly wider, though—in a town like Leicester where there were no industrial fortunes to be made—the peak of the pyramid may have gone no higher. The outstanding fact about the pyramid was that fully one-half of the population lived below or very near the poverty line, a dangerously large element in the town population.

* * *

For our knowledge of the occupational structure of the town in the Elizabethan period we must turn to the register of admissions to the freedom of the town, which forms a splendid directory of trades during this (and other) periods. Admissions to the freedom at this time were by inheritance from a freeman-father, or by seven years' apprenticeship to a Leicester freeman, and in all probability every trade in the town except that of the labourer is represented in the rolls. Between 1559 and 1603, almost nine hundred admissions were made, an average of about twenty a year. In order not to obscure any changes in the occupational structure that may have occurred during Elizabeth's long reign of forty-five years, the period has been divided roughly half-way in Table II on the following page.

There are a number of difficulties and arbitrary allocations in any classification like the above table. For example, shoemakers (who are a numerous class) have been classified under the clothing trades rather than the leather trades, and tailors under clothing rather than textiles. The distributive trades present a special difficulty. In the above table they include only merchants and mercers, carriers and chapmen, whereas it is certain that most of those in the food trades had retail shops and were distributors of goods. Even so a clear picture of the occupational structure of the town emerges. If we list also the

TABLE II: *Leicester Trades, 1559–1603*

	1559–80		1580–1603	
	Admissions	Percentage of total	Admissions	Percentage of total
Clothing trades	91	23	109	22
Food and drink trades	69	17½	98	19½
Leather trades	46	11½	53	10½
Textile industry	32	8	27	5½
Household goods	27	7	29	6
Building trades	24	6	29	6
Distributive trades	30	7½	30	6
Rural	18	4½	26	5
Miscellaneous	62	15	98	19½
	399	100	499	100

most numerous single trades in each period the picture grows clearer still:[10]

TABLE III: *Ten principal occupations, Leicester 1559–1603*

	1559–80	1580–1603
Tailors	32	35
Tanners	28	35
Butchers	25	38
Shoemakers	22	31
Glovers	21	22
Mercers	18	18
Weavers	18	12
Bakers	16	21
Chandlers	12	8
Smiths	8	12
	200	232

The ten leading trades in 1559–80 between them account for exactly a half the total number admitted to the freedom and in 1580–1603 for nearly a half (46 per cent). Even taken by themselves, they tell us a good deal about the economy of the town, but it will be best to consider them in relation to the preceding table also.

The markedly non-industrial character of the town emerges at once. Well over a half the occupied persons were engaged in the clothing, food and drink, household goods (cutlers, chandlers, ironmongers, etc.,), and building trades. If we include the distributive trades, just about three persons in five were engaged in directly providing for the consumer. The second fact that emerges is that so far as the town was acquiring any industrial character it was provided by the tanners, of whom no fewer than sixty-three are recorded in the period 1559–1603. They congregated largely in the north quarter of the town and particularly along the river just outside the North Gate. If Elizabethan Leicester could be said to have had an industrial quarter it was here, but we must not over-emphasize its development for the leather trades as a whole employed only about one person in every nine or ten. Possibly if we knew more about the labouring class, who are missing from the freemen's register, this proportion would be somewhat higher.

Another aspect of the town's economy which does not emerge so clearly perhaps, but is nevertheless a fundamental feature, is the high degree of dependence upon the surrounding countryside. This is brought out in a number of ways. In the period 1559–80, nineteen freemen are described as smiths, wheelwrights, husbandmen, and graziers; in 1580–1603, no fewer than twenty-six. The existence in the town of over a score of smiths and wheelwrights alone, in the second half of Elizabeth's reign, indicates to what an extent the town lived by providing goods for the countryman. Then, too, the high proportion of the occupied population engaged in providing clothing, food, drink, household goods, and building facilities (carpenters, glaziers, joiners, masons, and slaters) can only mean that they served a host of customers beyond the town itself. We can hardly envisage three people in every five selling consumer goods and services to the other two in the town. In fact the two weekly markets—on Wednesdays and Saturdays—held in the same place to this day, regularly attracted hundreds of country people; and the four annual fairs—two in the spring and two in the autumn—attracted thousands.

The great dependence of the town upon the surrounding countryside is shown above all perhaps by the number of townsmen who depended ultimately upon the neighbouring cattle pastures for their livelihood—the butchers, the tanners, curriers, whittawers, saddlers, and the glovers, not to mention the shoemakers. One tends to think too readily of the Tudor enclosure movement in terms of sheep-pastures and wool; but this analysis of the largest town in the East Midlands suggests that cattle-pastures were hardly less important, especially as other Midland towns, like Rugby, Birmingham, and Market Harborough, were all notable for their cattle and leather trades in this period. The well-to-do of Tudor Birmingham were the graziers and the tanners, rather than the smiths whom Leland noticed on his visit. At Leicester some of the most extensive enclosed pastures near the town seem to have been devoted largely to cattle (for example at Hamilton, Evington, and New Park), though further out on the uplands to the east and south sheep seem to have predominated.

An examination of the occupational changes between the beginning and the end of Elizabeth's reign is best deferred until the concluding section of this essay, but one curious aspect of the occupations of the town calls for notice here. That is the odd combination of trades which occasionally emerges from the Freemen's Register. The Newcombes, for example, constituted a regular dynasty of bell-founders, beginning with Thomas Newcombe, who died in 1520, and continuing through four generations down to 1612. The last three generations combined bell-founding with tanning, certainly from the middle of the sixteenth century onwards.[11] This curious combination of activities continued for more than fifty years. There is no obvious connection between the two trades. One must assume that bell-founding was a somewhat intermittent activity, perhaps more so after the Reformation, and that the Newcombes turned to tanning as the most profitable trade at hand. Again, in the freemen's roll for 1598–9 no fewer than eight 'chandlers and slaters' suddenly appear. No doubt the production of tallow candles was a seasonal occupation that fell off greatly in the lighter part of the year, and slating was a seasonal occupation for the better weather, but the combination seems an odd one

The Blue Boar Inn in Highcross Street: the most notable inn of Elizabethan Leicester. Its landlord (Thomas Clarke) was twice mayor of the town in this period

The courtyard of an Elizabethan inn: the Mitre and Keys in Applegate Street

for so many practitioners at once. The combination of chandler and haberdasher, which also occurs about this time, seems a more rational solution to the problem of seasonal under-employment.

*   *   *

Leicester had been governed by a mayor since the year 1250. Since 1489 the original twenty-four jurats had been supplemented by forty-eight of "the wiser inhabitants" who, together with the twenty-four, elected the mayor. The mayor, the Twenty-Four, and the Forty-Eight thus formed the single ruling body during the period 1558–1603. The machinery of local government was rudimentary. Of officials in the modern sense of the word, there was only one—William Dethick, the mayor's clerk, who first appears in the borough records in 1572 and who held office until 1608. He was virtually the town clerk. Though not the earliest occupant of this post, he is the first about whom we know much, by virtue of his long tenure of office; and he came to exercise considerable authority in the borough, much like a modern town clerk. The other "officials" —the bailiffs, the chamberlains, the coroners, the stewards of the fair, the auditors of the borough accounts, and the fish, meat, and leather testers in the markets, were all appointed from members of the governing body. It was one of the chores of office, and was unpaid. Finally there was the recorder, who was usually a local squire with a legal training—a Brokesby, Beaumont, or Farnham—and who spent more time outside the borough than in it.

The mayor received a fee of ten pounds yearly, fixed as long ago as 1379. This was increased in 1572 (because of the steep rise in the cost of living) to £13 6s. 8d. 'for and towards the better maintenance of his housekeeping'. The recorder received a fee of four pounds yearly all through the Elizabethan period. The mayor's clerk received only six shillings and eightpence a year, (raised to 26s. 8d. in 1572) but there were numerous perquisites of office, such as the fees for drawing up all indentures of apprenticeship within the borough. And the two chamberlains received forty shillings a year between them for their services. This was apparently the most unwanted office of all, for though a heavy fine of five pounds had been fixed for refusal to serve there were many such refusals. In the year 1560-1, for example, the borough funds benefited by fifteen pounds when John Wilne, Richard Ley, and Richard Rawly all declined the office.

The borough finances were simple and modest in scale.[12] Thus in the year 1558-9 (Michaelmas to Michaelmas) the total receipts were £57 14s. 4d., the total expenses £29 14s. od. This may be compared with the finances of the city of Exeter in the same year, where the receipts amounted to £431 (to the nearest £) and the expenditure to £385; or Bath in 1572-3 which received £148 (nearest £) and spent nearly £162, the chamberlains here being temporarily out of pocket to the tune of fourteen pounds odd.

At Leicester roughly half the revenue came from rents of town and country property, and the other half from miscellaneous receipts such as fees for admission to the freedom, fees from various trades for their ordinals, and fines for refusing the chamberlainship. The biggest single item among the receipts was rents at will and assized (fixed) rents in the borough, which produced £21 14s. 4d.; the second largest came from the eighteen admissions to the freedom, which yielded £8 15s. od. The town did not yet possess the fee-farm of the borough—it was remarkably late in acquiring this valuable privilege, not until 1589—so that its revenues from property within the town were still small.

Against this miserably small income, the largest items of expenditure in 1558-9 were fees to the mayor, recorder, and mayor's clerk, which came to nearly half the total expenses, and a payment of £4 to 'the bailiff of Leicester', acting for the Crown, for the rent of the sheep-pens.[13] Then there are minor items of expenditure such as mending the pinfold and the stocks, making the ducking-stool, and 'sweeping of the Corn Wall'. In some respects Leicester in 1558 was very like a village. And, finally, there were the gifts of wine to the auditors and justices, the high sheriff and the judges, and, 'to my lord of Loughborough', wine and a pound of the new delicacy called sugar.[14]

There was no system of local rating. Exceptional expenditure was usually met by special gifts, or by levies upon the governing body. When in 1573 the borough decided to refound and rebuild the free grammar school (which largely accounts for the sharp rise in receipts and expenditure in 1573–4), the earl of Huntingdon gave ten pounds and the Master of Wigston's Hospital £3 6s. 8d., and the Forty-Eight also contributed towards the cost. The Twenty-Four and the Forty-Eight were continually being called upon to dip into their pockets for one cause after another. In 1568, for example, it was ordained that every member of the Twenty-Four, upon getting married, should pay 2s. 8d. to the collectors for the poor in his own parish, and every member of the Forty-Eight 1s. 4d. Or, when in 1571 it was decided to get a clothier to settle in the town and set the able-bodied poor to work, the necessary loan of one hundred marks to the clothier—one Thomas Bradgate of Gloucester—was mainly raised by levying twenty shillings on each of the Twenty-Four and ten shillings on each of the Forty-Eight.

The purchase of the fee-farm of the borough from the Queen in 1589 greatly increased the borough revenues. The rent-roll rose from about £20 to £166. By the charter of that year the borough was incorporated, and all the crown and duchy lands granted in fee-farm. Much of the crown land had formerly been held by hospitals, gilds, and chantries, and the crown reserved considerable rents upon all of it. This largely explains why, after 1589, both the revenue and the expenditure rise sharply.

There was considerable speculation in the newly-acquired lands among the members of the governing body, some of which would not have borne close investigation. As a consequence there was much ill-feeling in the town and in the governing body. Some of the property was acquired by Thomas Clarke, landlord of the "Blue Boar", (and mayor in 1598), and rents formerly due to the Queen now became payable to him. In October 1597 Mistress Clarke came to the house of one Robert Cradock, cutler, to demand the rent. Cradock's wife answered that she knew not whether to pay her rent to the Queen or Mistress Clarke: no doubt a specious reply that angered the latter beyond control. "The Queen hath no need of my rent. The Queen should have a rope", she is alleged to have answered; and though the charge was never proved against her it was held *in terrorem* over her for years afterwards. Apart from this trivial incident, there had been ill-feeling for years. It was alleged that the mayor in 1589 had set the town seal upon certain sales without the consent of the Common Hall, and that the commissioners appointed to pay the debts incurred by the town in obtaining the fee-farm had sold property amongst themselves without the consent of the Hall. Charges and denials flew about for years. It was said among many other things that the poor were now worse off for their rents had been racked up by the new landlords, and the town as a whole had benefited nothing from the grant of the fee-farm. The matter got as far as the Privy Council, who in March 1593 directed that a committee of enquiry should be set up 'concerning the taking of lands to private uses which were granted by the Queen in fee-farm to the use of the corporation to support a preacher and a clothier, and to maintain the town'. No record of the commission's conclusions and recommendations has survived; and no restitution of the alienated lands ever followed.

The refounding of the free grammar school in 1573 was a notable event, if only because it affected a considerable part of the population in one way and another. The powerful and puritan Earl of Huntingdon, whose principal residence lay at Ashby de la Zouch castle nearly twenty miles off, had in 1569 bought a town house in the principal street, the Swinesmarket; and from this "Lord's Place" he kept a close watch upon the town, its governing body, and the townspeople at large. He had indeed exercised great influence in the town for a dozen years before this, for since 1557 he had administered the extensive possessions of the duchy of Lancaster in Leicestershire.[15] His hand is revealed in an ordinance passed by the corporation in 1562, compelling one person from each household in Leicester to listen to a sermon every Wednesday and Saturday morning from seven to eight o'clock. The drawing-up of the statutes for the refoundation of the school a few years later, under his personal direction, gave him another splendid opportunity of directing the mind of the town in the way it should go. A puritan schoolmaster was appointed, and the pupils were prescribed a thorough belly-full of "prophesyings" and sermons of the right sort. The upper forms had to rewrite the preacher's discourse in Latin verse or prose.

Leicester boys crept through the winter streets before seven in the morning—unwillingly to school indeed!—and just before five during the rest of the year, with a solid stretch of six hours' Latin or Greek ahead of them, and another four hours in the afternoon: six days a week with a possible (but not certain) half holiday on Thursdays. On Sundays all boys attended public worship in their own parish churches and were obliged to make notes on the sermon. Such early and long hours were not peculiar to schoolboys. At Coventry the journeymen cappers worked from six in the morning until seven in the evening from Michaelmas to Easter, and from five a.m. until seven p.m. during the rest of the year.[16] At Leicester it was enacted that no person, of whatever degree, should be abroad in the streets after nine o'clock at night, except officers and the watch. Such hours as this—up before five and in bed by nine or soon after— reflect in their own way the fundamentally country way of life that still marked the English towns in the sixteenth century.

There is much more one could say about the social history of the town—the frequent plagues and the regulations to limit its spread, the regulations concerning sanitation, lighting, and paving and so forth; but these things are well understood and amply recorded. Let us turn instead to consider the housing of the townspeople during this period, a subject about which there is much to be learnt.

For such a study we are largely dependent upon the inventories of personal estate drawn up for the purpose of proving a man's will and administering his estate according to his last wishes. At Leicester we have some forty inventories for the Elizabethan period, sufficient to enable us to form a good picture of all classes of house from the cottage of the journeyman to the more differentiated dwelling of the successful butcher or grocer. Most of the inventories list all the rooms of the dead man's house, together with their contents, and we can visualize from them the plan of the smaller houses—those, for example, that do not rise above a ground floor and an upper floor. The majority of Leicester houses were on one level only and contained two rooms, called generally the hall and the parlour. The hall was the general living-room, the parlour (despite its name) invariably the bedroom. Occasionally there were three rooms, the third being called a buttery or a "house". A growing number of houses by the late seventeenth century had risen to an upper floor, and here, too, the plan we can deduce from the inventories is reasonably clear. But where houses on a constricted site had risen by yet another floor it becomes increasingly difficult to deduce the exact plan, as the constriction of the site probably influenced the plan at all levels.

In London, Fynes Morison tells us (in 1617) that 'the houses of the citizens (especially in the chief streets) are very narrow in the front towards the street, but are built five or six roofs high, commonly of timber and clay with plaster, and are very neat and commodious within: and the building of citizens' houses in other cities is not much unlike this'. He further tells us that the richer citizens' houses are built 'all inward, that the whole room towards the streets may be reserved for shops of tradesmen . . . Great part of the towns and villages are built like the citizens' houses in London, save that they are not so many stories high nor so narrow in the front towards the street.'

These remarks about the houses in provincial towns (let alone the villages) are misleading, certainly for towns of the size of Leicester. Of the main streets of cities like Norwich, York, and Exeter they would be nearer the mark. But the precise topographical drawings by John Flower of Leicester in the early nineteenth century, done before the Victorian expansion and rebuilding swept away nearly everything of antiquity, show us that in this town at least it was rare for a sixteenth- or seventeenth-century house to rise above two floors. At the most, we find a small number of houses (as in the drawings of Shambles Lane, now St. Nicholas's Street, or of Southgate Street) in which the gables conceal a couple of attic rooms or a cock-loft on the third floor, and these do not appear to be lighted, on the street side at least. In this respect Leicester was less advanced, for example, than a city like Exeter, where drawings and inventories of Elizabethan houses frequently show or imply three floors, and occasionally even a fourth and a fifth floor. This is not surprising, for Exeter was a far wealthier and culturally more advanced town than Leicester. Out of fifty surviving Elizabethan inventories for Exeter people, seven reveal personal estate of more than £1,000 in value and four are above £2,000; whereas at Leicester the largest inventory which has survived for the same period shows a total of just over £600. And in 1543–4 Exeter had paid more than four and a half times as much to the subsidy.

Leland visited Leicester about the year 1540 and recorded that 'the whole town . . . is builded of timber'. The only brick-work to be seen was that in part of the abbey buildings and the enclosing walls, outside the town to the north, the work of Abbot Penny (1496–1509). Not until the last quarter of the seventeenth century was brick used for domestic building in Leicester. When John Evelyn rode into the town from Upping-ham on an August morning in the year 1654 he saw it as an 'old and ragged city . . . large and pleasantly seated, but despicably built, the chimney flues like so many smiths' forges'. This was much as it would have looked in the latter years of Elizabeth I. Before the 1590's it was indeed even more ragged and decrepit. A commission of enquiry into the state of the house-property belonging to the Crown disclosed, in the autumn of 1587, that there were no fewer than 235 tenements 'in great decay'. In addition there were 406 bays of buildings of which the timber, slates and plaster were 'wholly wasted, carried away, and utterly decayed'. At this date the total number of houses in the town did not greatly exceed six hundred, so that at least one-half the houses of the town were in serious need of repair. The commission reckoned it would cost £5,123 to repair and rebuild the houses belonging to the Crown. Possibly this frightening estimate helped to persuade the Crown to grant the fee-farm of the town to the corporation two years later, so handing over all responsibility for repairs but at the same time reserving a quite handsome annual rent upon all of it.

The details of forty-seven Elizabethan houses, for which inventories survive at Leicester, have been collected together in a table at the end of this chapter. The table has been extended to 1612 on the ground that most if not all the early seventeenth-century houses were standing in Elizabethan times; these houses range in size from the two-roomed dwelling of William Clarke, chapman (1612), to the eleven-roomed houses of William Manby (1586) and Philip Freake (1588). The range excludes the single-roomed houses, if there were any (and they are hard to detect), and also the large late-medieval houses which had been occupied by the wealthy Wigston family in the 1530's, and were probably still standing in Elizabethan times. Thomas Wigston's house in the Newarke had contained seventeen rooms, and William Wigston's at least seventeen besides the wool chambers, the brewhouse and meal-house, and the tavern. It also had a courtyard, and a barn and barnyard, and must have occupied a considerable amount of space off one of the central streets of the town.[17] With its wool chambers and chapel, and its extraordinary wealth of plate and jewels, it was the house of a great medieval merchant of the Staple, the like of which would never be seen again in the town. Its history after the death of Wigston's widow in 1541 is quite unknown: who could have been wealthy enough in Elizabethan Leicester to occupy such a dwelling? As for Thomas Wigston's house, it was replaced before 1601 by the so-called Skeffington house—the new town house of the Skeffingtons, who were well-to-do Leicestershire squires.[18]

The absence of one-roomed cottages from the sample of inventories is not surprising. The poorest class very rarely made a will, having little or nothing to leave; though now and then we come across a labourer who has prospered. The absence of any listing of rooms in some of the smallest inventories (e.g. Cecily Durrand, Roger Shuter, and William Burstall) may well indicate that there was only one room and therefore no need to distinguish where the household goods lay. Most of the poor probably still lived in sub-medieval cottages which consisted essentially of a single room—the hall or "house" —in which a lath and plaster partition towards one end formed a small second room known as the parlour and invariably used for sleeping. The chamberlains' accounts for 1559–60 show that such a single-bayed cottage could be built for just under five pounds. The carpenter was paid three pounds for erecting the timber frame; the 1,100 slates (from Swithland quarries, a few miles away) cost 5s. 10d. and the labour of slating eighteen shillings; the clay, straw, and lime for the walls, and the "torcher" (or dauber, who filled in the timber frame with the clay) cost 15s. 9d. altogether. The total cost of the cottage was

therefore £4 19s. 7d.[19] In the 1590's such cottages were being
leased by the corporation to labourers, poor weavers, and such-
like, at from four to seven shillings a year, rising to eight shillings
where there was a garden instead of merely a "backside".[20]

Where a third room was added it was usually a buttery. This,
too, was sometimes achieved by simply putting a partition
across the hall, as in Richard Ashehill's house (1591) where we
read of "the buttery within the Hall". A kitchen, however,
certainly involved the extension of the house in some way,
probably at the back of the hall. The fact that it involved the
addition of a room and not merely running up a partition inside
the existing house probably explains why a number of houses in
the above list have a buttery but no kitchen. For the average-
sized house above the cottage level, the addition of a kitchen
completed the ground-floor plan, though where there was a
yard on which to build there might be a brew-house, or a
bolting-house (for the sifting and storage of meal), and a
special "workhouse" according to the trade of the occupier.
Larger houses often had a wood-house and a stable. Where
there was no upper floor, the parlour was used for sleeping
with possibly an open loft over it for the children, reached by
means of a ladder.

Where "chambers" are listed in the inventories, they are
generally used as bedrooms (though some are storerooms) and
they almost invariably denote a second floor. The simplest
plan is that of hall, parlour, and buttery or kitchen below, and
one chamber above each, giving a six-roomed dwelling-house.
Where only one chamber is mentioned, it is probably a more or
less boarded-off loft above either hall or parlour, the mere
beginnings of a "bedroom floor". Occasionally a bedroom on
the ground floor is called a "chamber", as in Thomas Rams-
dale's house (1594) where we have "the Chamber next the
Shoppe". Edward Teylier's house (1594) had only one upper
room and that was over the kitchen. Here the hall and parlour
must have remained open to the rafters after the medieval
fashion. Indeed, wherever there are no rooms above, we must
assume that this medieval arrangement still survived, modified
here and there only by some planking which formed a loft in
the roof-space.

The glazing of windows in Leicester, a great advance in domestic comfort, can be dated fairly precisely from the inventories. When the town hall was being repaired in 1560–1 the upper range of windows were merely latticed in the old style, but the windows of the hall and parlour were glazed.[21] The windows of wealthy merchants like the Wigstons were partly glazed even in the late fifteenth century, but these were quite exceptional. Even in the 1560's, prosperous households had no glass windows. Unfortunately we have no inventories for the 1570's (and William Grene was admitted to the freedom of the town as a glazier in 1573), but two inventories in 1586 mention glass. Robert Rodes, shoemaker, had glass in his parlour windows, and William Manby had glass windows in an unspecified number of rooms. By the early 1590's there were four or five glaziers at work in the town, and glass windows soon ceased to be a novelty worthy of a special note in the inventories.[22]

The furnishings of the best Leicester houses show no luxuries at all comparable, for example, with those of the well-to-do merchants of Exeter. Philip Freake's house in Applegate Street (1588) contained cushions, pewter flower-pots, turned chairs, feather-beds, and a certain amount of silver and gilt plate: plenty of comfort but nothing like the house of Richard Bevys at Exeter (1603) which contained—besides all the usual furniture and furnishings—such fripperies as a pair of playing tables and bird-cages in the parlour, window cushions in the fore-hall, water-glasses in the buttery, a pair of virginals and a writing-desk in the "higher fore chamber", a looking-glass in "the little chamber over the Hall", and an extraordinary quantity of linen napery, and of gorgeous apparell. Leicester men were nearer the earth: their personal estate consisted almost entirely of the solid basic furniture, kitchen ware and fire-irons, tools of their trade and stock-in-trade, and, with the bigger men, cattle and sheep scattered over a few fields in the adjoining countryside. No nonsense like looking-glasses and bird-cages and musical instruments. Nor had the successful Leicester man yet graduated to a farm in the country like that of William Chappell, merchant of Exeter (1579), whose house five or six miles out was as large and comfortable as that of a good town house in Leicester at that date, or like that of Richard Bevys

(1603) a mile or so outside the city walls, houses which appear, from their contents, to have been used as summer residences and, no doubt, as convenient refuges from the plague from time to time.

*   *   *

By the end of Elizabeth's reign, considerable changes had taken place in the town of Leicester, not only in its physical appearance but also in its economy and social structure. The disappearance of the Wigstons by 1541 removed from the town a family who had dominated it economically for two or three generations. Their great business of wool-stapling dissolved into nothingness so far as Leicester was concerned, and left a hole that was gradually filled by a number of lesser families—the Reynoldses, Stanfords, Norrises, Tatams, and Herricks. The merchants of the Staple disappear,[23] and their place is taken by the butchers and the tanners. Cattle and not sheep became the economic foundation of Leicester. The excellent Leicestershire wool must have been drained off along other channels after the middle of the century without passing through Leicester at all, presumably going direct to the cloth-manufacturing districts instead of being collected in large quantities at Leicester, Melton Mowbray, and Stamford for export to Calais and the Low Countries.

The rise of the butchers and tanners is the most marked economic change in the town. It is made very evident when one observes that in the thirty-six years between 1559 and 1595 they filled the mayoral chair no fewer than seventeen times, whereas in the seventy-five years before that they had occupied it only three times in all. Nor was it merely a matter of a few successful families in the two trades. The number of admissions to the freedom of the town of butchers, tanners, and glovers shows a great rise between the beginning of the century and the end, while that of the mercers and merchants fell by nearly two-thirds between the first twenty years of the century and the last twenty. Another marked change, though less striking than that of the rise of the butchers and tanners, is the continued decline of the textile trade to the end of the century. Leicester had once had (in the thirteenth century) a considerable cloth industry.

Though much of this disappeared with the invention of the fulling-mill, it was not inconsiderable in the fifteenth century; and even in the first half of Elizabeth's reign about one freeman in every twelve worked or traded in textiles—weavers, shearmen, dyers, and "clothiers". During the second half of the reign the proportion was only one in eighteen—despite the prolonged attempt of the corporation to get a cloth manufacture going—and possibly even these were mainly engaged in the making of stockings by this date.

The rise of certain trades in the social scale, and of certain men within them, presented ticklish problems at times in a society which attached so much importance to degree and rank. In the parish church of St. Martin, attended by most of the successful, the churchwardens 'did place every man and woman according as they grew in substance and credit within the parish into their seats in the church', acting upon their own judgment, except that 'sometimes of their own goodwill' they would ask the Minister's advice when it came to removing difficult parishioners to another seat.[24] This did not save them, however, from the wrath of Mistress Joan Manby, the wife of William Manby, grocer, in 1575. Her husband had twice been mayor of the town—in 1556 and 1568—and was one of its wealthiest inhabitants; and Mistress Manby had been accustomed to sit, after her husband's mayoralty, in the seat behind the wife of the mayor for the time being. All went well as long as one moved forward in church, but when the inevitable time came to drop back a little not all the tact of the churchwardens saved them from being summoned to the Archdeacon's court by an irate woman. We do not hear the result of this suit, but the churchwardens made out a good case that for many years they 'had quietly removed and placed the parishioners of St. Martin's at their pleasure'.

Among the freemen of the town, sons followed their fathers with a high degree of regularity, especially towards the end of the century when the fluidity that had characterized the economic structure of the town in earlier decades solidified into a recognizable pattern and one could see how the new economy was shaping. Between 1580 and 1600, three sons out of four followed in their fathers' footsteps.[25] There is no discernible pattern among those who failed to follow suit. An ironmonger's son became a chandler; a chandler's son became a tanner; a smith's son became a butcher, and so on. The tanners and butchers appear to attract a few youths away from their fathers' trades, as we should expect, but the failure of a son to follow his father's line need not be explained by economic reasons in any generation.

Yet though sons so often followed their fathers' trades, it was rare for a Leicester business to last more than one hundred years. The exceptions stand out very noticeably in the town records. The Newcombes, already noticed, were bell-founders for four generations from about 1500 to 1612. The Herricks prospered as ironmongers from 1534 until 1633; the Tatams were tanners over three or four generations from Thomas, admitted to the freedom in 1526, to John Tatam who was still active in 1624. The Stanfords first appear as butchers in 1537 and continued as such until 1637. The Norrices, as tanners, had the longest run of all, from John Norres, who was elected as one of the four leather testers in 1494 and mayor in 1503, to John Norrice who became mayor in 1639. With his death in 1670 the tanning business ended, after nearly two hundred years. These appear to be the only five businesses which lasted as long as a hundred years in the sixteenth century.

The proceedings of the Common Hall at Leicester in the last year or so of Elizabeth's reign serve to show as well as anything what kind of town it was from one angle at least. In the autumn of 1601, the Hall were making further regulations for the prevention of fire and for the paving of the streets. Then there was the usual fear that "strangers" might come to live in the town and become chargeable to it. Landlords who took in such newcomers were required to enter into a bond that their tenants or lodgers would not become chargeable by reason of poverty; and every alderman was instructed to search his ward for strangers once a fortnight. The increasingly Puritan tone of the town is revealed in the same autumn when it was ordered that every alderman should cause all the ale-houses in his ward to be searched for tipplers in sermon-time and service-time. Some time later they discussed the Sunday closing of shops and warehouses.

The town waits were also taking up a good deal of the Hall's time. They had fallen out among themselves—apparently two fathers quarrelling over the playing of each other's sons—and in September 1602 the exasperated Common Hall, after bearing with months of wrangling, sacked the lot peremptorily A reconstituted company of five were admitted as the town waits on 28 January 1603, being 'skilfull in the knowledge and art of music'. They were to receive as quarterly wages sixpence from each alderman and threepence from each of the Forty-Eight, 'and of the other inhabitants and commoners what they in kindness and good will will give (them)'.

Before the magistrates there appeared the usual procession of petty offenders, charged with fornication, or stealing lead from a church roof, or cutting purses, and offering the same old excuses: Catherine Jervys, accused of cutting a purse in the housewives' market, and asked what she was doing there, replying that "she was agate to buy a pennyworth of salt". Or one Grasbruk, asked to account for a cloak and table napkin in his possession, saying that he bought them off a man who wore "a doublet of dunnish fustian, a grey frieze jerkin, blue nether-stocks, his breeches colour like french green and a blueish cloak and a black hat". And with this striking and improbable figure fresh in mind, we may take our leave of the streets of Elizabethan Leicester.

Houses in Elizabethan Leicester

Date	Name	Occupation	Rooms listed	Total of Inventory
1557	Edmund Carter	(not given)	hall, parlour, kitchen	£11 5 3
1557	William Smythe	saddler	hall, parlour, kitchen, 2 chambers, shop, brewhouse	£33 7 8
1557	William Taylor	smith	hall parlour, buttery, kitchen, 3 chambers, shop	£137 5 4
1557	John Wright	barber	hall, parlour buttery, 2 chambers, shop	£5 6 3

Date	Name	Occupation	Rooms listed	Total of Inventory
1558	Thomas Brown	(not given)	hall, parlour, kitchen	£3 16 0
1558	John Darker	shoemaker	hall, parlour, kitchen, shop	£7 0 8
1558	Edward Glossop	yeoman	hall, parlour, buttery, 3 chambers	£24 16 8
1558	Thomas Harcourte	curate (St. Leonards)	hall, parlour, buttery	£14 14 0
1558	Thomas Keckwick	fishmonger	(not given)	(not known)
1558	William Warde	grocer	hall, parlour, buttery, little parlour, kitchen, chamber, shop	£167 12 4
1563	Richard Woodward	innholder	hall, parlour, kitchen, buttery, 9 chambers, shop	£70 16 6
1564	Thomas Flemynge	butcher	hall, parlour, kitchen, buttery, chamber, maidens' parlour	£152 2 0
1586	Robert Rodes	shoemaker	hall, parlour, buttery, 3 chambers, cheese and malt rooms, brewhouse, shop.	(not given)
1586	William Manby	grocer	hall, parlour, kitchen, buttery, closet, 6 chambers, shop, brewhouse	£359 0 0
1588	John Tatam	tanner	hall, parlour, buttery	£13 10 0
1588	Philip Freake	butcher	hall, parlour, kitchen, buttery, nether parlour, 6 chambers, shop, brewhouse, milkhouse, boultinghouse, tavern	£624 19 6
1589	Roger Shuter	whittawer (tanner of white leather)	(not listed)	£10 1 2
1591	Edward Hyde	(not given)	hall, parlour, buttery, 2 chambers, woodhouse	£56 4 6
1591	William Winterscale	tailor	hall, parlour, kitchen, chamber	£86 0 0

Date	Name	Occupation	Rooms listed	Total of Inventory
1591	Richard Ashehill	'broad weaver'	hall, buttery, 3 chambers, warping chamber, workhouse	£13 16 1
1591	Thomas Woodland	chandler	hall, buttery, 2 parlours	£12 4 0
1583	Cecily Durrand	(widow)	(not listed)	£6 6 3
1593	Henry Bland	bellman of the town	(not listed)	£9 8 3
1594	William Burstall	husband-man	(not listed)	£5 5 0
1594	Thomas Ramsdale	weaver	hall, parlour, kitchen, buttery, 2 chambers	£66 15 2
1594	Edward Teylier	miller	hall, parlour, kitchen, chamber, 'yielding house'	£46 2 4
1594	Robert Molde	haber-dasher	(not listed)	£6 18 2
1595	Ralph Langley	'yeoman'	hall, chamber, 'house'	£61 11 0
1595	John Duce	shoemaster	hall, parlour, kitchen, buttery, 2 chambers, 'little tavern', shop, woodhouse	£39 9 9
1595	William Brewin	tailor	hall, parlour, kitchen, chamber	£19 19 8
1595	Richard Overend	fishmonger	hall, kitchen, buttery, 4 parlours, 3 chambers	£107 15 0
1597	William Hobby	wheelwright	hall, parlour, kitchen, 2 chambers, 'bolting chamber', shop	£120 8 2
1599	Henry Halpennye	chandler	hall, kitchen, buttery, 3 parlours, 2 chambers, shop, brewhouse, inner and outer workhouses	£148 3 2
1600	William Baylie	(not given)	hall, 2 parlours, kitchen, buttery, 3 chambers, 'boultinge house'	£17 10 4
1600	Henry Hauldefeyle	(not given)	hall, parlour, kitchen, buttery, 2 chambers	£21 4 0

Date	Name	Occupation	Rooms listed	Total of Inventory
1602	John Ludlam	chandler	hall, 2 parlours, buttery, chamber, workhouse, limehouse	£54 5 8
1602	Thomas Baylie	salter	hall, 2 parlours, kitchen, buttery, 3 chambers, salthouse	£21 8 4
1602	Eleanor Harvey	(widow)	hall, parlour, chamber, shop	£9 11 1
1602	John Rodes	yeoman*	chamber only	£254 1 4
1603	Christopher Needham the elder	locksmith	hall, buttery, 2 chambers, shop, tavern	£37 7 4
1606	William Wootton	haberdasher	hall, parlour, kitchen, 2 chambers, cellar, shop	£179 15 4
1606	Richard Brewin	butcher	hall, parlour, chamber, slaughter house	£40 18 8
1606	Thomas Walker	glover	hall, parlour, kitchen, buttery, 2 chambers, workhouse	£32 18 4
1612	Margaret Hawes	(widow)	hall, parlour, 'little house'	£24 5 10
1612	John Osseter	carpenter	hall, parlour, buttery, 2 chambers	£27 5 0
1612	Roger Brookesby	tailor	hall, kitchen, buttery, 3 chambers	£28 9 2
1612	William Clarke	chapman	hall, parlour	£8 0 0

* Probably retired from active farming. Hence the one room in a son's house. Most of his estate consisted of cash in hand and money due to him.

NOTES

[1] These remarks about the population of certain Elizabethan towns are based upon various episcopal returns to the Privy Council made in 1563. The surviving returns are to be found in B.M. Harl. MSS. 594, 595, 618.

[2] M. S. Henderson, *Three Centuries in North Oxfordshire* (1902), pp. 258–61.

[3] M. Bateson (ed.) *Records of the Borough of Leicester* (Cambridge 1899–1903), i, pp. 129–45. The total taxed population in the four quarters of the walled town was 570, in the suburbs 116.

[4] D. Charman, 'Wealth and Trade in Leicester in the Early Sixteenth

Century', *Trans. Leics. Arch. Soc.* XXV (1949), p. 74. These figures are based on the number of taxpayers in 1524–5.

⁵ Reproduced as a frontispiece to Bateson, *op. cit.* iii.

⁶ P.R.O., E.179. 133/144 (1543, first payment); E. 179. 133/139 (1544, second payment).

⁷ The payments made by thirty-three towns in 1576 are listed in B.M., Stowe MS. 570, no. 11, f. 106. The list is evidently not complete but allowing for the exclusion of Newcastle, Coventry, and Reading (all wealthier than Leicester) Leicester comes out 30th on the list.

⁸ Charman, *loc. cit.*, p. 84.

⁹ These open spaces were not retained simply for pleasure; merchants and big-scale traders in general needed room for their warehouses, workshops and stables. There was no separation of house and business until a much later date.

¹⁰ This table lists all trades in which there were twelve or more admissions to the freedom in either period.

¹¹ Robert Newcombe, who died about 1558, was the first to do this. The accounts of his executors speak of bark, leather, an ox hide, etc. (Bateson, *op. cit.* iii, p. 97).

¹² What follows is based upon an examination of the annual accounts of the chamberlains among the borough records (Leicester muniment room). The accounts are complete from 1555–6. The borough receipts and expenditure (to the nearest £) from 1558 to 1603 are given in the table on the following page.

¹³ These were let in turn by the borough for eight pounds a year, so showing a profit of four pounds annually.

¹⁴ Sugar first appears in the accounts for 1531–2. It cost 15d. to 16d. a pound at Leicester in the 1550's.

¹⁵ The substance of the following remarks is taken from M. C. Cross, *The Free Grammar School at Leicester* (Department of English Local History, University College, Leicester, Occasional Papers, no. 4.).

¹⁶ *Tudor Economic Documents* (ed. R. H. Tawney and E. Power, 1924), i. p. 108 (1520).

¹⁷ Thomas Wigston's house is described in an inventory dated 18 August 1537 (Leicester muniment room, 1 D.50.ix/5) and William Wigston's (inventory dated 26 July 1536) in *Wyggeston Hospital Records* (Leicester 1933), ed. A. Hamilton Thompson, pp. 39–46. The latter house is described again in his widow's inventory, dated 1541 (Leicester muniment room, 1 D.50.ix/9).

¹⁸ The new house is shown on Speed's map of the town. Sir Thomas Skeffington was sheriff of the county in 1576, 1588, and 1599, and was very active in Leicester. The house probably dates from his time.

¹⁹ I deduce that the cottage was a single-bayed dwelling from the fact that in 1587 it was reckoned that it would cost six pounds to rebuild a single bay of a house (Bateson, *op. cit.*, iii, p. 239). The difference between £5 and £6 is accounted for, of course, by the rise in building costs (like all others) since 1560.

[20] Leicester muniment room. Deeds, 20 D.52 (various).

[21] Chamberlains' accounts, 1560–1, *loc. cit.*

[22] Hoskins, *Essays in Leicestershire History* (Liverpool 1950), pp. 111–12.

[23] The admission of a Merchant of the Staple to the freedom as late as 1582–3 was due only to the special invitation of the corporation of Leicester who were still vainly trying to establish a cloth manufacture in the town.

[24] Leicester muniment room: Archdeaconry Court Proceedings, 4/113 and 4/156 (1575).

[25] Out of sixty-two examples where the facts are known, sons followed fathers in forty-six. In the 1570's, out of twenty examples, eleven sons followed suit, nine did not; but the sample is perhaps too small to be worth comment.

Year	Receipts*	Expenditure	Year	Receipts	Expenditure
	£	£		£	£
1558–9	58	30	1580–1	197	136
1559–60	74	44	1581–2	147	128
1560–1	89	39	1582–3	85	74
1561–2	101	39	1583–4	125	120
1562–3	120	55	1584–5	76	101
1563–4	126	85	1585–6	55	67
1564–5	88	67	1586–7	68	80
1565–6	120	84	1587–8	58	67
1566–7	103	61	1588–9	60	63
1567–8	110	71	1589–90	92	97
1568–9	127	82	1590–1	207	199
1569–70	161	97	1591–2	194	210
1570–1	161	87	1592–3	177	223
1571–2	161	114	1593–4	267	264
1572–3	117	119	1594–5	218	186
1573–4	230	187	1595–6	359	340
1574–5	134	85	1596–7	251	228
1575–6	136	90	1597–8	327	266
1576–7	165	183	1598–9	440	430
1577–8	89	76	1599–1600	367	358
1578–9	111	88	1600–1	398	389
1579–80	79	72	1601–2	353	382
			1602–3	363	387

* Including the surplus of the previous year (if any). In 1558–9 the sum of £9 4s. 10½d. was brought forward from the preceding year.

III

The English Woman,
1580–1650

WALLACE NOTESTEIN

III

Most of those scholars who have by means of books and manuscripts taken up residence and settled down in the late-sixteenth and early-seventeenth-century England would admit, I suspect, that they have never felt wholly at home. They have found themselves among strangers with whom they could never become intimately acquainted and about whom they could not form assured judgments. The men of those days had backgrounds and traditions, ideas and standards, so removed from ours that they remain to us shadowy figures. Much more shadowy are the women. Only a few women left diaries or autobiographies; not many wrote letters that have been preserved. Our knowledge of women comes largely from the incidental mention of them by men who seldom took pains to characterize and individualize them. But it is as individuals that we must know them, if we are to understand them as members of a sex. For such knowledge we must always be on the look-out even if we find less than we would. To get at the inwardness of the every-day life of a past generation we need to know as much about the women as about the men. If we could attain to some comprehension of a good many women in every group of society in the early seventeenth century we might see through a glass less darkly.[1]

For such a study more materials exist than can be explored thoroughly in this brief essay. The diaries, autobiographies, and letters already alluded to are fundamental, but records of almost every kind contain references to women. Even local documents have their use: household inventories, churchwardens' accounts, orders of quarter sessions, and minutes of boroughs.

Literary sources must be examined as well. Fortunately the dramatists put women in their plays, and more women, as time went on. It will at once be asked, how trustworthy are the plays as evidence. The New York or London theatrical performances of today would offer a warped representation of American or English life. The same is true of the late-sixteenth and early-seventeenth-century plays as to their time. The plots were drawn, many of them, from Italian, and some from Spanish and classical sources, and were often improbable and even fantastic; they were full of violence and cruelty, of adultery and murder. Those plots we may leave out of account as having little resemblance to English everyday life. What interests us is the occasional and incidental remarks about women. One has indeed to read scores of plays to collect enough comment to add up to any body of social criticism. The comments are, of course, those of the dramatists themselves, of men. But these men knew not a little about their wives and sisters and female cousins, and were furthermore men of more than usual intelligence. Some of them were better informed of the trends of the time than the political figures. Their judgments as to society and the changes taking place in it, are often amply supported by other evidence, and, if there are enough of those judgments, and if they are in agreement, they cannot be overlooked. Even then they must be used with caution. Literary men tended to exaggerate social differences and sometimes to make a rare instance seem a custom. They used certain literary conventions and they drew upon older literary sources that may be wide of the mark for the early seventeenth century.

The romantic poetry of the time ought to afford information about women. In innumerable lyrics we read of Phyllis, of Delia and Daphne, fancy shepherdesses, who played Theocritan parts in an English setting, and who had expressive eyes and lovely complexions, and other bodily assets, and were, according to convention, hard to win. One can read hundreds of poems written by competent versifiers with some gift of phrase and metre and by such good poets as Robert Herrick and Samuel Daniel and others, and yet learn little about women. The effusions of the poets on that subject seem artificial and dull. Even the more intellectual of them, like Ben Jonson and John Donne, limited themselves largely to extolling the graciousness and goodness and piety of the female sex, though Donne sometimes indulged in profaner thoughts. The reader looks eagerly to find allusions to what women had to offer their mates, and looks in vain. It was otherwise in Scotland where the lyric poets of the fifteenth and sixteenth centuries sang of the well of womanhood, of love's observance, and of the "joy inwart" afforded men by their partners. Their beautiful and profound expressions of the feminine resources of spirit have never been bettered. It is a strange fact and one that bears thinking about that the English lyric poets of the early seventeenth century, unlike the dramatists, had little of interest to say about women.

The pamphlets and booklets of the time are full of references to women and their ways. Women were fickle, foolish, and given to making cuckolds of their husbands. The writers remind us of Rosalind's old religious uncle who railed against the female sex. When Orlando asked what were the principal evils with which her uncle charged women, Rosalind replied: 'There were none principal; they were all like one another . . . every fault seeming monstrous till his fellow fault come to match it'. Those slurs by the scribblers of the time, "spent poets", and "superannuated bachelors," were not the outcome of careful observation, but a kind of standard patter, with which it was easy to fill pages, secondhand stuff derived from Italian sources and from medieval and ancient writings.[2] The student of the period picks up book after book, hoping to find interesting comment, and comes upon long narratives of female inconstancy and folly designed to appeal to sex interest. There was so much literature of that kind that it might well seem to the casual reader the fashion of the time to underrate women.[3]

However lightly such complaints were to be taken, the censure of women in the more serious writings of the time, especially in the letters of men, was another matter. That women were less mature than men was asserted. They were as wise at fifteen as at fifty, wrote an embittered but thoughtful earl in a long letter of advice to his son. 'Our wives', wrote another man to a friend, 'as well as other men's must be children', and added that what they wanted they must have at once. A young diplomat whose sisters caused him worry, suspected that women were stirred with less wind and given to passionateness, and this opinion of the sex was not uncommon. To men who cherished a Roman ideal of pursuing the mean, or moderate course, passion was a form of childishness. The quarrelsomeness of women, as another indication of their immaturity, was deplored by a generation of men who were always carrying on family feuds or challenging their fellows to duels.

Women were believed to be more humorous than men, that is, more capricious and temperamental. Rosalind outlined to Orlando what he must expect in a wife:

> I will be more jealous than a Barbary cock-pigeon; more clamorous than a parrot against rain, more new-fangled than an ape; more giddy in my desires than a monkey—I will weep for nothing . . . and I will do that when you are disposed to be merry. I will laugh like a hyen, and that when you are inclined to sleep.

She went on to remark of her sex, "the wiser the waywarder", a comment that makes us think of George Meredith's Marian.

The charge that women had not enough to do was levelled against the great ladies of court and the wives of well-to-do business men in London and in country towns. Such women could procure nurses for their children and find among their less fortunate kin gentlewomen to manage their households for them. They were to be seen on the street going from one shop to another and chatting with their friends. The city women who cross the pages of John Chamberlain's letters were obviously hard put to it to fill in their days. The country women in those letters were less restless but occupied themselves with elaborate gardens. Now and then a woman dabbled in medicine, or music, or painting, or even astrology. It might be said in defence of women that most of them up to the age of forty-five were too busy bringing children into the world to need other occupations. It was possibly the elder ladies who impressed the public with their idleness and restlessness.

It was asserted that women were more conventional than men. They followed precedents and custom, said the Earl of Northumberland already mentioned, they did what others did, and not what was fit for them. No doubt women were inclined to accept the codes of their class. Even in the days of her poverty Alice Thornton, who never forgot whose daughter she was, was determined to live up to the old conventions of the gentry. Not

far behind her in subservience to the standards of her group was
Lady Harley of Bryan Brampton Castle. Whether the gentlewomen whom John Chamberlain met on his visits to the
country were more conventional than their husbands I cannot
say. The seventeenth-century gentleman was seldom given to
"novelties" and he kept in step with his well-born neighbours.
If once in a while an eccentric gentleman in a remote country
house caused whispers over the countryside, even his odd ways
were likely to follow ancestral patterns. The eccentric woman,
unless of great birth, would not have been readily tolerated.
Women were not allowed the leeway granted to men.

It was said on the other hand that women were less conventional than they should be. When young women were involved in the business of mating they were sometimes thought
to be wanting in conformity to established standards. Three
hundred years before Bernard Shaw made his discovery about
the female sex, it was written that women were the wooing sex,
and in many a play they were so represented. Do we not know,
says a character in a play, that women are most wooers,

> Though closest in their carriage.

Heywood makes a woman say:

> This is the fashion that's but late come up
> For maids to court their husbands.

In Wit Without Money both the portly widow, a "woman of
presence", and her sister did the courting and in the grand
manner. John Chamberlain marked the way of a maid with a
man, and particularly the ways of widows, and his letters would
convince any reader that women were often the pursuers.

Their unconventionality went further. Women allowed
themselves now and then to become the talk of the neighbourhood. Sir Francis Willoughby of Wollaton Hall had a self-
willed daughter about whom the mother wrote to the father:
'She is so great with Mr. Candish's son that she is fully minded
to have him . . . Whether you like it or not it must go forwards
and be a match.' The mother was bound to London and had
been told by a servant that both the daughter and young
Cavendish planned to go along, and 'the riding, flawning,

roisting, and flirting by the way will be such that every ostler will talk of it'. Of a widow Chamberlain wrote that she would play cards with Tom Hatton till midnight, and twice a week would be in his rooms before he was up. 'I know not', commented the staid bachelor, 'what to say to the widows of this age, nor what privileges they pretend.'

Hoydenish young women were to be found in all classes and appear in many types of records. Sometimes they gave parents anxiety. Marry your daughters betimes lest they marry themselves, was a saying in the shires. Most of the less conventional young women settled down with marriage. Bearing a child almost every year was a taming experience. But other young women, like their brothers, had a coltish streak in them and were not easily broken to harness. Now and then a young woman of good stock, the daughter of a gentleman or of a citizen, might become the lady of delight of some nobleman or country gentleman, bear him a child or two, and live at some remote dwelling. Once in a while such a young woman drifted to London and fared worse. The fate of Shakespeare's talented sister, as imagined by Virginia Woolf, was not improbable.

The criticism of women was not lessened by the behaviour of the great ladies of the Court, who took advantage of their position and were seldom called to account. Unlike other women of the time they sought the spotlight and rendered themselves often unpleasantly conspicuous. At masks and fancy-dress parties they imbibed too freely and sometimes ruined the costumes of those near them and had to be carried out; a few of them in recesses of balconies behind screens took liberties. Their goings-on afforded rare gossip for Paul's walkers and opportunities to be censorious for the writers of moral tracts and of less moral plays. Slowly the stories of a vulgar Court, however hushed up, reached the ears of quiet gentlemen in Nottinghamshire and Devonshire and no doubt confirmed them in the old opinion that women needed a strong hand over them.

The praise of women is as significant as the blame. When Milton wrote of his late-deceased wife,

> Love, sweetness, goodness in her person shined,

he hit upon those qualities most commended in women. The

tenderness and affection they bestowed upon their mates were celebrated in funeral sermons and epitaphs, in autobiographies and plays.

There is no comfort in this world,

wrote Deloney, compared to women that are kind, and this judgment is to be found throughout the literature of the time. In *The Taming of the Shrew* Hortensio says:

> Kindness in women, not their beauteous looks,
> Shall win my love.

Shakespeare, Massinger, and other dramatists have left us heroines memorable for their devotion to their partners. Patient Griselda in the ballad and in the play and Celia in *The Humourous Lieutenant* displayed a loving adhesiveness that was not unwelcome. So much emphasis did men place upon warmth of feeling in their wives that when Lord Harington proposed his son for Salisbury's daughter, the great minister answered in an amazing letter that his own daughter promised little real affection.

The affection women offered gave men freedom from care. They cheer us, said an Elizabethan, when we are melancholy and redeem us from the gates of hell, that is, I suppose, from fits of depression. They are sovereign cordials, it was declared, and renew men as spring renews the year.

The quiet behaviour of women was reckoned one of their graces. They were expected to keep in the background. In a play it was put thus:

> A retir'd sweet life,
> Private and close, and still, and housewifely,
> Becomes a wife, sets off the grace of woman.

Even today there is the English woman who has little to say in the presence of men, unless called upon. Her type was more common in the early seventeenth century. Silence in women was esteemed a great virtue by poets, playwrights, and biographers.[4]

Women were constantly praised for their good housekeeping. In many a church it is set down on a brass against the wall that the wife had maintained a well-ordered household. To do so a woman had to be thrifty, a virtue not overlooked by the makers of epitaphs, to keep children and servants under control, to provide clean and sweet linen, and to be ready at all times for guests. In an occasional autobiography a man gave his wife credit for good management; visitors at country houses observed it in their hostesses. It was the result of an attention to detail which Thomas Fuller had the wit to recognize as a gift of womankind.

For nothing were they more extolled than for obedience to their lords and for the patience that went with obedience. Biographers liked to expatiate on this virtue in wives, and clergymen in funeral sermons alluded to it, perhaps with a glance towards a certain pew. Mothers instructed their daughters in the duty and set an example to them. The young Margaret Lucas, writing to her future husband, the then Marquis of Newcastle, seemed to feel pleasure in thinking of her future obedience to him. In a Dekker play a woman admires her husband because he makes her obey, and in a Heywood play a character exclaims of a wife-to-be, "A perfect wife, already meek and patient". The dramas *Patient Grissil* and *The Taming of the Shrew* were in line with old traditions and must have been well received by husbands.

So prevalent was the social prejudice in favour of feminine subordination that men were wary of allying themselves with strong-minded ladies. In a play Vitellius shows himself greatly attracted by Clara but is reluctant to marry her, and warns her that she is of so great a spirit that he would have to wear the petticoat and she assume the breeches. She hastens to reassure him; love hath expelled all but her softness; every day she will grow more pliable. Her admirer decides to hold out no longer. The story of John Pym is similar but with another ending. He was encouraged by a "brave-spirited gentlewoman", but was fearful of her "greatness of spirit," and looked another way. Yet in plays now and then women of great force of character, like Bonducca (Boadicea), were held up for admiration on account of their masculine virtues.

Women were seldom praised for their charm, a word little used at that time, but they were represented by dramatists as behaving in what we would regard as charming ways. In our day the word is overworked to cover many feminine qualities. It is used of women who draw men out to talk of themselves, who persuade them to think better of themselves, and who sympathize with them in their troubles. No doubt women in the seventeenth century must have understood such wiles but they were seldom represented as resorting to them. It was their liveliness, their high spirits, and their natural friendliness that rendered them charming. Robert Burton, a donnish old bachelor who wrote *The Anatomy of Melancholy*, must have come upon attractive women for he quoted Fonseca with approval: 'There's something in a woman beyond all human delight, a magnetic virtue, a charming quality, an occult and powerful motive'. We all recall the Egyptian queen who was extolled for her infinite variety, and perhaps not so readily the other lady in a play of whom it was said:

> She will drive
> Tediousness out of time with her sweet character.

Who could have been more charming than Rosalind, or Miranda, or Celia in *The Humourous Lieutenant*, or Bessie Bridges in *The Fair Maid of the West*? Mary Lady Wroth could lure Ben Jonson to her Essex home, and Lady Winwood and Lady Fanshawe were magnets to get John Chamberlain on horse for the country, away from his beloved City. When we think of charming women we must never forget Sidney's sister, Pembroke's mother; nor Penelope Rich, for whom Sir Philip Sidney made hymns of immortal praise, and whose sins men could not but condone; nor the most adorable of all seventeenth-century women, Dorothy Osborne.

It will not have escaped the reader that both the blame and praise of women were based in most instances upon the assumption of their intellectual inferiority and of their subordination to the ruling sex.

That they were intellectually inferior, which is far from saying that they were mentally inferior, may well be admitted by those who have read the letters of the women of that time. Women wrote of their household affairs, of the illnesses of their children, of their troubles with servants, of recent marriages and christenings, and of their own pregnancies, matters that fell naturally

within their purview but that seldom lead the reader on with
suspense. They were matter-of-fact, as were indeed most men.
Few women were able in writing to express lively personalities.
They must not be too much blamed. Writing was an effort;
some of them did not form script easily; not many were adept
at framing a good sentence; most of them wanted something
in clearness and cogency of statement. Anne Lady Clifford was
a great lady who presided eventually over five castles in the
North, a determined woman, who feared neither king, nor
secretary of state, nor archbishop, nor the weakness of age, nor
the angel of death. But her letters, ill spelled and ill put
together, reveal little of the power of her personality. What
shall we say of the epistles of less vivid gentlewomen but that
few of them would repay a second reading, except by the intent
scholar?

About the talk of women we know little except from plays,
and few dramatists were as yet able to present natural talk, or to
develop a character by showing her way of speaking.[5] It was an
old opinion that women did not stick to the point, but would
bring up twenty tales nothing to the purpose. That weakness
was of course the result of their want of education, to be discussed later. They were blamed with being repetitious in their
conversation, 'for few varieties can flow from few knowledges'.

If the women of the more fortunate classes seem to the
modern reader not overly interesting, what are we to expect of
the women in country villages? About them we have unhappily
less information than we could wish. Sir William D'Avenant,
who was used to good company, makes an unflattering allusion
to such females:

> I choose
> None of your dull country madams, that spend
> Their time in studying receipts to make
> Marchpane and preserve plums, that talk
> Of painful childbirth, servants' wages, and
> Their husband's good complexion and his leg.

Glapthorne has an even more scornful picture of village
women at a christening with the parson's wife leading the conversation. The dramatists may have been a little hard on women
whose experience was limited. One must suspect from some

acquaintance with country districts today that even in the seventeenth century an occasional village woman was earthy and even racy. Some of Shakespeare's humbler women were by no means commonplace.

The assumption of the subordination of women, implicit in the blame and praise of them, hardly needs other justification. It is best revealed in the letters women wrote their husbands; they were eager to please them, they leaned upon them as having superior judgment, they were often afraid of them. But in no way was their subordination more evident than in their want of influence over them. Too fearful they were of their lords and masters to venture upon disagreement. When Lady Harley wished her husband to do something she would ask her son at Oxford to raise the question with his father. Philip Stubbes admired his wife and wrote: 'She would never contrary him in anything, but by wise counsel and politic advice, with all humility and submission, seek to persuade him'.

Occasionally in a play a woman would implore her husband to take another course, usually a less risky one, but with no success. The man knew best. When women in real life attempted to reform their errant spouses they faced even greater odds than women in a like situation in our time. We do happen upon two instances where women succeeded in that effort. One comes from John Aubrey, whose gossip was not completely dependable, and the other from a family mentioned in the *Verney Papers*. It was a time when women who could have held out a steadying hand would have been useful. Young men, who had perhaps inherited from feudal forebears a touch of wildness, or who had been brought up the darlings of their families and of the servants, were likely when they came into their inheritances to go their own furious ways and ruin themselves and possibly dissipate their holdings. Someone at home they dearly needed to restrain them and above all to laugh at them, a rôle seldom allowed to women.

The women of all classes suffered in varying degrees under handicaps. Their want of education was possibly their fundamental disadvantage. To realize the difference of opportunity between boys and girls we have to recall the thorough grammar school education given the young males. From seven or eight to

6

fourteen or fifteen a considerable proportion of boys was put through a hard disciplinary drill in Latin. They had to learn to read and write the language, to compose essays, to form close-knit arguments and to debate in it. It was no doubt a narrow training but unequalled for developing the power of orderly thought. Furthermore, it opened to young men, at a time when they had no large body of English literature at hand, the wisdom and history and traditions of the ancient civilized world.

For the sisters of those boys few schools were available and those of inferior quality. We know little about the schools for girls.[6] Some of them were managed by French and Dutch immigrants who made a living in England by setting up schools in and around London. In such schools the girls were taught to play on musical instruments, to sing and dance, to do needle-work, to read, and possibly to talk French. Here and there were women like the Countess of Huntingdon and like the grand-mother of Sir John Bramston, who took in the daughters of their friends and gave them training. There is no reason to believe that in such schools or in other schools the girls had a chance at Latin. It is true that girls were sometimes tolerated among the "petties" in the grammar schools, but only up to the age of nine. If given Latin at all, they would only have made a beginning at it. There was opinion indeed that they should not be taught Latin. Among the proverbs listed by George Herbert was one to take heed of a Latin-bred woman. The Elizabethan Earl of Cumberland provided carefully for the education of his daughter, Anne Clifford, but stipulated that she was not to be taught Latin, though that young woman would have enjoyed Seneca and Horace. Ralph Verney, not one of the conventional men of his day, wrote his uncle about his god-daughter: 'Let not your girl learn Latin'. Nancy did not agree. She wrote her godfather that she meant to outreach him in Hebrew, Greek, and Latin.

No doubt Miss Nancy had a tutor. Among the more cultivated gentry the father might retain a curate, or the vicar, or his own chaplain, or an intelligent gentlewoman to teach his daughters, and the clerical instructors would have found it a hardship not to give lessons in the language they had mastered.

Few women, however, were so fortunate. Not to be able to read Latin was to go in blinkers. The ancient modes of thought and the ancient wisdom familiar to the intelligent gentry, to the better lawyers, and to clergymen and physicians, were beyond the ken of their wives. In his *Forest Promiscuous* Dudley North hit the nail on the head when he wrote:

'Tis but your education keeps them blind.

Another handicap of women, closely related to their lack of education, was that in many cases they had little association with their husbands in their interests and activities. It is often said that women enjoy men's talk and miss it when they are deprived of it. The early-seventeenth-century woman found herself sometimes almost cut off from the male world. If her husband were a reading man, familiar with the Roman writers, she could not hope to live on the same plane with him. If the husband were of the more common type, a hunting gentleman who spent the day in the fields and some of his evenings over a bottle, his partner had little chance of companionship with him, unless he happened to be idle.

The gentlemen saw much of one another, at assizes and quarter sessions, at fairs and markets, and on occasional hunts; they lunched with neighbours in the county at inns recognized as rendezvous. They went visiting their kind, which included many families within the shire, only now and then taking their wives with them. In high feudal days men had gone off to war and left the women in the castle. Castles had given way largely to unfortified houses, but old habits remained, and men were still those on horseback, the roving sex. It was a man's world, and few imagined any other. Slowly through the decades of the seventeenth century, women were drawn more into the community life. More often women were accompanying their husbands on visits, even going with them to London; not for a long while yet did they go hunting with them. We are talking, of course, of gentlemen and their mates, about whom we know most, and who did after all set the standards of the time. About the humbler folk we had best say little. Their men were, of course, less mobile and thus thrown more into association with their wives.

But even when men and women were at home together there was often a dividing line. The business and political affairs of men were for men. It was an old notion that the prudent man looked after his property interests and determined his conduct and policies himself, consulting possibly a few friends and male relatives, but that he did not take into his confidence the distaff side of the house. Women, it was widely believed, could not keep secrets. When Portia in *Julius Caesar* implores Brutus to tell her what is worrying him, he puts her off, and most of the audience at the play would have thought he did well. But among those present there would have been some ready to feel the justice of Portia's words:

> Tell me, Brutus,
> Is it excepted I should know no secrets
> That appertain to you . . .
> Dwell I but in the suburbs
> Of your good pleasure? If it be no more
> Portia is Brutus' harlot, not his wife.

For there were gentlemen not a few who did talk over their most intimate affairs with their partners.

A third handicap of women was the subordination imposed upon them as children. The little people were in most families taught to be silent before their elders and utterly submissive. Aubrey declared that in his young manhood parents were as severe with their children as schoolmasters, and schoolmasters as severe as masters in a house of correction. Sir William D'Avenant blamed parents for abusing their authority over their offspring, frightening them out of their wits and enforcing rough discipline. He added that as children grew older the parents made strangers of them, and such a policy was exactly what many parents believed wise. Philip Stubbes urged fathers to keep austerity and distance between themselves and their children, and his opinion would have been that of many fathers. No wonder that few of those who have left narratives of their childhood looked back upon it with pleasure. It was of course worse for daughters than for sons, who were often away at school. Moreover mothers, who were no doubt kinder than fathers, deemed it their duty nevertheless to bring up their daughters to be "pliable", and utterly obedient,[7] so that they would be more readily sought in marriage. Frances Coke wrote to her husband of a young woman that she had been brought up by her mother to be of a very mild disposition and not uneasy to be governed. In *The Maid's Tragedy* Aspasia says:

> We fond women
> Harbour the easiest and smoothest thoughts.

They had been bred to do so. In another play Flavia says:

> Our sex is most wretched, nurs'd up from infancy
> in continual slavery.[8]

A fourth handicap of women was that they were often married by the arrangements of their parents, and thus had limited opportunities or none to experience romance at the mating age. Young men suffered in the same way but they were less bound down to the home and could readily evade the plans of their fathers for them.

It must not be supposed that young women did not have their own ideas about their future mates. Those ideas were seldom stated in letters, for the young women wrote few, but the playwrights afford us information on the subject that may be worth something and that is occasionally confirmed by the letters of parents.

The girls were often worldly then as now, and sought in their future mates wealth and sovereignty, lordships and manors, and those outward symbols, coaches and horses. Some of them desired above all things to be "ladified", that is to wear a title. Strangely enough, it was rare that a young woman craved a husband who was going to thrive. In one instance a young man was recommended in a letter as a matrimonial prospect because his law practice was on the increase, but we may doubt whether the daughter to be married would have been greatly interested. Good acres in view were safer than success in the future. In a Shirley play, however, Lucilla, who seems hardly a proper seventeenth-century young woman, inquires closely about her suitor's thrift and plans, remarking:

> 'Tis an age
> For men to cast about them.

Possibly daughters of citizens in London and in the larger towns might have shared Lucilla's notions. The widow in Plymouth hoped that her wooer, the sea-captain, would bring home honour and rich prizes, but was going to marry him in any case and pay his debts.

Other young women in the plays were more conventional. They looked for husbands of valour and honour, for men who did not talk too much nor too boastfully. They valued comeliness in the man, handsome attire, and a dignified bearing.

Many young women demanded the sober virtues. In a Marston play Rosaline craves a partner

> Of steady judgment, quick and nimble sense.

Steadiness was valued most by parents, but also by daughters in plays and in letters. A young lady of high birth was unwilling to marry either of two great nobles of the time because they were young and fantastical. An older man who had settled down was more to her liking. Some of the women in plays hoped for mates who would give them content; more spoke of kindness as the essential desideratum in a partner. Margaret Verney wished goodness in a man and so did many a female character on the stage.

A few young women in plays were romantic. To be loved for herself alone and not regarded merely as a piece of household furniture was the aspiration of one young woman. Some girls put it the other way round, that they would forgo riches and rank for one whom they loved for himself alone. A woman declined a suitor in these words:

> You're for greatness:
> I dare not deal with you. I have found my match,
> And I will never lose him.

The romantic hopes of young women, at least in the moneyed classes, were seldom realized and those who desired in their husbands good looks and seemly attire, or the solid virtues, had sometimes to compromise with their ideals. The women who had worldly aspirations had more chance of gaining the helpmates they craved. The marriages arranged for them by parents were based largely on property considerations, with rank and old family not overlooked. The reader of Elizabethan and early Stuart letters hardly recovers from his astonishment at the mercenary way in which parents planned the marriages of their children. They were the more inclined to take pains in such matters because many of them were subject to old feudal tenures that were an anachronism but still on the statute books. Among feudal incidents was the right of the king to the wardship of heirs, to take for himself their incomes during their minorities and to marry heiresses to the highest bidder. The Court of Wards caused gentlemen great expense and worry about their heirs or heiresses and tended to make them matchmakers. Moreover they were bound by community opinion to busy themselves about the marriages of their sons and daughters. Those who failed to make good matches for their progeny, or who left a daughter unbestowed, were censured by the neighbours and indeed by the children themselves. There was another good reason why parents came to the fore in all the marital plans for their children. It was they who had to make settlements upon their sons and provide dowries for their daughters. Young people in the propertied world were not supposed to marry without an income.

As soon as a girl approached a marriageable age, say fifteen or sixteen, her parents were likely to write letters to other families in the county or in the next county, or elsewhere, proposing the daughter for a son of the other family. It was deemed not in the least unbecoming for Sir Thomas to suggest to Sir George that his daughter Jane would make a suitable wife for Sir George's son, Philip. In offering his daughter as a possible wife Sir Thomas was expressing his good opinion of Sir George's family. Sir George might fall in with the proposal or he might answer that he had other plans or had made other arrangements already.

The proposals for a family alliance were often made through intermediaries. The Countess of Bedford constituted herself a matchmaker among her friends in London. Marriage brokers may now and then have been employed. But it was more usual for a father or mother of a marriageable daughter to ask a common friend to sound out another family as to the possibility of a marriage arrangement. 'A business of this nature', wrote

a contemporary, 'is first to be treated of by friends.' Lady
Verney asked John Coke to deal with the Naunton family on
behalf of her daughter, Moll, and, if Moll were out of the
question, for Nan. Occasionally the steward of the family was
given authority to look out for a match. Now and then friends
pressed their services upon a family.

The settlements and dowries were reckoned closely and the
family lawyers were called in. Social position and financial
status were reckoned realistically and balanced carefully. A
merchant who married his daughter to the heir of an old and
well-known county family was expected to offer a handsome
dowry.

What part did the young people concerned play in these
negotiations? They had been brought up, especially the
daughters, to believe that in such matters father and mother
knew best, and that it was a religious duty to obey them. But
they were human beings and now and then they fell in love.
Some of them had read narratives of

> Old loves and wars for ladies done by many a lord,

and had caught romantic notions from them.[9] They were as
romantic as the young women already mentioned who had
their existence in plays. The ballad-makers and the romancers
were in favour of the lovers[10] as against designing parents.
A contemporary composer of ballads, Thomas Deloney, told
how a father had compelled his daughter, in spite of her sighs
and sobs, to marry where was gold and silver. The union
resulted in continual strife, the girl consented to the murder of
her husband and was executed. The dramatists were as opposed
as the ballad-makers to enforced marriages. 'Made marriages
prove mad marriages', declared one of the persons in a play. In
another play Mendoza spoke

> As one that knows inforced marriage
> To be the Furies' sister.

Enlightened parents were aware of the rising opinion against
such marriages. Some of them moved slowly in mating their
children and took into account the wishes of the young people.
Such parents became more in evidence towards the mid-

seventeenth century. Not uncommonly in the bargains they made about the matches of their children they put in a saving clause, if the young people, after seeing one another, develop a "liking", or a "kindness". Other parents were from the beginning of negotiations willing to allow their offspring a negative. The knowing Anne Clifford at the age of fifteen gained a promise from her father that her mother, whom she counted her ally, should have a veto about her marriage.

If parents failed in making the arrangements they deemed suitable for their daughters, they resorted occasionally to other measures, and those measures afforded the daughter more opportunity to make a love-match. A girl was sent away to be a kind of honourable maid-in-waiting to some great lady in London or in the country. There she could learn courtly manners and meet young gentlemen in attendance upon his lordship, or visitors at the castle or house. Other methods of marrying daughters were used, if necessary. Sir John Oglander had a daughter whom he regarded as the loveliest in the Isle of Wight. The possible men in the Island had been carefully considered and none had been deemed worthy. At length Sir John wrote to his son at Gray's Inn, telling him that the family was sending the daughter to visit her aunt in London and suggesting that possibly the son could find a proper mate for his sister. The son acquiesced readily in the scheme, not a foolish one. We read in the records of the time of young women who married the friends or room-mates of their brothers at the university or at one of the Inns of Court. That young women at home in country houses had few opportunities to meet young men of their own status might well have been given as a reason why arranged marriages were necessary.

Arranged marriages, whether necessary or not, worked a special hardship in cases where older men were joined to very young women. The rate of mortality among young wives meant that many a man married three or four times. In the third or fourth venture he might be intent upon finding a mate young enough to assure him of a male heir. Hence it was not uncommon for a man of forty-five to marry a girl of eighteen. It was not hard for him to command such a bride and from his own class. Parents were in many cases only too glad to bestow their daughters upon a man of settled habits and of an assured income. If the bride seldom fell in love with her husband, or indeed remained always afraid of him, as she had been of her father, that was her misfortune.

A fifth handicap of women was that they spent the years from eighteen to forty-five in the business of bearing children.[11] That meant that they were unwell much of the time. If they survived the perils of childbirth, and the illnesses that followed frequent pregnancies, they bore from eight to fifteen children (including stillbirths). To the reader of family letters it would appear that women were always in a state of expectancy. John Chamberlain was constantly alluding to the great bellies—a common and wholly proper phrase then—of his feminine friends. John Donne, who ran away with and secretly married the daughter of a well-known Surrey gentleman, Sir George More, had twelve children by her in the sixteen years of their married life, she dying at thirty-three. Justice Bramston wrote of his wife: 'She was the mother of ten children in the twelve years that she was a wife, though when she died she left only two sons, one of whom survived a short time'. Frances Clark wrote to her father, Sir John Oglander, 'This day month . . . I was brought abed with a son, which is my tenth child, and pray God . . . it may be my last'.[12]

Women were always facing the possibility of death at the next accouchement.[13] Mrs. Thornton was terrified before the arrival of her children. Her sister, Lady Danby, died at thirty, after bearing sixteen children, including six still-births, and received her approaching change with much satisfaction. The story of what happened to women is written in stone in many an English church.

The women had to endure more than childbirth and the fear of it. Again and again their hearts must have been wrung with the deaths of their infants. Statistics on infant mortality would be hard to collect and impossible to verify. I suspect, if stillbirths be included, that women lost two-thirds of their children before the children were four years of age. They watched at the bedsides of those little things as they died of convulsions or of some inexplicable illness, and, if they mentioned the blow in a diary or letter, recorded it in a matter-of-fact way. Only once in a while can we catch the anguish of the mother.

They had to witness also the deaths of many daughters who survived babyhood and then between the ages of fourteen and twenty died of what was called consumption. The cold and unventilated houses made for tuberculosis. The men escaped because they were out of doors much of the time.

A sixth handicap of women arose from the artificiality of manners imposed upon them. The formal treatment of women as exalted beings, a relic of chivalry, implied their weakness, assumed their inferiority, and made natural conversation with men difficult. Shakespeare makes Hermione say:

> Cram us with praise and make us
> As fat as tame things

Aspasia was cynical in her advice to her sex:

> Learn to be flattered, and believe and bless
> The double tongue that did it.

A self-respecting woman must have grown weary of all the compliments paid her sex, many of them less than sincere. She was compelled to play a part and her thoughts were sometimes far from what she said. It could not be otherwise. Married in many cases without affection, she had afterwards to pretend to it:

> Alas! poor wenches . . .
> Go learn to love first, to lose yourselves.
> . . . .
> Make a faith out of the miracles of ancient lovers.

The woman, if she were to keep the home smooth, learned to be an actress. She was expected to accept the friends of her husband, even his female friends, to ignore unfaithfulness, and to make the best of unhappy situations.

A seventh handicap of women is closely related to those already mentioned, their own realization that they were inferior beings, "men's shadows" as a nobleman put it to his wife, "lumps and undigested pieces, licked over to a form by our affections". The subordination of women has already been discussed and we are concerned here only with its effect upon them. They had to endure the attitude most maddening of all, the patronage of the other sex. Nicholas Breton makes a character advise about the management of an unlearned wife:

> Commend her housewifery, and make much of her carefulness and bid her servants take example at their mistress; wink at an ill word . . . Sometime feed her humour . . . at board be merry with her, abroad be kind to her, always loving to her, and never bitter to her, for patient Grizell is dead long ago.

In other words treat your unlearned wife as a child. An Elizabethan pamphleteer was more moderate:

> If thou be a husband govern so your wife
> That her peevish means work not thy strife:
> Give her not too much law, to run before,
> Too much boldness doth work thy overthrow:
> Yet abridge her not too much by any mean:
> But let her still be thy companion.

That was no doubt a fairly precise statement of the ideal of many husbands, to control their wives without showing too much control. Such a policy may have suited women who would fain lean on a strong shoulder, but must have sometimes proved a hardship to those of force and intelligence.

Perhaps they were not as much irked by the realization of their position as we would today suppose. Their lower status was an old story, told by the parson, set forth in the Scripture, and sanctioned by custom. Women of character knew how to accept their situation gracefully and yet hold their heads high. Mrs. Hutchinson thought it belonged to her honour and pride to obey her husband, but maintained a great dignity. Margaret Russell who became Countess of Cumberland had a bad time with her wayward Earl but flew her flag high. Brilliana Lady Harley was afraid of Sir Robert, but, like ladies of the manor in nineteenth-century novels, gave orders to everyone else in the community and played the part of the great châtelaine.

Other women rose not only above the handicaps of subordination but above all their handicaps. Lady Winwood was devoted to the friends of her husband and spent her excess energy in multifarious gardening. Lady Oglander looked after her household with utmost pains and met her husband at the outer gate when he came home from official duties. Lady

Verney had to take charge of everything at Claydon House because Sir Edmund was away most of the time in the King's service; she kept him informed of what she was doing and could act with decision because she knew that he relied completely upon her. Such women were possibly the happier for accepting gracefully the duty of showing deference. If men controlled them without seeming to do so the women had often their way without seeming to expect it. Advantages there were in such a system. The women avoided those quarrels in which the strong-minded females of a later age became involved, and a few of them, like Lady Verney and Johanna Lady Barrington, had the pleasure of power without its pains.

Yet now and again the handicaps proved too much for the woman. In sets of family letters we come upon marital dissensions that shook shires. The famous Bess of Hardwick in late Tudor times made herself the talk of the Midlands and must have proved a continuous cross to her husband. She was indeed a woman to be pitied, almost as much as her partner. So was the Elizabethan Lady Willoughby whose running fight with her mate over many years makes a harrowing story. Alice Thornton's married life ran smoothly only because she was determined to make the best of a stupid and worthless man, even at great expense of spirit. Anne Lady Clifford was desperately unhappy in both her matrimonial adventures. At Wilton there is a group painting of the Herbert family in which the Countess of Pembroke looks out from the frame a figure of misery. The two great houses in which Lady Anne lived had been to her but "gay arbors of anguish". No happier had been the wife of the sixth Earl of Rutland of whom Beaumont wrote:

> Marriage was to thee
> Naught but a sacrament of misery.

In some of these cases the worthlessness of the man or the ingrained quarrelsomeness of the woman was no doubt an essential factor. Yet neither the trouble-making Bess, nor the self-pitying Alice, nor the masterful Lady Anne was intended for any subordinate rôle. What is more significant is that most women were inclined to believe that a woman who quarrelled with her husband was in the wrong.

The attentive reader will have noticed that the country gentlewomen have held the centre of the picture, for the reason that their husbands left in their muniment rooms letters and records and that some of the women themselves wrote diaries and autobiographies. We know less about the wives of the successful lawyers, of the well-to-do physicians, and of the higher clergy. It would be a good guess that in the country they were not in a very different situation from the women of the gentry. In towns they may have been better off, as respects their subordination to their husbands, and more in the position of the wives of the business aristocracy.

Those women, the consorts of the merchants in London and the larger towns, figure in Chamberlain's letters as important people. 'In all banquets and feasts', wrote a traveller from the continent, 'they are shown the greatest honour; they are placed at the upper end of the table, where they are first served.'

The smaller business people, the tradesmen in London and country towns, have left few individual records. We do know, however, that the wives of those people lived in most cases above their shops with their husbands, and thus learned the business. Some of them were little less than partners. 'Your citizens' wives are like partridges,' it was said, 'the hens are better than the cocks.' That may have been often true. Women were likely to be good at details and more regularly on the job. They were not only shopkeepers; they sometimes played a part in the town. When we look over the records of boroughs, more of which are being published, we find women increasingly mentioned. They complained of abuses in the town; they asked for a better schoolmaster; they proved themselves sometimes zealous Puritans and an embarrassment to the vicar.

About the wives of yeomen we have only incidental information. The helpmate of the farmer was associated with her husband in a common enterprise. If she were more interested in the dairy and the female help, if he were more concerned with the fields and the farm labourers, both of them went to markets and fairs and bought and sold commodities. They had much to consult about together. No doubt some farmers maintained their male authority but we may imagine that in many cases there was a kind of working partnership. In matters of their children the yeomen were sometimes as money-minded as the gentry. They economized to provide dowries for their daughters and expected that their sons should receive dowries with their wives. Shakespeare makes Suffolk complain:

> So worthless peasants bargain for their wives
> As market men for oxen, sheep, or corn.

Yet the daughters of the yeomanry came in natural contact with the young men about the farm and the neighbouring farms, and had a better chance than girls in the country house to follow fancy, as they would have put it.

If we go down in the scale and inquire about the wives of husbandmen, or small farmers, of petty artisans, and of farm labourers, we have almost no evidence upon which to form judgments. Here and there a ballad and some doggerel verses deal with women of the humblest classes and make them out as sometimes too strong-minded for their mates. We need not take such evidence too seriously, but we must remember that the husbands and wives in those families were close to the instant need of things and would have been almost forced to cooperate. They would either work closely together or quarrel sharply. We look hopefully at court records, trusting to find men and women of the hard-driven groups, and we do meet many of them, usually the less worthy. Unhappily we learn too little of the relations between men and women of those groups. What we do find is that among the very poor were women of character and courage, women who had not been beaten down by hardships. I think of one young woman with a baseborn baby on her hands, who pleaded her pitiful case before the justices in quarter sessions so unforgettably that she might have been a Hardy heroine ahead of time. Poverty and misfortune do not always degrade people; sometimes they serve to develop strong characters. Such characters might well have been able to hold their own in the war of the sexes.

All that has been said about women of other than the moneyed and ruling classes has been somewhat conjectural and even speculative. The women we know most about were handicapped beings, subordinated to their mates, unfitted by either training or experience to play any considerable rôle. They were the ancestors of those Victorian women to be found in memoirs and novels whose acquiescence in the domination of their masterful and unreasonable mates seems incredible. If the seventeenth-century woman did not feel her shackles so painfully because she was less aware of the world, she was in the same unhappy position.

Having said so much, we turn to Shakespeare and the other dramatists and find ourselves in another and very different milieu. We are introduced to Portia, Beatrice, Helena, Hermione and other women of liveliness, spirit, initiative, and even of heroic quality. Dekker, Heywood, Massinger, Marlowe, Marston, Middleton, and Beaumont and Fletcher put on the stage women of character, charm, intelligence, and spontaneity, occasionally indeed of greatness. Furthermore the playwrights, especially Shakespeare, Dekker, and Heywood, bring before us women of all classes, and some of the humblest prove characters not easily forgotten. Were the dramatists fashioning women out of their imagination? Of course. But their imagination was working from pictures in their mind, revamping to suit their purposes women who had been part of their experience. Kipling in his poem, 'The Craftsman', has explained something of the methods of the creative artist.

Who were the playwrights and what had been their experience? Shakespeare had grown up in Stratford-on-Avon, a not uncivilized country town, and had been associated through his middle-class family with interesting people. No doubt he had seen scores of young women of the middle classes and of the small artisan group; he knew about women from them. The other playwrights had similar backgrounds. Massinger had been a boy in Salisbury, when his father was steward of the Herberts three miles away. He may have talked to the great ladies of Wilton and no doubt talked many times with the wives of tradesmen in Salisbury. Heywood was country-born but lived in London. Dekker was a Londoner who knew the streets and shops and taverns. Marlowe, who came from Canterbury, where his father had been a member of the shoemakers' guild, proceeded to Cambridge and then was in and out of London. Beaumont grew up in a country house in Leicestershire and, as the son of a judge, had chances to know many

Mary, Lady Verney, by Vandyck

Mary, Lady Clitherow, wife of a Lord Mayor of London

kinds of people. Fletcher, who was perhaps as much interested in women as any dramatist, unless Shakespeare, was the son of an eminent clergyman who became bishop of London. Middleton was the son of a London gentleman. Marston was of small Shropshire gentry. In other words the dramatists were men who knew many aspects of English life in London and in country towns and were likely to have drawn their female characters in some degree out of their experience.

They and other less-known dramatists have set before us a wide variety of women, and have offered many illustrations of the attitudes of men and women to one another; they have furnished indeed a large body of comment upon women and their ways, more than is to be found in any other type of source. Could we but use the dramatists without reservations, we should be able to say a good deal about the women of the time.

The dramatists lend support to the idea already broached that the women of the business world, both in town and country, at the upper level of the great merchants, and at the lower level of tradesmen, were the most emancipated of all women in that time. Thomas Dekker makes Birdlime say that the country gentlewomen learned from the City wives how to check and control their husbands. In the old play of *Timon* Callimela says:

> I'll subject my neck
> To no man's yoke . . .
> . . .
> The wives of citizens do bear the sway,
> Whose very hands their husbands may not touch
> Without a bended knee . . .

Davenport in *The City Nightcap* puts into the mouth of the clown these words:

> And where have women most their wills? Oh, City.

The playwrights overstated matters, of course, but they knew the ways of merchants' wives.

Throughout the plays those women were putting themselves forward; in London they were coaching their husbands in the proper behaviour towards courtiers and in country towns

7

reminding them of their obligations to their partners. Vulgar and pretentious they seemed to the dramatists, and so they seemed to John Chamberlain who knew the type well and could compare them with their betters in country houses.

The playwrights were interested in courtship and marriage. We have already observed that they displayed an increasing antipathy to marriages arranged by parents. Sometimes they arrayed themselves almost militantly on the side of youth. They were no doubt influenced in part by the old romances but probably also by what they had seen. They presented young women who had a part in choosing their husbands, parents notwithstanding, and who thoroughly enjoyed being courted and were making the most of the experience. The girls poked fun at their suitors, they called them names and bid them play with pages, they angled with them as if on a line. At long length they picked one "made to be loved", and "loved extremely". Married they were different creatures:

> How fair we grow, how gentle, and how tender.

The same playwrights, or some of them, thought of marriage as a partnership. In a play just quoted a woman is made to say:

> I know you are young and giddy,
> And till you have a wife can govern with ye,
> You sail upon this wor[l]d-sea, light and empty;
> Your bark in danger daily; 'tis not the name neither
> Of wife can steer ye; but the noble nature,
> The diligence, the care, the love, the patience,
> She makes the pilot, and preserves the husband,
> That knows, and reckons every rib he is built on.

Such an encomium upon marriage is indeed unusual among dramatists. But the notion of the sympathy and equality that went with it is to be found here and there. In Ford's *The Lover's Melancholy* Palador is made to utter these words:

> The music
> Of man's fair composition best accords
> When 'tis in consort, not in single strains.
> My heart has been untuned these many months,
> Wanting her presence, in whose equal love
> True harmony consisteth.

You will note the word *equal*. In another play the lovers are addressed:

> There's equality
> In this fair combination . . .
> . . .
> There's music in this sympathy.

Another dramatist put into the mouth of Laxton even more significant words: 'The raising of the women is the lifting up of the man's head at all times'.

Middleton was not more forward-looking about women than others of his craft. They allowed their characters to praise the minds of women. Of Pulcheria in a Massinger play it was declared:

> Her soul is so immense,
> And her strong faculties so apprehensive
> To search into the depths of deep designs,
> And of all natures . . .

However little the conceptions of the playwrights as to women correspond to what is to be found in biographies, letters, and diaries, we may be sure that the ideas they set forth were in the air and known to many more than those who had to do with the theatre.

We find, indeed, as we move into the last years of James I and on towards mid-century, that memoirs and letters give some support to the portraits of women presented on the stage. We come upon Mrs. Hutchinson, upon the Duchess of Newcastle, whom we have already met as Margaret Lucas, upon Lady Harley, the Countess of Warwick, Anne Viscountess Conway, and Dorothy Osborne, women as lively and spirited, as intelligent and strongminded as those in plays. Perhaps they represent a new type of woman. Social changes of several kinds were taking place between 1580 and 1650, medieval notions were being slowly discarded. It is possible that among the changes was one in the way men—and women—regarded the female sex, or that a change long in process was beginning at last to make itself evident.

That husbands had certain obligations to their wives had been recognized of old, but from the reign of Charles I we hear more about those duties, possibly of course because we have more information. 'There be certain times due unto our wives . . . and must be wholly observed by us', wrote a husband as early as 1613. Husbands were expected to comfort their wives in times of illness, to be at home when their wives bore children, and to be present at the christenings that followed. In the thirties and forties of the seventeenth century men were constantly apologizing to their wives for their enforced absences, as if they recognized an obligation to be at home much of the time. Some husbands thought it their duty to support their wives in their differences with servants and stewards. In an earlier generation men were known to take sides with their stewards against their wives. If a wife died, it was thought becoming that the widower should not marry at once, but this scruple was rarely taken seriously. The duty of faithfulness in marriage was occasionally urged by fathers upon their sons. Here and there in autobiographies we come upon men who declare that they had been entirely faithful to their wives, as if such faithfulness were unusual.

I have alluded to the praise of women in late Elizabethan and early Jacobean days. That was becoming less conventional. Members of the female sex were sometimes praised for strength of intellect. Henry Hastings, fifth Earl of Huntingdon, wrote of his wife to his sons that she had a masculine understanding and one that was predominant. Men might have believed that of their wives in an earlier time but would not have boasted of it. Anthony Ashley Cooper, later the Earl of Shaftesbury, wrote of his partner that her wit [intelligence] and judgment were expressed in all things. The biographer of Lady Falkland spoke of her perspicacity of understanding and clearness of judgment and said that in debate she would give ready submission to the best reasons, an openmindedness not common. When Lady Wroth wrote of women in her *Urania* she praised those of wit and was herself an example. William Habington admired a noblewoman because he found

> In the interior province of her mind
> Such government.

Women, said Dudley North, were the winning commonwealth and society of this our world.

The views about marriage seem to have been undergoing some slight alteration. Even among the gentry, as I have indicated, there had always been some examples of romantic marriages. My impression is that, as we go towards the middle of the seventeenth century, such marriages were becoming more common. In the circle in which Mrs. Hutchinson moved before her marriage we come upon young people consorting together at Richmond, the parents not too much in sight, with marriage in the back of the minds of the young people. One thinks forward to the young people at Bath in Jane Austen's novels. In an account of Lettice Lady Falkland's marriage it was said of the couple,

A Soul with soul, and mind here match'd with mind.

The matching of minds on the part of married people is more or less assumed by Lady Coke and her husband, Sir John. They made plans together and in every detail considered one another, as if entirely equals.

The diaries, autobiographies and letters of men from the 1620's on seem to make more mention of wives and sisters and mothers than they did earlier. Sir George More wrote his son-in-law Sir John Oglander: 'I am now my wife's secretary as at all times I am her servant', and his son-in-law would have realized that the jest was half in earnest. His own wife was the most important factor in his existence. Sir John Bramston had a great deal to say about his female relatives; they were competent women who looked after financial affairs with skill and held families together in times of crisis. John Aubrey in his *Brief Lives* gives women their due as helpmates. As we get into the second third of the seventeenth century we run into whole sets of family correspondence and the letters often indicate real comradeship between husbands and wives. There could have been no more delightful partnership than that between Sir Ralph Verney and Mary Lady Verney. When he was exiled in France she was sent over to negotiate with the Oliverian government because it was believed by his friends that she would be more successful than he, and their belief was justified. Sir Roger Twysden called his wife the saver of his estate. Moreover, there was a new tone in letters. Husbands addressed their wives with affection and informality, sometimes with pet names, and indicated in many ways their confidence in the understanding and judgment of their helpmates. As for the women, they seemed less afraid of their husbands and behaved more nearly as equals.[14]

It is a further sign of the growing estimation of women that now and then husbands were granting allowances to their wives for household expenses. In 1636 Hayne, an Exeter merchant, was giving his wife 3*li* a fortnight for running the home.[15] Other men were beginning to grant fixed sums. Moreover women were asking for many services. In Jasper Mayne's *City Match* Dorcas says:

> I do expect it, yes, sir, and my coach.
> Six horses and postillion; four are fit
> For them that have a charge of children; you
> And I shall never have any . . .
>   Then I'll have
> My footman to run by me when I visit
> Or take the air sometimes in Hyde-park.

One could quote letters to the same effect.

If there were some slight change in the attitude towards women between the last years of Elizabeth and the time of Cromwell, if medieval conceptions were a little losing their hold we may well ask why.

It is easier to mark a possible change than to explain it. But some suggestions may be offered.

In the decades that followed the death of Elizabeth the growing appreciation of her statecraft must have done something to raise the estimation of women. As men watched the misgovernment of James I and the futility of Charles I they could not but look backwards to what seemed a golden age. If a mere woman could show judgment in choosing her subordinates, prescience in estimating forces, and courage when the mighty seemed gathered against her, it was time to take a more favourable view of the female sex.

Undoubtedly one of the reasons why women were figuring more was because a larger number of them could read and write. John Aubrey speaks of the old days before women were readers. Now we know that between mid-Elizabethan and the

Long Parliament there was an enormous increase in the literacy of women. They did not have, as we have seen, the schooling given men, but the wife of the townsman and the wife of the farmer wished to read the Bible and the sermons that were being published, and managed somehow to master the skill. When women could learn from books, as their fathers and brothers and husbands had been doing, they were bound to have more share in affairs and to be taken more into account.

The playwrights of the early seventeenth century played possibly a rôle not unlike that of novelists in the nineteenth century; they were in some slight degree the teachers of their generation. We may remember that the young women of two generations ago devoured the novels of George Meredith and set out to be Meredithian heroines. It is a fair presumption that men and women of the seventeenth century were affected by what they saw on the stage, especially when the plays were less taken up with Italian scenes and were beginning to touch upon English life, and to picture gentlewomen, wives of merchants, and even waitresses in taverns. As wives in the audience watched the heroines of plays, they could hardly avoid forming a better opinion of themselves as part of the human scene. Possibly their husbands modified a little those notions of women inherited from their progenitors.

The prevalence of rich widows did something for their sex. Not all early deaths were those of women. In an age when medicine was guess-work and when the plague and smallpox were prevalent, many men died in the twenties and early thirties. Some of them were successful business men, who had done well in the "First Industrial Revolution", and their widows were often able to carry on the business. Helen Manning of Devonshire employed hundreds of people in her clothing industry. England was full of widows who managed large and small enterprises, and often well. Other men died who left large landed estates to their widows. When a wealthy widow came into the market there was hurrying and scurrying among gentlemen who wished to be married, and younger sons who needed an endowment, and on the part of family solicitors and stewards on behalf of their clients. Suitors appeared on every side, and the widow in her weeds found herself not a pitied figure but a centre of attraction among manœuvring men.[16] She could marry whom she liked with none to say her nay. It was pleasant to be sought after, and she took her time and consulted often her whole connection, and especially her male relatives, and made a close bargain in which she was able to retain some control over the money she brought to the union. She had had her interval of independence, and knew its sweets, and even when she accepted a husband, as she usually did, she was not always a submissive member of the partnership. In the letters of John Chamberlain the rich widows who have married again figure largely, and not in a minor capacity.

The growing wealth of England resulted almost necessarily in "society", the natural sphere of women. The rich fabrics of the Low Countries and of the Italian cities, the furs of Muscovy, and the jewels of the East were to be seen in London shops. The gentlemen and the merchant princes wished their wives to show something of their affluence and dignity, and their partners were seldom unwilling to please them in that respect.

'Since our women must walk gay and money buys their gear', was as true then as now. We have already observed the display by the great ladies of the Court. All those women who wore fine clothes aspired to society and served to create it.

Society was beginning to appear also in the country. The gentlewoman, when she was allowed to do so, went with her husband to London and brought back word of London doings and of the power of London women. Moreover, many of the gentry were leasing houses in the larger towns for the late winter and early spring, as they had long done in some degree, and mixing with the well-to-do townspeople, and marrying their children to the sons and daughters of those people. In Exeter and in York and other towns a kind of society was forming, the opportunity of women.

The influence of Puritanism in ameliorating the position of women cannot be overlooked. We have noted the considerable rôle allowed women by the business classes in London and in the larger towns. Those classes had become largely Puritan before the end of Elizabeth's reign and were in the next two reigns the backlog of the Puritan movement. It will be said at once that the Puritans looked to the Bible for their opinions and found in the Old Testament and in the Epistles full support for the subordination of the female. It might be added that the great Puritan poet, Milton, insisted in his prose writings upon that subordination. Yes. But the Puritans were inclined to lay stress on the obligations of the husband to his wife. William Gouge in his *Domesticall Duties* took a somewhat advanced and generous view as to those obligations. The Puritans exalted family life and the association of men and women in the home. The Puritan biographers were always talking of the man's wife and of her share in the service of God. They were not mentioning the equality of men and women but emphasizing their partnership. That partnership was to be seen in practice in many Puritan households.

NOTES

[1] This paper was first given in briefer form as the Henry L. Stimson Lecture at Goucher College, Baltimore. I am grateful to the President of Goucher College for permission to publish it in this book.

[2] 'These cuckooish songs of yours of cuckolds, horns, . . . by tradition delivered from man to man, like scarecrows, to terrify fools from this earthly paradise of wedlock.' Chapman, George, *All Fools* (circa 1605), act iii, sc. 1, Dodsley (London, 1825), iv, p. 149.

[3] Heale, William, *An Apologie for Women* (1609), pp. 1–2. Heale's interesting little book was a reply to William Gager who had defended the thesis that it was lawful for husbands to beat their wives. Like other writers of the time Heale draws on Scripture and classical works for his arguments, but he does more than that, something unusual, he goes to nature in order to make his case. The males in the animal kingdom treat their females well. Cf. Speght, Rachel, *A Mouzell for Melasyomus* (1617).

[4] See, for example, Davenport, Robert, the *City Night-Cap* (circa 1624), act i, sc. 1, Dodsley, xi, p. 268; Daniel, Samuel, *Works*, ed. Grosart (1885), i, p. 215; Stubbes, Philip, *A Christal Glasse for Christian Women* (New Shakespeare Soc. 1877–9), p. 198; Aubrey, John, *Wiltshire Topographical Collections* (Devizes, 1862), p. 370. In Webster's *Appius and Virginia*, act i, sc. 2, *Complete Works of*, ed. F. L. Lucas (1927), ii, p. 159, Icilius says, as he takes Virginia's hand:

> Here I hold
> My honorable pattern, one whose mind
> Appears more like a ceremonious chapel
> Full of sweet music, than a thronging presence.

Sweetness rather than an overpowering personality seemed to be what Icilius wished in a wife.

⁵ To judge from plays and from occasional pamphlets the conversation of ordinary people was often filled up with old sayings and proverbs but not a great deal of individual observation. Miniona (*The Soddered Citizen* (*circa* 1623), act ii, Malone Soc. Reprints (1936), pp. 27–28) is made to say:

> To heare the chat
> Of those illiterate and barbarous people
> Would grind one's brains to dust.

Dudley Carleton complained that the talk of the time (he was thinking no doubt of the Court) was spent in discourse of quarrels and marriages. Carleton to Chamberlain, 25 Dec. 1605, P.R.O., State Papers, 14/24 no. 29.

⁶ From casual reading I feel sure that there were more schools for girls than the monographs indicate. Such schools are often mentioned in the memoirs, which have not been carefully enough gleaned.

⁷ On the other hand there were parents, as in the Verney, Coke, and Sidney families, who gained great pleasure from their children. The children of some of the relatives of Lady Jane Bacon (Lady Jane Cornwallis) were made much of by their parents. That there were not a few such parents appears from the constant complaints that fathers and mothers spoiled their offspring. See notes in Stubbes, *Anatomie of Abuses*, p. 265 and Hall, Joseph, *Works* (1625), p. 394.

⁸ *Albumazar*, act ii, sc. 9, Dodsley (1825), vii, p. 154. In *Mother Bombie* (Lyly, John, *Works*, iii, p. 180), Livia says that parents when children grow to years of judgment 'deprive us of the greatest blessing . . . the liberty of our minds . . . because their fancies being grown musty with hoary age, therefore nothing can relish in their thoughts that savours of sweet youth; they study twenty years together to make us grow as straight as a wand, and in the end by bowing us, make us crooked as a cammock'.

⁹ Some young women were much influenced by the romantic stories they had read. I suspect Dorothy Osborne, who pored over French romances, was one of them. Even writers of that day recognized the influences on the young:

> Of ballads that entreat of nought but love,
> Of plaints, unkindness, and of jealousy,
> Which are of wonderful effects to move
> Young people's minds that read them to folly.

Francis Thynn, *The Debate between Pride and Lowlines*. Shakespeare Soc. (1841), p. 67.

¹⁰ Aubrey reports Dr. William Harvey as saying: 'A blessing goes with a marriage of love upon a strong impulse'. Dick, O. L., *Aubrey's Brief Lives* (1949), p. 130. Cf. Almira's statement about Love (Massinger, *A Very Woman* (1634), act v, sc. 5, *Works*, iv, p. 340):

> Thou art feign'd blind
> And yet we borrow our best sight from thee.

¹¹ It was said that women were the rarest works of nature (Marston, *The Insatiate Countesse*, act iv, *Works*, ed. Halliwell (1856), iii, pp. 155, 156), and that they were the instruments of nature (D. North, *A Forest Promiscuous*, p. 66). It was implied that their part was a matter for pride and not for reticence (*The Dutch Courtesan*, act iii, Marston, *Works*, ed. A. H. Bullen (1887), ii, pp. 47–50).

In general the seventeenth-century woman was not given to reticence, but there were interesting cases to the contrary.

¹² *Nunwell Symphony*, p. 115. Lady Bacon (Cornwallis) feared her accouchements. See *The Private Correspondence of Lady Jane Cornwallis* (1872), pp. 59–62. Mary Lady Rich feared giving birth to many children lest she spoil her looks. See her *Autobiography*, ed. by T. C. Croker (Percy Soc. 1848), pp. 32–3. Mrs. Stubbes, wife of Philip Stubbes, had what she regarded as a revelation that she would die in her first childbirth and died, as she predicted, not without courage. See *A Christal Glasse for Christian Women* in the back of Stubbes' *Anatomie of Abuses* (New Shakespeare Soc. 1877–9), pp. 200–201.

¹³ An epitaph in a Wiltshire church runs as follows:

> How faithful thou hast been to me,
> And haddest six children dear,
> Within six years, a marvel to see,
> All born one time of year.
> The seventh also in like manner,
> If death had not them let.
>
> *   *   *
>
> Alas, how should it chance so bad
> To little babes so young.

> Aubrey, *Wilts. Topographical Colls.* (Devizes, 1862), p. 88.

¹⁴ These generalizations must be made with reservations. The body of family letters is so much greater.

¹⁵ T. N. Brushfield, 'Financial Diary of a Citizen of Exeter'. *Devon. Trans.* xxxiii, p. 209. Musophil (Barnaby Riche), *The Description of a Good Wife* (1619), urged a man to make his wife his treasurer.

¹⁶ Scores of examples could be cited from family letters. Framlingham Gawdy was advised of several possible widows and of their incomes. Mingay writes him about their various qualities and especially about their lands. On 20 Nov. 1637 he wrote: 'If a widow happens to fall in the mean time, she shall be kept in syrup for you'. Gawdy MSS (H.M.C.), p. 166. Sir John Eliot's friend, Sir Henry Waller, suggested the possibility of a certain wealthy widow, whose kinsman he knew, as a wife for Eliot. Eliot asked no questions as to her character, but reposed himself confidently in Waller's judgment: 'I shall guide myself with all due observation of your honour'. See Eliot's *Letter Book* (ed. Grosart 1882), pp. 15 *et seq*. Eliot is remembered as a martyr to free speech and is counted a hero in the parliamentary struggle. But he left so important a matter as his second marriage to a friend's negotiation.

IV

Comedy in the Reign of Charles I

———

C. V. WEDGWOOD

IV

ON 2 SEPTEMBER 1642 the London theatres were closed by an ordinance of the Lords and Commons, phrased in terms which would not have disgraced a tragedy:

Whereas the distressed Estate of Ireland steeped in her own Blood and the distressed Estate of England threatened with a Cloud of Blood by a Civil Warre, call for all possible meanes to appease and avert the Wrath of God appearing in these Judgments . . . and whereas publike Sports doe not well agree with publike Calamities, nor publike Stage playes with the Seasons of Humiliation, this being an Exercise of sad and pious solemnity, and the other being Spectacles of pleasure, too commonly expressing lascivious Mirth and Levitie: it is therefore thought fit and ordeined by the Lords and Commons in this Parliament Assembled, that while these sad Causes and set times of Humiliation doe continue publike Stage playes shall cease and bee forborne.

There was as much policy as moral reprobation in the decision of Parliament to close the theatres. Political and social comment, by no means always favourable to the government, had become increasingly common on the stage during the first half of the seventeenth century.[1] During the Ship Money disputes Massinger had put these words into the mouth of a tyrannous King:

> Moneys? We'll raise supplies what ways we please,
> And force you to subscribe to blanks in which
> We'll mulct you as we shall think fit.

Before the play was licensed the King marked this in the margin: 'This is too insolent and to be changed' so that the offending words never reached the public[2] but it is an interesting comment on the amount of liberty allowed to dramatists that Massinger introduced them at all. On other occasions the

King's policy had come under open criticism from the theatre. During the religious troubles with Scotland the players at the Fortune Theatre introduced into one of their plays a mockery of the Laudian ritual which was received with great enthusiasm by the audience until the government prohibited the performance and confiscated the properties. Undeterred, the company retaliated by putting on a play called *The Valiant Scot* which dealt with the heroic resistance of Sir William Wallace to Edward I. The modern analogy was perfectly understood by the Londoners who sympathized with the Scots in their current rebellion against King Charles and the Laudian liturgy.[3]

Since the accession of King Charles I the taste for topical comedy, immensely stimulated by Ben Jonson earlier in the century, had become fully established. Dramatists like the veteran Philip Massinger and Richard Brome, the one-time servant and assiduous imitator of Ben Jonson, as well as the fashionable James Shirley and a number of lesser men, both amateurs and professionals, made use of contemporary incidents and contemporary controversies in their comedies. Davenant, in his *Platonic Lovers* (1636), Brome in his *Court Beggar* (1632), Chapman and Shirley in *The Ball* (1632) exploited subjects of current interest and Thomas Heywood in *The Late Lancashire Witches* (1634) took his material almost unaltered from the accounts of the famous witch trial in Lancashire in the previous year. The realistic representation on the stage of familiar places of public resort—as in Brome's *Covent Garden Weeded* and Shirley's *Hyde Park* (1632)—underlined the contemporary character of stage comment on manners, morals and even politics. The closing of the theatres was thus an obvious counsel of prudence on the part of Parliament when serious trouble began. Puritan prejudice against these 'sinful heathenish lewd ungodly spectacles and most pernicious corruptions'[4] provided a moral justification for an act of policy. The players, as the abstract and brief chronicles of the time, were far too dangerous to be left at liberty to utter what they would to excitable London audiences during the Civil War.

The fifteen years before the Civil War is not one of the great epochs of English drama. The veteran Ben Jonson complained that amateurs were spoiling the stage:

> Now each Court Hobby horse will wince in rhyme;
> Both learned and unlearned, all write plays.[5]

Shackerley Marmion, a professional playwright of a younger generation, complained of "this licentious generation of poets" who troubled the peace of the whole town by turning everything that happened into a play. So that a scrivener could not lose his ears,

> Nor a Justice of the Peace share with his clerk,
> A lord can't walk drunk with a torch before him,
> A gallant can't be suffer'd to pawn's breeches
> Or leave his cloak behind him at a tavern,

but the poets would be writing about it.[6] The chief sinners, in James Shirley's estimation were the young university men who would come up to London 'like market women with dorsers full of lamentable tragedies and ridiculous comedies'.[7]

Certainly, but for the three great plays of John Ford, the thirties were not remarkable for poetry on the stage. Both tragedy and pastoral were blown out with wordy pretentiousness and had come to depend too much on over-ingenious intrigues, on magnificent costumes and on scenic effects imitated from the masques.

> In scene magnificent and language high
> And clothes worth all the rest . . .

complained Richard Brome, thinking perhaps of the insipid works of writers like Ludovic Carlell or the courtier Sir John Suckling's absurd *Aglaura*. But Brome was hardly fair in suggesting that the clique which admired such plays had taught the public to

> . . . despise all sportive merry wit
> Because some such great play has none of it.[8]

To judge by the number of comedies written, the demand for comedy was as strong as ever. If the public sometimes had a mind to sugared kickshaws and wished to see imaginary Kings, Queens, knights and ladies performing improbable actions, at other times it robustly clamoured for the beef and bag-pudding of topical comedy.

The comedies of this time are not of course, purely topical. They share a number of stock situations and stock characters— often frank plagiarisms of Ben Jonson—with the comedies of the two previous generations and some with the comedy of all time. The pert page, the sly waiting woman, the talkative old nurse belong to comedy through the ages. The comic Justice of the Peace, and the stupid constable are peculiar to England, though not to one decade rather than another. Justice Bumpsey, Justice Testy, Justice Cockbrayne are followers in the tradition of Jonson's Overdo and Shakespeare's Shallow. If these gentle-men had fairly represented the average ability of the Justices of the time it would be hard to understand how the administration functioned, more especially if they were seconded by Con-stables of the line of Dogberry. Constable Busy in *A Match at Midnight* (1633) locks up 'twelve gentlewomen, our own neighbours, for being so late at a woman's labour'. He will have none of their excuse for going out at night; their friend should have 'cried out at some other time'.[9]

The comic Frenchman—usually a dancing master—the comic Dutchman, drunk and valiant, the comic Welshman, fiery and boastful but good-humoured and brave, were all popular figures. So were the low life characters—the bawds, the cut-purses, the confidence tricksters, and the unemployed soldiers living by their wits. These latter have a long pedigree in English comedy but they became more common in the comedies of the thirties just as their prototypes were becoming more common about the streets of London. England stood neutral in the wars of Germany and the Netherlands; and both, or rather all, sides recruited indifferently in the British Isles. The officer from the foreign wars, known by his "taff'ta scarf and long estridge wing" was a familiar figure in the London taverns. The indifference of the professional to the cause which em-ployed him was now and again the subject of comment. Young Palatine in Davenant's *The Wits* (1634) mocks a more scrupu-lous warrior with

> What is't to thee, whether one Don Diego
> A Prince, or Hans van Holme, fritter seller
> Of Bombell, do conquer that parapet
> Redoubt or town, which thou ne'er saw'st before? [10]

But Justice Cockbrayne, in Brome's *Covent Garden Weeded*, probably overdid the part when he disguised himself as a soldier and boasted: 'I have seen the face of war, and serv'd in the Low Countries, though I say't, on both sides'.[11]

While the stock types still continued popular in the reign of Charles I, the introduction of some new figures and the development, or the more frequent appearance, of certain older ones, point to the pre-occupations of the time. The decayed gentleman or dispossessed landowner (Dryground, Monylack), the city usurer (Bloodhound, Hornet, Vermin, Quicksands), the feckless courtier living by his wits, the tradesman—and occasionally the yeoman—turned gentleman, the citizen's wife with ambitions beyond her station: all these turn up with almost monotonous regularity.

The comedies do not present an exact picture of what was going on, but by the exaggeration of some elements in the social situation and emphasis on others they clearly reflect the prejudices and anxieties of the audiences who watched them. Wealth was changing hands; the structure of society was being steadily modified by the upward thrust of yeomen and tradesmen into the gentry, while the intelligent gentry consolidated their position by engaging in trade. Examples of this shifting and coalescence of classes are repeatedly given in the comedies of this period, sometimes with a direct, sometimes with only an implied comment. 'I am a gentleman', claims one Startup in Shirley's *Constant Maid* (1640), 'my father was a yeoman, my grandfather was a nobleman's footman.'[12] Sir Paul Squelch the Justice of the Peace in Brome's *Northern Lass* (1632) is the son of a rich grazier and the grandson of a ploughman.[13] Massinger in *The City Madam* (1632) comments on the invasion of trade by the gentry:

> masters never prospered
> Since gentlemen's sons grew prentices: when we look
> To have our business done at home, they are
> Abroad in the tennis court.[14]

But there is one surprising characteristic of the social commentary of this period. The Puritans are let off very lightly. In King James' reign Ben Jonson had dealt ruthlessly with them in *Bartholomew Fair* and in *The Alchemist*. But Zeal-of-the-Land Busy, Tribulation Wholesome, and Ananias have few imitators, perhaps because it was felt that no better could be done. During King Charles' personal rule, when the anti-Puritan stage might have been expected to pursue the godly with relentless ridicule, few comic Puritans are to be found. There are references to them of course, allusions to silenced ministers, and to preaching sectaries of both sexes, mockery of their attitude to love-locks, Sunday pastimes and maypoles. But the criticism is on the whole good-natured, and lacks entirely the bitterness and bite of Jonson's attack. In Davenant's *News from Plymouth* (1635), Cable, the sea-captain wooing a widow of Puritan sympathies, tells her

> I know
> You love to frequent the silenc'd parties;
> Let but their lungs hold out, and I'll listen
> Till my ears ache.

In case this should not prove his sincerity he gaily adds a promise to cut down his mainmast because it resembles a maypole. In Davenant's *Wits* occurs that description, much quoted by modern economic historians, of the 'weaver of Banbury that hopes to entice Heaven by singing to make him lord of twenty looms'.[15]

Cartwright, himself an Anglican divine, makes the strongest attack on the Puritans in *The Ordinary*, but even this hardly goes beyond the bounds of good nature. In the last scene the gang of rogues who frequent *The Ordinary* from which the play has its name, decide to seek their fortunes in New England. The inhabitants, who have

> one eye
> Put out with Zeal, th'other with ignorance

ought to be easy game. The tricksters will need only to cut their hair to the right length and

> Nosing a little treason gainst the King,
> Bark something at the Bishops,

and garnish their talk with 'now and then a root or two of Hebrew'.[16]

It is fairly evident from this mild treatment that the public, while ready to laugh at the excesses of fanatics, was no longer in the mood to think Puritan-baiting as funny as it had been twenty years before. The King was doing too much of it and the sympathies of the Londoners were not with him.

The treatment of the Anglican clergy had scarcely altered since Shakespeare's time. The curate appears only as a comic figure or as a necessary convenience to the plot, like Sir Boniface the down-at-heel pedant who marries runaway couples in Heywood's *Wise Woman of Hogsden* (1638). Frequently he has not even a name and appears at the foot of the Dramatis Personae among servants and supers as *Curate*. When he is given a name it will be something unflattering like Quailpipe, my lord's chaplain in Brome's *The Antipodes*. His wife, when he has one, fares no better. Davenant paints her unkindly

> Mother Spectacles, the curate's wife
> Who does inveigh 'gainst curling and dyed cheeks,
> Heaves her devout, impatient nose at oil
> Of jessamine, and thinks powder of Paris more
> Profane than th'ashes of a Romish martyr.[17]

Two of the least reputable clergy appear in Cartwright as 'clubbers at the Ordinary'. Sir Christopher, a rather low church divine whose wordy sermons Cartwright parodies in the play, declares bitterly that 'poor labourers in divinity can't earn their groat a day'. His companion, Vicar Catchmey, a "singing man" out of a job, is equally poor and both are represented as hovering in want and bewilderment very near the edge of the criminal classes.[18]

This attitude to the unfortunate Anglican clergy reflects the popular opinion of the time. Lack of respect for the ministers of the established Church was quite as great a block in the path of Laudian policy as the active opposition of the Puritans.

The religious controversy was a theme too dangerous and too inflammable to be openly touched on by the dramatists. But the social problem, the changes in society, the pretensions of the new rich and the troubles of the new poor were freely discussed. Even the King's financial shifts were treated as the subject of comedy and the sale of titles provided good material for jokes.

In Shirley's *Love in a Maze* (1631) the foolish new-made knight Sir Gervase Simple is contemptuously described

> one that has
> But newly cast his country skin, come up
> To see the fashions of the town, has crept
> Into a knighthood, which he paid for heartily,
> And, in his best clothes, is suspected
> For a gentleman.[19]

In John Carvell's play, *The Soddered Citizen*, the title buyer is a lord, but

> He's of our city breed . . . he bought
> His raw green honour with the overplus
> Of what his father left, of purchasing,
> Got in his shop, by 's "What dee lack?" and fawning.[20]

The great number of the new knights who came into being when the King, to increase his revenues, revived the old knighthood fees, could hardly pass without comment. In Brome's *The Damoiselle* these ordinary knights are compared to cob nuts—

> He was one of the cob knights in the throng
> When they were dubbed in clusters.[21]

An unpleasant young snob in Shirley's *The Ball* (1632), who can go nowhere without boasting that he is cousin to a lord, shows his mettle by announcing:

> I care no more for killing half a dozen knights of the Lower House, I mean that are not descended from nobility, than I do to kick my footman.[22]

Davenant makes use of the royal sale of honours to mock the pretensions of ladies who elevate their chambermaids into "waiting gentlewomen". Widow Carrack in *News from Plymouth* tells her maid Smoothall:

> I may make thee a gentlewoman, though thy mother
> Was Goody Smoothall, and do it by my lord's patent
> When I am a baroness: 'tis now in fashion
> To metamorphose chambermaids. The King
> Dubs knights, and new stamp't honour creates gentry.[23]

Neither the dramatists nor the audience held the view that rising in the world, acquiring an estate or buying a title,

was in itself wrong. Worth deserved a material reward and
wealth that had been honestly earned was wholly respectable.
In Brome's *The Damoiselle* a citizen who has acquired gentility
by acquiring land is thus defended against the criticisms of a
born, but impoverished, gentleman:

> Land lordship's real honour
> Though in a tradesman's son: when your fair titles
> Are but the shadow of your ancestry:
> And you walk in 'em, when your land is gone
> Like the pale ghosts of dead nobility.[24]

But the honest acquisition of wealth as a theme, the success
story of the old Dick Whittington variety, was out of fashion.
On the contrary plays were now more often written on the
theme of successful dishonesty, as in Mayne's *City Wit* or
Davenant's *The Wits*.

Bewildered as they usually were by the operations of
capitalism which surrounded them, the dramatists and the
great majority of the audience were disposed to think that any
transaction by which money was made to multiply, without the
labour of the owner, must be dishonest. Usurers, goldsmiths,
lawyers, scriveners and all such as dealt in loans and mortgages,
were natural villains on the stage.

> That man who has the readiest way to cheat
> Wins all the glory, wealth, esteem, grows great,

reflects the villainous goldsmith in Carvell's *Soddered Citizen*.
He next enters into an ingenious plot with a friend. They will
buy an estate jointly. One of them will then dispose of it to
some unsuspecting innocent. After the sale, the other will make
his appearance with title deeds showing that the estate was
jointly owned and has been sold without his permission. The
victim will be forced either to relinquish the estate or to buy
him out. In either case there will be proceeds to share.[25]

The most famous of all the blood-suckers is the veteran
Massinger's tremendous creation, Sir Giles Overreach, the dark,
overshadowing villain of *A New Way to Pay Old Debts* (*c.* 1623).
Beside him, financiers like Brome's Vermin and Shirley's
Hornet are mere pygmies. Massinger, whose boldness, force

and colour belonged to an earlier generation of dramatists, was a much more violent satirist than the younger men who rose to fame in the sixteen-thirties. Overreach shared his Christian name and some of his characteristics with Sir Giles Mompesson, a financier once greatly favoured at Court, who had been attacked by Parliament and had crashed to ruin in 1621. One of the relatively few references to enclosure occurs in this play, where Overreach is described as 'the grand incloser of what was common'. The younger generation of dramatists tended to write almost exclusively about London, where enclosure was not a topic of the first interest. Massinger and his generation still drew on the whole countryside for their themes, and Overreach is not a city figure, but one of the new financier-landowners who, by fair or foul practices, were building up large estates in the country.

Overreach, like all the successful rich men of the epoch, has to establish his social position and plans to do so by marrying his daughter to a lord. To make certain of this alliance he suggests to the girl that she should lure the lord into a compromising position so that he can be compelled to marry her. The girl's innocence and the lord's shining virtue prevent any such thing happening and Overreach is effectively over-reached in the last act.

The theme of intermarriage between the children of the self-made and the decaying nobility and gentry could be, and was, variously handled. James Shirley, in *The Witty Fair One* (1628), expressed pity for the young women and contempt for those who sought this way of bolstering up their fortunes:

> not a virgin
> Left by her friends heir to a noble fortune
> But she's in danger of a marriage
> To some puffed title[26]

A character in Shackerley Marmion's *A Fine Companion* takes a more severely practical view, "Why, sir, your citizens' widows are the only rubbish [i.e. rubble] of the kingdom, to fill up the breaches of the decayed houses".[27] Celestina in Shirley's *Lady of Pleasure* (1635), a young rich widow herself, although anxious not to be carried off too soon, has no great aversion to the probable fate which will overtake her, when the court gentleman

> Claps in with his gilt coach and Flandrian trotters
> And hurries her away to be a countess.[28]

William Davenant, a courtier, regrets the necessity which compels the 'female issue of our decay'd nobility' to

> quarter arms with the City
> And match with saucy haberdashers' sons.[29]

The opportunities for comedy afforded by the more innocent and more absurd pretensions of the new rich, and especially their wives, were freely exploited. In Massinger's *City Madam* (1632), the rich citizen's wife has turned her house into a little court. She will have only French or Italian cooks to dress her meat and scorns her poor husband who thinks he has done very well in engaging the Lord Mayor's cook to prepare her a banquet. When three sucking pigs, fattened on muscadine and costing twenty marks apiece, are set on the table she waves them away as not good enough for her. Her husband expostulates with her on her extravagance, reminding her of earlier days when

> you wore
> Satin on solemn days, a chain of gold,
> A velvet hood, rich borders, and sometimes
> A dainty miniver cap, a silver pin
> Headed with a pearl worth threepence, and thus far
> You were privileged and no man envied it:
> It being for the city's honour that
> There should be a distinction between
> The wife of a patrician and plebeian.

But now with her 'Hungerland bands and Spanish quellio ruffs' his wife will be as fine as a Court lady: she spends forty pounds on a nightgown and when she receives her gossips after lying-in has the baby in a rich canopied crib like a young prince.[30] The dramatists usually saw to it that such proud ladies ended humble and penitent, well content to go back to their miniver caps, velvet hoods and threepenny pearls.

Massinger's *City Madam*, like Chapman and Marston's *Eastward Ho* a generation earlier, developed, with modern trappings, the time-honoured theme of the over-proud woman. But a new element was introduced into the treatment of city wives by the younger generation of dramatists. The citizen's wife is now not merely pretentious but anxious to show her quality by having a lord for a lover. This was not difficult to manage because the young sparks at the Court were—the dramatists of the thirties are wonderfully in agreement on the subject—very willing to seduce a citizen's wife so that they might get their hands into her husband's coffers. The first step was usually to smuggle her into the gallery at a Court masque and make love to her in the dark.[31]

A city beauty of this kind, Alice Saleware, in Brome's *The Mad Couple Well Match'd* (*c.* 1638), sits in her husband's shop 'more glorious than the Maidenhead in the Mercer's Arms, the Nonpareil, the Paragon of the City, the Flower de Luce of Cheapside . . .' She has several Court admirers and she cleverly persuades her doting husband that if he wishes to appear like a gentleman he must not hang over her all the time or even share a room with her—'that were most uncourtly'.[32] Her plans are, however, brought to nothing by an unexpected turn of events. Her Court lover becomes virtuous.

The reputation of King Charles' Court and of elegant society in general is somewhat ambiguously reflected in these plays. Prynne's attack on the morality of the stage and his supposed reflections on the Queen in *Histriomastix* (1633) caused both Brome and Shirley to come to the defence of their own profession and of the innocent amusements of the Court. Prynne had declared 'delight and skill in dancing a badge of lewd lascivious women and strumpets'. Several of Shirley's plays seem designed to do little else but prove the contrary to be the case, and even Brome, who was far less favourable to the Court than Shirley, introduced a scene into his *Sparagus Gardens* (1635), with the sole purpose of defending the reputation of the Court.

Sparagus Garden was an expensive pleasure ground on the south bank of the river, where asparagus and fresh strawberries were served, with sugar and wine, at exorbitant prices. The place had walks, lawns and arbours, and private rooms could be hired in the adjoining eating houses. The Garden had a dubious reputation but was patronized by some of the Court. Brome in his play brings the usual gang of tricksters, gulls and citizens' wives to this resort. They are at once much impressed to see three Court ladies—'Every lady with her own husband: what a virtuous, honest age is this'. Shortly after, the Court party re-appears; they engage in dull conversation, and dance a stately measure 'to help digestion'. The dance ended, one lady priggishly cries out that she sees some 'wicked ones' approaching, to which her virtuous gallant replies:

> May the example of our harmless mirth
> And civil recreation purge the place
> Of all foul purposes . . .
> We seek not to abridge their privilege
> Nor can their ill hurt us; we are safe.[33]

If Brome had depicted any more of the Court's 'harmless mirth' in this style he would soon have brought it into ridicule, but this type of scene—which is apparently intended seriously—does not recur.

Shirley, a more consistent defender of the royal reputation and policy than Brome, offers a well-deserved compliment to the King and Queen in his *Lady of Pleasure*. His heroine, congratulating a courtier-rake on his reform, attributes it to the truth and innocence

> which shine
> So bright in the two royal luminaries:
> At Court you cannot lose your way to chastity.[34]

This high opinion of the Court was not shared by the Londoners in general. It must be remembered that most of the eulogies of King Charles' Court, with which we are familiar, were written after the King's death when its virtues shone all the more brightly by comparison with the disorders of the exile and the Court of Charles II. This posthumous reputation makes it difficult to form a dispassionate estimate of the opinion in which contemporaries held it, but comedies, especially Shirley's, throw an interesting light on the question.

Many of these comedies turn on the misinterpretation or slandering of innocence. This is a time-worn theme, but when it was used by the playwrights of an earlier generation the innocent person was almost invariably the victim of a plot—like the unfortunate Hero in *Much Ado*. In the plays of the sixteen-thirties on the other hand, the innocent have only themselves to blame: they persistently conduct themselves with an indiscretion that cannot but cause comment, and indulge in the most dubious manœuvres. The young people of *The Ball*, *The Lady of Pleasure*, *Love in a Maze*, all behave with the utmost freedom and pour scorn on the malicious comments of a censorious world.

Celestina, the young widow in *A Lady of Pleasure*, takes a house in the Strand and announces her intention of leading a gay but virtuous life. She encourages admirers and when one of them ventures on a dishonourable proposal she magnificently—but a little unreasonably—turns the tables on him. She suggests to him that he should sell his coat of arms for money and when he indignantly refuses, declares that her honour, like his, cannot be bought and sold:

> think, think, my lord,
> To what you would unworthily betray me,
> If you would not, for price of gold or pleasure,
> (If that be more your idol) lose the glory
> And painted honour of your house.[35]

In *The Gamester* an unfaithful husband is reformed by being deceived into a belief that his virtuous wife has been unfaithful too. She herself is a cheerfully consenting party to this deception which goes on for several acts. The plot is an adaptation from a story in *The Heptameron*, but Charles I himself seems to have suggested it to Shirley for a play and he was delighted with the way in which Shirley had handled it. In Brome's *The Damoiselle* an impoverished knight advertises a raffle of his daughter and sells tickets at twenty pounds a piece. This unspeakable conduct turns out to be an ingenious trick to collect a dowry for her while making her beauty and innocence shine the brighter.

The theme which emerges from all these complicated intrigues is simply that virtue and innocence are to be judged by the inward intention, not by the outward appearance. This idea was the foundation of the practice of Platonic love which had recently come from France and was fashionable at Court. In Davenant's *Platonic Lovers*, which makes light-hearted fun of the convention, the avowed Platonic lovers Theander and Eurithea are allowed to be in each other's company at all hours unchaperoned without giving rise to scandal because they are

> lovers of a pure
> Celestial kind, such as some style Platonical,
> A new court epithet scarce understood:
> But all they woo, sir, is the spirit, face,
> And heart: therefore their conversation is
> More safe to fame.[36]

Platonic love was all very well at Court where the conventions were accepted, but it made a very different impression outside the charmed circle, and the Queen's willingness to be the central star in this whole planetary system of courtly love gave rise to a great deal of groundless gossip and malicious scandal.

On the stage, at least by the conventions of the time, the innocent had only to declare themselves for all slanders to vanish away. In real life it was not so, and the misunderstandings which thickened about King Charles, his Queen and his Court during his personal rule played their part in undermining the position and power of the Crown.

The extravagance of the Court was another cause for complaint. Courtiers were not noted for punctuality in meeting their obligations, and the special privileges which protected them from arrest for debt were very unpopular. A similar privilege, protecting members of Parliament came to be hated no less bitterly after 1640. Davenant set his play *The Unfortunate Lovers* in an imaginary Italy, but the experiences, and the conversation of the gay young courtier Rampino belong none the less to Whitehall. In the first act, he shows some visitors over the palace, asking them to walk boldly and not slink about or they will be taken for city spies trying to collect debts. Later, when he cannot pay his tailor, Friskin, he offers to get him court preferment, and perhaps a rocker's place to the next young prince or princess for the sempstress to whom he also owes money. The tailor, a man of ambition, is delighted with this and begins at once to boast of the future glories of the House of Friskin.[37]

It was a serious weakness in King Charles and in some of his advisers—notably the Earl of Strafford—not to realize that a bad reputation, however undeserved, and a scandal, however baseless, can be dangerous to the government. They persistently tried to suppress criticism, where they should have removed its causes.

The King, and his father before him, had always striven to prevent their subjects from indulging in "idle talk", in loose or scandalous speeches. But Charles appears to have believed that the ordinary tendency of human nature to speculate on public affairs, or on the private affairs of public men, could be stifled by stopping up the sources through which the public gained its information. Without news, he calculated, there could be no gossip about public affairs. When criticism of his foreign policy became too vocal, he accordingly prohibited the importation of the foreign news letters, the *corantoes*, out of which his people gleaned their knowledge of what went on in the great world. (With a far clearer understanding of human nature, Cardinal Richelieu at the same time in France took charge of the press and fed it plentifully with such news as he wished the people to have. King Charles only learnt this trick during the Civil War when he had the sense to start an official newspaper, *Mercurius Aulicus*, at Oxford.)

The prohibition of the *corantoes* and the discouragement of newspapers generally, is several times mentioned in contemporary plays. Lucina, in *The Ball*, declares scornfully that people with nothing better to do will fall back on private scandal "when *corantoes* fail". Thomas Heywood, in the prologue to *The Late Lancashire Witches* excuses himself for taking up this domestic and local theme, because of the lack of more significant subjects—

> Corantoes failing, and no foot post late
> Possessing us with news of foreign state.[38]

That the news in the *corantoes* was inadequate and often false was generally known—Ben Jonson had mocked at them in an earlier generation—but they provided a contact with the outside world, they fed the public interest in the fate of the

Protestant Cause in Europe and they were extremely popular.
Therefore they continued to be smuggled into the country and
were supplemented by handwritten sheets, circulated by enterprising newsmongers. Some of the sources used by these
underhand journalists were moderately reliable; most were not.
Shirley declared that your professional journalist 'will write
you a battle in any part of Europe at an hour's warning, and
yet never set foot out of a tavern'.[39]

Davenant devoted the sub-plot in *News from Plymouth* to dis-
crediting the newsmonger. Sir Solomon Trifle, a Justice of the
Peace, supplements his income by compiling a newsletter which
he distributes through various agents, one of whom is a Puritan
called Zeal. When his creatures call on him, he explains his
manner of business to a friend:

> They come for news; man's nature's greedy of it.
> We wise men forge it, and the credulous vulgar,
> Our instruments, disperse it . . .
> News of all sorts and sizes, I have studied hard
> And from the general courants and gazettes,
> Public and private, letters from all parts
> Of Christendom, though they speak contraries,
> Weigh'd and reduc'd them to such certainties
> That I dare warrant 'em authentical
> Under my hand and seal . . .

His authentical news follows :

> Rome is taken
> By the ships of Amsterdam, and the Pope himself
> To save his life turn'd Brownist . . .
> . . . The Spanish fleet
> That anchor'd off Gibraltar, is sunk
> By the French horse . . .
> . . . From the Low Countries
> Antwerp is plundered, Brussels burnt, the cannon
> Brought before Lovaine, and the Prince of Orange
> Stands to be Emperor.

At this point the sceptical listener interrupts:

> The Emperor lives!

Not in the least put out, Sir Solomon continues:

> But is to die the tenth of October next,
> And he has it in reversion. From France:
> Rochelle recovered by the Huguenots,
> And the fifth July last, yes, 'tis the fifth,
> The Cardinal Richelieu as he slept in his tent,
> Had his head cut off with an invisible sword
> By the Great Constable's ghost.[40]

This monstrous newsmonger is very properly arrested in the last act for holding unlawful intelligence with foreign princes. Less properly, he is threatened with the rack to divulge his sources of information.

James Shirley as well as the courtier playwrights and most of the university amateurs—Davenant, Mayne, Cartwright—supported the royal policies in so far as they mentioned them at all. Massinger and Brome on the other hand could be critical, Massinger sometimes so broadly—as in the case of the King's demands for money mentioned before—that the offending passage had to be deleted. Brome in *The Court Beggar* took up the abuse of monopolies and patents, which was one of the King's most fruitful ways of raising money during his unparliamentary rule. The satire is conceived in general terms and owes a great deal—as Brome usually does—to his master's, Jonson's, treatment of a similar subject in *The Devil is an Asse*. The Parliament of 1624 had made monopolies illegal, but they had crept in again under the transparent disguise of patents. Monopoly rights were granted to those who claimed to have some special process or invention or some interesting experimental scheme for trade or industry. Projects, as they were called, were put forward in great numbers by hangers-on of the Court. In Brome's play a country knight, Sir Andrew Mendicant, comes to London and wastes his fortune trying to procure a grant of this kind. The Court is represented as being surrounded by sharks who will, for a consideration, suggest hopeful schemes to men like Sir Andrew and share the proceeds with him, if he can get a grant to operate them. These "projectors", who follow Sir Andrew about in a babbling chorus, have plans which they assert will bring in fifty thousand

The Piazza at Covent Garden from the etching by Wenceslaus Hollar

Two Ladies of Fashion: winter, with Cornhill in the background, and summer, with one of the London parks, from etchings by Wenceslaus Hollar

pounds a year to them, twice as much to Sir Andrew, and
£64,783 7s. 9d. to the Crown. When one of them is asked to change
a shilling for two sixpences he has no ready money about him.
This, to an audience who still had the gravest suspicion of all
credit transactions, was proof positive that the fellow was a fraud.

Among the projects suggested to Sir Andrew is a monopoly of
wig-making in the interests of the nation's health, an imposition
of a fourpenny tax on any gallant wearing a new fashion on
the first day he puts it on, and the establishment of a floating
theatre on barges in the Thames so that the watermen may
get back some of the custom recently lost to hackney coachmen
and the carriers of sedan chairs.[41]

Brome covered himself for this attack on one aspect of the
royal policy by strongly defending another part of it in his play.
The King in 1632 had issued a proclamation forbidding country
gentlemen to come to London except on business. Sir Andrew
Mendicant, who is one of these absentee landlords, is up-
braided by his daughter for having abandoned his rural seat:

> Your aim has been to raise
> Your state by court suits, begging as some call it,
> And for that course you left your country life
> To purchase wit at Court . . .
> And for the exchange of a fair mansion house,
> Large fruitful fields, rich meadows and sweet pastures,
> Well cropped with corn and stocked as well with cattle,
> A park well stored with deer too, and fish ponds in't,
> And all this for a lodging in the Strand . . . [42]

Shirley, with considerable eloquence, in several comedies
depicts the folly of country gentlemen and their wives who
waste their fortunes in London. But though he can write
persuasively of the pleasures of the countryside, he knew the
other side of the question. Lady Bornwell, newly arrived in
London with her husband, exclaims

> I would not
> Endure again the country conversation
> To be lady of six shires! The men
> So near the primitive making they retain
> A sense of nothing but the earth; their brains

9

> And barren heads standing as much in want
> Of ploughing as their ground. To hear a fellow
> Make himself merry and his horse with whistling
> Sellenger's Round! To observe with what solemnity
> They keep their wakes and throw for pewter candlesticks![43]

To leave the boredom of the country was one thing, but there was no need to run to the other extreme, and Lady Bornwell's husband complains with some reason of

> Your charge of gaudy furniture, and pictures
> Of this Italian master and that Dutchman,
> Your mighty looking glasses, like artillery
> Brought home on engines . . .
> Fourscore pound suppers for my lord your kinsman,
> Banquets for t'other lady aunt and cousins,
> And perfumes that exceed all: train of servants
> To stifle us at home, and shew abroad
> More motley than the French or the Venetian
> About your coach . . .
> I could accuse the gaiety of your wardrobe
> And prodigal embroideries, under which
> Rich satins, plushes, cloth of silver dare
> Not show their own complexions . . . [44]

The lure of the town sometimes reached the rich yeoman. In Brome's *Sparagus Garden* the foolish Tim Hoyden from Ta'anton arrives with 'four hundred pounds, sir, I brought it up to town on purpose to make myself a cleare gentleman of it'. He falls at once into the hands of the decayed knight Moneylacks who, under pretence of teaching him the ways of the world, removes most of it. Starvation on what he is assured is court fare, provokes a spirit of rebellion in Hoyden: 'Marry, I feel that I am hungry, and that my shrimp diet and sippings have almost famished me and my purse too; slid, I dare be sworn, as I am almost a gentleman, that every bit and spoonful that I have swallowed these ten days, has cost me ten shillings at least'.[45]

Crosswill, the captious country gentleman in *Covent Garden Weeded*, gets off more lightly. His humour being always to cross everyone, he came up to London because 'the Proclamation of Restraint spurred him on'.[46] But he was very well able to take care of himself when he got there.

The theme of this play is a direct imitation of Ben Jonson's
Bartholomew Fair, modernized and made topical by being trans-
ferred to the new and much talked of region of Covent Garden.
Cockbrayne, a Middlesex Justice of the Peace, who describes
himself as a near relation of Justice Overdo of *Bartholomew Fair*,
disguises himself and mingles with the inhabitants of Covent
Garden in order to discover and reform their sins. He meets
with much the same adventures and misfortunes as did Justice
Overdo at *Bartholomew Fair*. Brome's play falls behind Jonson's
in every respect, but it has a bustling liveliness and is full of
topical allusions. In the first scene Justice Cockbrayne admires
the new buildings:

> I, marry sir! This is something like! These appear like buildings!
> Here's architecture expressed indeed! It is a most sightly situation
> and fit for gentry and nobility! . . . Yond magnificent piece the
> Piazzo, will excel that at Venice, by hearsay, (I ne'er travelled).
> A hearty blessing on their brains, honours and wealths, that are
> projectors, furtherers and performers of such great works . . . The
> Surveyor (whoe'er he was) has manifested himself the master of
> this great Art. How he has wedded strength to beauty, state to
> uniformity, commodiousness with perspicuity. All, all as't should
> be.[47]

The inhabitants, however, are not all as they should be and
Justice Cockbrayne's expedition among them does little to
improve them. Although the nobility and gentry hastened to
take houses in Covent Garden as soon as it was built, so did the
fashionable ladies of pleasure. Soon the new Covent Garden
rivalled the Strand as the place where richly dressed young
women, alluringly seated on balconies could

> angle up
> The gay peripatetics of the Court.[48]

The setting of comedies in recognizable places was obviously
an attraction to audiences, especially no doubt to those who
either could not afford, or did not like, to venture in such places
themselves. From the opening scene of *Covent Garden Weeded* it is
clear that the buildings must have been represented on the
stage—"these appear like buildings". No doubt the walks and
arbours of *Sparagus Garden* were also fairly well imitated on the

stage for that play too, so that citizens who could not afford the prices charged at such a resort could get a very good idea of what it was like for their sixpenny or twelvepenny seat at the theatre.

Shirley attempted great realism in his representation of a race meeting in his play *Hyde Park* (1632). The runners in the foot race—one of whom is called by the name of a famous Irish champion—actually cross the stage twice. Although Shirley could hardly do the same when it came to a horse race, he contrives in the dialogue to give a wonderfully vivid impression of the mounting tension as the race is run. The audience could hear the seventeenth-century equivalent of the cry "They're off!" and listen to the shortening odds shouted by excited gamblers as the race was run. The excitement spreads to a group of ladies in the front of the stage who begin to lay bets among themselves—

> What odds against my lord!—
> Silk stockings—
> To a pair of perfum'd gloves? I take it.—
> Done. I'll have them Spanish scent—
> The stockings shall be scarlet. If you choose your scent I'll choose
> my colour. [49]

Gambling ladies were probably not approved of by the majority of the audience but that would merely add spice to the scene. Incidentally, Shirley has another gambling lady in his play *The Example* (1634). The representation and the description of extravagant and fashionable pleasures is a marked feature of these plays which, in taste as well as time, stand midway between the Elizabethan and Restoration drama. Restoration drama is directed to a society audience which itself indulged in expensive pleasures, took them for granted and needed no explanations. But the public of the sixteen-thirties was still the mixed public for which Shakespeare had written. The explanatory character of some of the descriptions in Shirley, Brome and others suggest that in their time it was a popular function of the theatre to provide the humbler members of this mixed audience with glimpses of a "high life" which was something of a mystery to them and of which they already in some measure disapproved.

Another fashionable craze, more innocent than gambling and racing, which figures in the comedies, was that of collecting. The serious interest in antiquarianism of the later sixteenth and early seventeenth century had by this time spread to less scholarly enthusiasts, who fell an easy prey to fraudulent pedlars of antiques. Veterano, in Marmion's *The Antiquary* was such a one, although he begins sensibly enough with the statement that ancient things 'are the registers, the chronicles of the age they were made in, and speak the truth of history better than a hundred of your printed commentaries'. He talks like a good book but behaves like a fool; on being offered a very dilapidated manuscript he recognizes it at once as one of the lost books of the *Republic* penned by Cicero's own hand.[50]

Cartwright introduces an antiquary into *The Ordinary*. He has been deeply infected with the current passion for Anglo-Saxon studies and uses such phrases as "I ween" and "Waes hale" in his conversation. From his lips comes the faked folk rhyme which of recent years has been a popular subject for poker work in Olde Tea Shoppes, being—who knows?—perhaps taken for the genuine article.

> St. Francis and St. Benedight
> Blesse this house from wicked wight
> From the Nightmare and the Goblin
> That is hight good fellow Robin.
> Keep if from all evill spirits,
> Fayries, Weezels, Rats and Ferrets,
> From Curfew time
> To the next prime.[51]

These comedies are light, frivolous, essentially ephemeral stuff and their charm lies in the incidental intelligence that they give of the things of everyday life in this period of calm before the Civil Wars.

Those who lived through that epoch were in later life to look back on the halcyon days before 1642 with much the same nostalgia that some now living feel for the legendary time before 1914. The survivors of the Civil Wars, of whatever party, could not but feel that those lost years, which had in truth been restless, depressed and rather unhappy, had been infinitely

sweet. In retrospect the inestimable blessing of peace made that
whole epoch bright. 'God Almighty send us a happy end of all
our troubles and peace in this poor kingdom again'; Sir
Thomas Knyvett writing in the midst of the Civil Wars uttered
the prayer that was in the hearts of most honest Englishmen.

Something of this feeling about the interlude before the Civil
War inevitably communicates itself to the historian. That epoch
has the air of heightened peace and stillness which belongs to a
time immediately preceding catastrophe. We know that there
was much amiss, that there was distress and unemployment,
trouble over enclosures, persecution of the Puritans, a bad run
of plague in London and much else to darken those years. But
there was also much poetry, much singing, wakes, whitsun ales
and harvest festivals, jollity in taverns, learned talk in common
rooms; crops ripened and were garnered in peace and the
housewife and husbandman need fear no enemies save the
weather and the gypsies. Life went on normally from day to day
with no more than the ordinary anxieties and pleasures.
England was by no means all a sunlit garden but there was a
kind of truth in Marvell's poignant cry:

> Oh thou that dear and happy isle
> The garden of the world erewhile
> Thou Paradise of the four seas
> Which heaven planted us to please . . .
> Unhappy! shall we never more
> That sweet militia restore
> When gardens only had their towers
> And all the garrisons were flowers,
> When roses only arms might bear
> And men did rosy garlands wear?

The beauty of these plays is that they fix, in phrase after
phrase, the vivid ephemeral details of that time, the ordinary
pleasures which became so sweet in retrospect simply because
they were ordinary: the holiday expeditions to "the city
outleaps", Islington, Newington, Paddington, Kensington, to
eat prunes and cream; the busy bustle of Hyde Park on a
summer afternoon with a milkmaid leading round her red cow
to offer drinks to the ladies, and the gentlemen sending their
pages hurrying to 'Grave Maurice's Head' for ale; the

'booths and bagpipes upon Banstead downs'—though these we have still; the country bumpkins throwing for pewter candlesticks; the citizen's wife bringing her baby home from nurse with her coach stuffed with hampers of fruit and cheese cakes; the common hangings on the walls, The Prodigal Son and the Story of Joesph; the thumbed copy of Foxe's *Martyrs* on the country gentleman's hall table for his tenantry to read while waiting. Out of the comedies we can hear the long silenced voices talking of everyday things: laughing at the new portable chairs—'the handbarrows, what call you 'em?—Sedans', marvelling at the handsome pocket watches—'you have not a gentleman that's a true gentleman without one'; the worldly ladies shopping in the Dutch shops of the New Exchange; the godly ladies trooping to church each with her prayer-book in its green dimity bag.

Take away the improbable intrigues and the ingenious entanglements, and a whole society with its petty pleasures and preoccupations starts into life from the pages of these comedies. It is their real claim on our remembrance; the best that can be said of them was said by Alexander Brome, writing commendatory verses to the plays of his namesake Richard during the Commonwealth:

> we may be glad
> To see and think on the happiness we had.

NOTES

[1] See L.C. Knights, *Drama and Society in the Age of Jonson*, London (1937), for a general exposition of the social tendencies of the drama during the first forty years of the century and Gerald Eades Bentley, *The Jacobean and Caroline Stage*, Oxford (1941), for all information concerning companies and players.

[2] *The Dramatic Records of Sir Henry Herbert, Master of the Revels, 1623–73*, ed. Joseph Quincy Adams, Newhaven (1917), p. 23.

[3] *Calendar of State Papers Domestic, 1639*, p. 140; Leslie Hotson, *Commonwealth and Restoration Stage*, Cambridge, Mass. (1928), pp. 3–4.

[4] William Prynne. *Histriomastix*, London (1633), title page.

[5] Ben Jonson, ed. Herford and Simpson, Oxford (1947), VIII, p. 410; the literary characteristics of the drama in all its forms during this epoch are fully analysed by Alfred Herbage in *Cavalier Drama*, *Modern Language Association of America*, New York (1936).

[6] Shackerley Marmion, *A Fine Companion*, Prologue, *Dramatic Works*, Edinburgh and London (1875), p. 106.

[7] James Shirley, *The Witty Fair One*, Act IV, Scene II, *Dramatic Works*. ed. Dyce, London (1833), II, p. 332.

[8] Richard Brome, *The Antipodes*, Prologue, *Dramatic Works*, London (1873), III, p. 232.

[9] Anonymous, *A Match at Midnight*, Act V, *Dodsley's Old English Plays*, ed. W. Carew Hazlitt, London (1875), XIII, p. 85.

[10] William Davenant, *The Wits*, Act II, Scene I, *Dramatic Works*, Edinburgh and London (1872), II, p. 122.

[11] Brome, *Covent Garden Weeded*, Act III, Scene I, *Works*, II, p. 42.

[12] Shirley, *The Constant Maid*, Act II, Scene I, *Works*, IV, p. 467.

[13] Brome, *The Northern Lass*, Act II, Scene I, *Works* III, p. 23.

[14] Philip Massinger, *The City Madam*, Act V, Scene II, *Plays*, ed. Arthur Symons, Mermaid Series, London (1887), I, p. 487.

[15] Davenant, *News from Plymouth*, Act V, *Works*, IV, pp. 184–5; *The Wits*, Act I, Scene I, *Works*, II, p. 124.

[16] William Cartwright, *The Ordinary*, Act V, *Plays and Poems of William Cartwright*, ed. G. Blakemore Evans, Madison (1951), p. 349.

[17] Davenant, *The Wits*, Act II, Scene I, *Works*, II, p. 174.

[18] Cartwright, *The Ordinary*, Act III, Scene V, *Plays and Poems*, p. 314.

[19] Shirley, *Love in a Maze*, Act I, Scene I, *Works*, II, p. 277.

[20] John Carvell, *The Soddered Citizen*, Act II, Scene I, Malone Society Reprints, Oxford (1936), p. 26. The introduction to this edition of the unique surviving manuscript of this play gives reasons for attributing it to John Carvell rather than Shackerley Marmion.

[21] Brome, *The Damoiselle*, Act I, Scene I, *Works*, I, p. 384.

[22] Shirley, *The Ball*, Act I, Scene I, *Works*, III, p. 7.

[23] Davenant, *News from Plymouth*, Act I, Scene II, *Works*, IV, p. 17.

[24] Brome, *The Damoiselle*, Act I, Scene II, *Works*, I, pp. 390–1.

[25] Carvell, *Soddered Citizen*, Act I, Scene VI, pp. 24–5.

[26] Shirley, *The Witty Fair One*, Act I, Scene I, *Works*, I, p. 278.

[27] Marmion, *A Fine Companion*, Act II, Scene II, *Works*, p. 130.

[28] Shirley, *The Lady of Pleasure*, Act II, Scene II, *Works*, IV, p. 31.

[29] Davenant, *The Wits*, Act III, Scene II, *Works*, II. p. 173.

[30] Massinger, *The City Madam*, Act I, Scene I, Act II, Scene I, and Act IV, Scene IV, *Plays*, I, pp. 402, 421, 475.

[31] Anonymous, *A Match at Midnight*, Act IV, and Jasper Mayne, *The City Match*, Act IV, Scene III, *Dodsley's Old English Plays*, XIII, pp. 77, 277.

[32] Brome, *A Mad Couple Well Match'd*, Act III, *Works*, I, p. 59.

[33] Brome, *Sparagus Garden*, Act III, Scenes V and VI, *Works*, III, pp. 160, 166.

[34] Shirley, *The Lady of Pleasure*, Act III, Scene IV, *Works*, IV, p. 81.

[35] *Ibid.*, p. 97.

[36] Davenant, *Platonic Lovers*, Act I, Scene I, *Works*, II, p. 17.

[37] Davenant, *Unfortunate Lovers*, Act III, *Works*, III, p. 353.

[38] Thomas Heywood, *The Late Lancashire Witches*, Prologue, *Dramatic Works*, London (1874), IV, p. 169.

39 Shirley, *Love Tricks*, Act I, Scene I, *Works*, I, pp. 8–9.
40 Davenant, *News from Plymouth*, Act IV, Scene II, *Works*, IV, pp. 167–8, 170.
41 Brome, *Court Beggar*, Act I, *Works*, I, pp. 182–4.
42 *Ibid.*, p. 187.
43 Shirley, *Lady of Pleasure*, Act I, Scene I, *Works*, IV, p. 5.
44 *Ibid.*, pp. 7–8.
45 Brome, *Sparagus Garden*, *Works*, III, pp. 140, 167.
46 Brome, *Covent Garden Weeded*, Act II, Scene I, *Works*, II, p. 19.
47 *Ibid.*, Act I, Scene I, pp. 1–2.
48 Carvell, *Soddered Citizen*, Act II, Scene III, p. 36.
49 Shirley, *Hyde Park*, Act IV, Scene III, *Works*, II, p. 518.
50 Marmion, *The Antiquary*, Act II, *Works*, pp. 228, 252.
51 Cartwright, *The Ordinary*, Act III, Scene I, *Plays and Poems*, p. 303.

V

Daniel Finch,
2nd Earl of Nottingham:
His House and Estate[1]

H. J. HABAKKUK

V

BURLEY-ON-THE-HILL stands on a high prominence over-looking the Vale of Catmose in Rutland. Defoe came this way in the early eighteenth century, not very long after it was built, and was moved to say 'There may be some extra-ordinary places in *England*, where there are so many fine ones, I say there may be some that excel in this or that Particular, but I do not know of a House in *Britain*, which excels all the rest in so many Particulars, or that goes so near to excelling them all in everything'.[2] Since the builder of the house had been responsible for imprisoning Defoe in 1704, this must be counted an unbiased tribute. In 1815 the Duke of Wellington thought of buying it, and of building on the site an entirely new house or palace. A friend, Mr. H. B., 'ventured to say that Burleigh was among our finest houses, and much too good to pull down. . . . They cannot build anything as good as Burleigh is at this moment for £200,000; and I much question whether they will build him so handsome and commodious a mansion.'[3] Burley-on-the-Hill is one of the country houses of the second rank, smaller than the Leviathans like Blenheim and Castle Howard, but in the same class as Easton Neston or Nuneham Courteney. It was built between 1694 and 1708, and it belongs therefore to one of the great periods of English house-building, for though it is difficult to plot with precision the number and size of great houses built at various times, it is a common and reasonable impression that the end of the seventeenth century and the first half of the eighteenth were times of exceptional activity. Today the glory has departed from these houses; many have been pulled down, many put to alien uses and those that still survive in the hands of the families for which they were built do so mainly by grace of the shillings of curious visitors and govern-ment subvention; and they survive as relics of a society, not indeed distant in time, for our grandfathers knew it, but strange and remote. They may soon be as obsolete and curious as the cromlechs. Yet in their day they were the centres of an active social and political life, the homes of a ruling class. For what sort of men were they created? Why did men desire to live in such great and remote mansions? Who designed and built them? How were they paid for? Or rather, since our field must be limited, what are the answers to these questions in the case of this single house of Burley?

A contrast is often made in social history between old and new landed families, the former long seated in the countryside, the latter establishing themselves for the first time with the gains of law, trade or government service. The man for whom Burley was built—Daniel Finch, second Earl of Nottingham—does not fall easily into either category. He belonged to a cadet branch of a landed family long established in Kent which acquired substantial estates by a series of lucrative marriages. Early in the seventeenth century, the representative of the family at that time, Sir Moyle Finch, married the daughter and heiress of an Essex landed family, the Heneages, and this coalescence of estates raised the main line of the Finches out of the substantial squirearchy into the aristocracy. Daniel Finch's grandfather was a younger son of this marriage who, like many another younger son, went in for the law; he became Recorder of London and Speaker of the House of Commons. His eldest son, Heneage, Daniel's father, was also a lawyer, one of the most successful of his day, who ultimately became Lord Chancellor and was created Earl of Nottingham. This cadet branch had been endowed with estates brought into the family by the marriage with the Heneage heiress. Younger sons were not, in ordinary circumstances, lavishly provided for, but where the mother had property of her own she sometimes settled all or part of it on a younger son, and this had happened in the Finch family. Daniel's father, Heneage, inherited from his grandmother a substantial estate at Ravenstone in Buckinghamshire, which in the 1670's yielded about £1,200 a year, and another at Daventry which yielded about £700.[4]

Heneage, the first Earl, was in his day a man of considerable importance and from his legal practice and the salary of £4,000

which he received while Chancellor, accumulated a substantial
fortune. He did not, however, greatly extend his landed estate.
Early in his career he acquired from his younger brother the
house at Kensington which their father had bought in the early
seventeenth century, and he probably purchased some property
in London. But his landed income at its height was only some
£3,000 a year, a modest income for his rank. Above all, he
never took the decisive step of acquiring a country seat. There
was a decayed manor house at Ravenstone, but though
Heneage built almshouses there and was buried in the local
church, it was not a country seat; it was a farm-house let to a
local farmer. The family lived in their house at Kensington.
Kensington in the seventeenth century was a pleasant and
healthy village—it did not begin to fill up until William III
acquired a residence there—and it contained a number of large
mansions, Holland House and Campden House for instance, as
well as many smaller ones. But the Finch property there was
not in the proper sense of the term a country estate. The total
property was small. It seems to have covered nearly all the lands
of the modern Kensington Gardens, that is to say it was about
two hundred acres; part of this was let to a farmer and the rest
probably consisted of gardens—rather elaborate gardens, for
when Pepys went there in the summer of 1664, 'seeing the
fountain and singing there with the ladies', he thought it 'a
mighty fine cool place . . . with a great laver of water in the
middle, and the bravest place for musick I ever heard'.[5] The
house itself, the core of what is now Kensington Palace, was of
some architectural interest. It was in the form of a compact
rectangle, and it has been regarded as 'the fore-runner of a
whole series of plans leading to a typically eighteenth-century
villa plan and marking the final breakaway from medieval
tradition'. But it did not contain many rooms. It had three
main storeys with attics above; on the ground floor there was a
hall, a parlour, probably a chapel, and one or two lodgings; on
the upper floor was the Great Chamber, the Gallery and two
lodgings or bedrooms. There was some sleeping accommo-
dation for guests or servants in the attic, and in the basement
were the kitchen and servants' room. On the two main floors,
that is, there were probably eight rooms, excluding the Chapel.[6]

Heneage does not seem to have made any substantial alterations to the house, and never appears to have contemplated moving from it, or building a country house at Ravenstone. His main efforts were devoted to launching his sons, and particularly his eldest son Daniel. For him, in 1673, he secured a marriage, both lucrative and socially advantageous, with one of the three daughters and heirs of Robert, Earl of Warwick, one of his neighbours at Kensington. Her share of the Warwick estates consisted of the island of Foulnesse and of a number of manors in Essex, and to win so well-endowed an heiress Heneage made a very generous settlement, and, in pursuance of this settlement, helped his son in 1677 to buy a substantial estate at Milton in Buckinghamshire, not far from the family property at Ravenstone.[7]

I. THE ESTATE

Daniel succeeded his father in 1682. In 1685 he married for the second time, Anne, daughter of the old cavalier, Viscount Hatton of Kirby, who brought with her a portion of £10,000.[8] In 1686 he began to look out for a place to live in the country, either to purchase or to rent. Occasionally he dealt directly with potential sellers, but as a general rule he negotiated through Robert Clayton, the foremost scrivener of his day, who probably knew more about estates for sale than anyone else in the late seventeenth century. It was a bad time to buy an estate; and Nottingham further limited his choice by confining himself to Northamptonshire, Buckinghamshire and Rutland, in which area lay not only the estates he had inherited from his father, but those of his father-in-law. It is a comment both on the small number of estates available for purchase and on the seriousness with which contemporaries regarded the reported intention of James II to confiscate the former monastic lands that Nottingham should write to his father-in-law on June 30, 1688, 'I have no scruples about Abbey-Land, but on the contrary think those the best purchases, because there are fewer rivals and consequently will be the cheapest, and there are so few things now to be sold, that every man that has money to lay out is very ready to hearken to every offer of that kind'.[9]

If he could not buy, Nottingham was prepared to lease.

A Northamptonshire squire, Sir Thomas Samwell, offered him his spare manor house at Gayton, but it was too small: 'he tells me twill hold 40 in family, but mine exceeds that number by near twenty, so that I fear it will be too little'.[10] The other properties available to him were all estates in the hands of more or less heavily indebted landowners, and there was some defect in each of them. Nottingham negotiated for an estate at Boughton in Northamptonshire which belonged to the Earl of Banbury, a young profligate 'who always failed at his appointments',[11] but Banbury asked too much—22 years' purchase for his land of inheritance, 16 years' purchase for lands he leased from the Savoy, £7,000 for the woods and £2,000 for the house. Hanslope Park in Buckinghamshire was another possibility; it lay conveniently enough, 'but the house has cost him [i.e. the then owner] so much money he will value it highly in the purchase and 'tis so very bad and so ill contrived that I shall give but very little for it'.[12] Here again negotiations broke down on the price. There were also prospects of his buying an estate at Salden, in Buckinghamshire, from the Fortescue family, and Moulton Park in Northamptonshire, but they came to nothing.

On 8 October 1689, Nottingham got the details of the estate of Burley in Rutland 'and if it be possible to compass it', he wrote, 'I shall not think of any other purchase'.[13] This was an estate which had belonged to the second Duke of Buckingham who died in April 1687, leaving his properties heavily encumbered. The Duke had been very heavily indebted almost from his youth. As early apparently as 1671 he had settled all or most of his estates on trustees who were to pay him £5,000 a year for life and out of the rest to raise money to pay his debts. After that he borrowed further large sums and incurred heavy expenses in buying the estate of Cliveden and building a great house there. Already before his death his creditors had obtained decrees in Chancery for the sale of his property, and after his death the creditors obtained an Act of Parliament providing for the immediate sale of the Duke's estates at Burley, at Helmsley in Yorkshire and at Whaddon in Buckinghamshire. There were delays in obtaining the Act, so many and conflicting were the claims of Buckingham's creditors, and it was not until July 1693 that Burley was put up for sale and not until February of the following year that the purchase was certain.[14]

There is a tradition that Nottingham was first interested in the estate at Helmsley, but that while on a journey to view it he passed by Burley, was pleased with its amenities and decided to buy it. Family tradition often preserves a core of hard fact, but it does not seem so in this case. All Nottingham's previous negotiations had been for estates not far distant from Ravenstone and Daventry. From the first time he saw particulars of Burley he regarded it as a highly desirable purchase, and from his point of view it was indeed an ideal estate and in just the right part of the world. Nottingham's fear was that Charles Duncombe, the great banker, who was also looking for a substantial estate, would bid against him for Burley. Duncombe 'promised not to rival with me in the purchase of Burleigh'. Nottingham was nervous that Duncombe would break his words 'and play me a trick', but Duncombe kept his bargain, and purchased the Duke of Buckingham's estate in Yorkshire.[15] Thus,

> Helmsley, once proud Buckingham's delight,
> Slides to a scrivener and a city knight,

and Nottingham acquired Burley. The purchase was completed in the summer of 1694, at a price of approximately £50,000. The price seems to have been calculated at twenty-years' purchase, which was a modest valuation for an estate in this part of the country, a compact estate moreover, which made Nottingham the largest landowner in Oakham and in several of the surrounding parishes. One peculiarity the estate had; it included no mansion, for the great house of the Buckinghams had been burned by a Parliamentary garrison during the Civil War, and only the stables—'the noblest of their kind in England'—had escaped the flames.

II. THE HOUSE

Nottingham had sold his house in Kensington to William III in June 1689, and during his term of office as Secretary of State his family had lived in a rented house in London. He resigned his office in November 1693, and there was no longer any need to live the year round in London. 'I am resolved', he wrote, 'to

go into the country, though I live in the stables at Burleigh.'[16]
So drastic a course did not prove necessary for he obtained a
lease of the great house at Exton, which belonged to the Earls of
Gainsborough, and moved his family there in the summer of
1694. Almost immediately the purchase was completed,
Nottingham set about preparing to build a house.

There is no known architect of Burley, and it has been con-
jectured that he was his own architect, like his friend Sir John
Lowther at Lowther Castle and his uncle Lord Conway at
Ragley. In 1665, when he was 18 years old, he had spent a year in
Italy; at that time Bernini's colonnade in front of St. Peter's in
Rome was nearing completion, and it has been suggested, as
evidence that he was his own architect, that this was the in-
spiration of the colonnade which is so extraordinary a feature
of Burley. He clearly discussed his project with other landowners who had experience of building great houses, and with
knowledgeable men in London.[17] In his correspondence there is
a brief and tantalizing reference to a conversation with Wren,
in April of 1694; 'I find', he writes to his father-in-law, 'Sir
Christopher Wren agrees with your Lordship's opinion that oak
timber is not so good as fir for floors, for its own weight will
warp and bend it.'[18] It is conceivable that he sought advice
from officials of the Office of Works, with whom he may have
come into contact when he was Secretary of State. In July
1695, when the main work was about to begin, somebody,
presumably his superintendent of works, on his behalf asked Sir
Henry Sheeres, surveyor of the ordnance, for an opinion
'touching some general rules for building'.[19] He also had a
model of the house constructed for him by Thomas Poulteney,
the joiner employed on many of the city churches.[20] But the
absence in the many letters that survive of any reference to a
designer of the building, the absence, in his accounts, of payment to anyone who might be identified as architect, the very
detailed attention which Nottingham himself paid to every
operation and aspect of the building, and the numerous
occasions on which he refers to his intentions and schemes—all
these circumstances make the conjecture plausible that
Nottingham designed his own house. Though in this period,
when the professional architect had barely emerged, and

architect-like functions and abilities were widely diffused among
the men who took part in a building, this may not have meant
much more than that he had clear and exacting ideas of what
he required from the masons, joiners, carpenters and so forth
who worked for him.

At this period a man had a choice of three methods of
arranging the building of a house: he could employ the builder
directly on time rates; at the other extreme, he could contract
with a single builder to build the house at a fixed price; or, a
method something between the two, he could arrange with the
master-masons, joiners, etc., to do specified sections of the work
at so much per foot or whatever was the relevant measurement.
Nottingham adopted the last of these methods.

This laid a very heavy burden on the man who superintended
the building operations and calculated the various payments
due. Henry Dormer, who performed these functions for
Nottingham, had already acted for him in the survey of Burley
made on behalf of Chancery before the final completion of the
purchase; he is known to have made designs for the rebuilding
of the chapel of St. Mary in Arden, near Market Harborough,
in 1693, and he may conceivably have had some hand in
designing Burley, or at least in giving precision and practical
form to some of Nottingham's general ideas. Dormer continued
to control operations until April 1697 when he was succeeded
by John Lumley of Northampton, who remained in charge
until the house was completed, and who continued to come to
Burley for some days each year so long as any of the supplementary work remained to be done. It is not clear why this
change of overseer was made. There had been many difficulties
over the building in the winter of 1696–7 and it may be that
there was some unrecorded breach between Nottingham and
Dormer. More probably, by 1697 the work was entering a stage
which required the supervision of a man more experienced in
ornament and decoration. All we know of Dormer, besides his
design for St. Mary in Arden, is that in 1706 he made a model
of a new steeple for the church at Burton Overy in Leicestershire, and he is not known to have taken part in the building of
any other great house. Lumley was evidently more skilled in
ornament, for he did work on the first Earl of Nottingham's

tomb at Ravenstone, and made marble and stone urns for Lord Ashburnham's house at Ampthill.[21]

Nottingham originally intended to build his house entirely of stone, but, as a result probably of Sheeres' advice, decided to use brick for 'the case or carcase of the building', and to confine the use of stone to the foundations, the outer covering, and ornamentations. Brick, Sheeres argued, was more durable and a lighter burden to the foundation, but the argument that presumably appealed most strongly to Nottingham in his haste was that 'stone work ripens by so slow degrees in comparison to brick, that the one in a year or two may afford a tolerable habitation, while the other in thrice the time will continue green, moist, cold and unfit to dwell in'.

Preparatory work started in May 1694 when Nottingham started to arrange for a supply of stone. Clipsham was a few miles away and he decided to build the outside walls of the house in Clipsham stone. There is no evidence that the presence of good building stone in the neighbourhood influenced Nottingham in his choice of estate, but it certainly proved a great advantage that he did not, like the Duke of Marlborough at Blenheim in the next decade, have to go far afield for his stone. At first, indeed, Nottingham had some difficulty in making satisfactory contracts with suppliers.

> The prices Wilkinson demands are higher much than Sir Jo Lowther pay'd or Mr Bertie to whom Wilkinson himself furnished the stone, but I hope to be in the country time enough to adjust all matters preparatory to my building: and that those I shall deal with will not ask more than they do of others; the quantity of my building may be a reason for them to take less of me: I am sure tis a good reason for me to get everything as cheap as is possible: so as it be good & substantial.[22]

But eventually he made arrangements with a number of Clipsham men, who owned or leased quarries, to supply him with stone and he made contracts with several Clipsham masons to do the necessary masonry work in and around the house. The great colonnades on the flanks of the house, he planned to build of stone from Ketton, which was some ten miles away towards Stamford, and for this he contracted with a partnership of Ketton masons headed by Miles Pomeroy.

Although, according to Miss Pearl Finch, over fifty masons are mentioned, the main work was in the hands of a small number of master craftsmen, many of whom worked in partnerships. The principal masons were Bray, Richard Hide, Toplis and Swindall, Halliday, Jackson and Rice, and Wigson and Rowbottom. Most of the masonry on the main walls of the house was done by this last partnership.

The bricks were made on the spot, by Matthew Child, Nottingham's old tenant at Kensingston, and by brickmakers who came mainly from Nottingham and London. And most of the brickwork was done by two partnerships—Varney and Baker, and Hurst and Reading—who probably came from either London or Reading.

The masons were all local men, from either Clipsham or Ketton. Some of them owned or leased quarries but some did not. Conversely, many of the men who supplied stone, including some who supplied a great deal and some who supplied little, did none of the actual masonry. The masons who did most of the work worked in partnerships, and from the frequency with which the names changed, they seem to have been flexible, or at least impermanent. The accounts suggest that many of them were short of capital. These masons were not specialists in the mansions of the great. Samuel Halliday of Stamford, a descendant of the Nathaniel Halliday who worked on Burley, was still engaged as master-mason and quarry-owner early in the present century. He 'restored churches and country houses and built rectories, gate lodges, stables, estate cottages and other buildings over a wide radius of the three counties whose borders meet at Stamford',[23] and the masons who built Burley probably spent most of their time on a similar range of buildings.

There is no mention of difficulty in obtaining masons for building the house; but the masons themselves had some difficulty in procuring adequate labour, partly, no doubt, because of the speed at which Nottingham was attempting to build. In May 1696 he wrote to his father-in-law:

> I am now very well provided of builders, but my great want is of freemasons to work and prepare the stone, without I shall make very little progress this year, nay I must in a very short time give over. Mr Sharp of Clipsham can't, as he says, procure men, which

makes me trouble your Lordship with this to entreat your favour in recommending this work to the Weldon men: Sharp will give a good mason that can work the mouldings from 10 to 12 shillings a week to Mich and from Mich to Lady day 9^s. And he would give 1$\frac{1}{2}$^{d} p foot for working rustic ashlar & 1^d per ft for the plain ashlar, & rather than fail 1$\frac{3}{4}$ & 1$\frac{1}{4}$: and he would want 10 or 12 men at least for the first sort of work about the mouldings. Yr. L. will greatly oblige me to order Mr. Horton to speak with as many as are or can be speadily at liberty to come to Burley & to know the rates which they require & if Yr L. cld prevail with them to come upon the abovesaid terms, or so much under those rates as you think reasonable because Sharp at present does not give so much, I might hope to get my house up this year which is of so much importance to me.[24]

Most of the other important craftsmen employed were men who are to be found employed on similar work elsewhere. The glazier's work was done by Isaac Eeles, and some of the joiner's work by Charles Hopson; Eeles had been engaged on the glasswork at Greenwich Hospital,[25] Hopson in 1706 was appointed the King's Master Joiner, and both were employed at Blenheim.[26] Most of the joiner's work was done by Matthew May, and the painting by Charles Blunt of Nottingham, and most of the plasterer's work by James Hands of London. The fireplaces were made by Richard and Edward Chapman of Bedford Square, London, who supplied the chimney pieces for Winslow Hall, built for the secretary of the Treasury, William Lowndes, between 1699 and 1702 and attributed to Wren.[27] Thus Burley, as probably the other great houses of the later seventeenth and eighteenth centuries, represented a fusion of local with London talent; it combined the work of men whose normal occupation was local domestic building with the work of men who contributed to the greatest buildings of the age.

Preliminaries for the work were started in 1694 but very little actual work was done in that year or the next. In July and August 1695 labourers were digging the foundations and Dormer was buying timber for scaffolding. The main structure of the house was put up in 1696, 1697 and 1698. By the end of 1696 or the beginning of 1697 the first floor was roofed over, and late in 1697 the bricklayers got to the top of the house. The years 1698 and 1699 saw the greatest activity by the joiners, the glazier, the plasterers, the painters. By the beginning of 1700 the house itself was completed, though a considerable amount of work remained to be done to the interior and to the grounds.[28] At least it was completed sufficiently for the family to move in. They gave up their tenancy of Exton in December 1699 and moved to Burley probably a little before this, though in the early months life there must have been bleak. 'Though I have lain here this fortnight,' writes Lady Nottingham from Burley, 'I can't say we are more settled than when we first came for we still eat at Exton and I'm afraid must do so for some time.'[29] But though the house was habitable, much remained to be done. The library floor was not finished until the middle of 1704, and work on the painting and decorating of the interior of the house continued for several years after the family had taken up residence. Gerrard Landscroon, a native of Flanders who came to England and assisted Verrio and Laguerre, painted the walls of the main staircase with scenes representing the history of Perseus and Andromeda, and the principal rooms of the house were hung with tapestries. In these years, too, the gardens were laid out, and large numbers of workers were employed to level out the great terraces that front the house. Outbuildings had to be added, and after a fire in 1705, the great stables, the last remnant of the Duke of Buckingham's house, were rebuilt and enlarged. Altogether, a third of the total cost was incurred after the fabric of the house was completed and the family had moved in.

When he was about to start building, Nottingham estimated the probable cost of the house at about £15,000, but Burley took longer to build than he expected and the actual cost greatly exceeded the estimate. The fact must have been notorious, for Defoe notes that the house was built 'at a very great expense and some years of labour'.[30] Nottingham himself complained of it and writing from Burley in 1701 to his neighbour, Lord Normanby, he says that he is engaged in building 'which is a pleasure your lordship will not envy me when once you have tried it'.[31] Miss Pearl Finch suggests that the final cost came to £80,000.[32] Calculations of cost vary of course according to the items included; some estimates cover only the bare fabric of the house, others include the furniture and internal decorations, the outbuildings and the gardens. It is also difficult, when the cost has to be reconstructed from the landowner's general accounts, to identify with certainty the payments made on account of the building. But £80,000 is a figure it is impossible to reconcile with Nottingham's finances. My own calculations, covering all the items, suggest a cost not greatly in excess of £30,000.[33]

Total Building Expenses

	£	s.	d.
1694	1,184	3	10½
1695	954	11	3¼
1696	2,006	10	6¼
1697	4,608	12	8
1698	2,658	9	0¼
*1699	4,297	17	6¾
*1700	2,509	2	6½
*1701	1,128	0	3¾
*1702	676	13	8
1703	858	16	6½
1704	1,113	12	7
1705	2,500	17	3¾
1706	1,362	1	8¼
1707	1,452	11	0
1708	1,880	16	3¼
1709	914	17	0¼
1710	549	12	9¼
	£30,657	6	7½

It was not unusual in the eighteenth century for the cost of great houses to exceed their original estimate. The most notorious instance is Blenheim, but that unhappy story is only an epic version of a not uncommon experience. Bubb Doddington, for example, was left £30,000 to finish the great house at Eastbury, which is said to have finally cost £140,000.[34] The divergence between estimated and actual cost was often due to major changes of plan once the building was under way— the imaginations of architects tended to soar as their creations took shape—but there is no evidence that this happened at Burley, though the gardens may have been more elaborate than Nottingham originally intended. There may have been a change of plan but it does not look like it. Some of the additional cost was possibly due to the speed at which the house was put up. Part may have been due to difficulties in obtaining satisfactory stone; there was a "hard course" in the middle of the rock at Clipsham, so that stone raised in frosty weather perished, and there were exceptionally hard frosts in the winter of 1696.[35] Part of it was certainly due to the fire in the stables in 1705 which made necessary some expensive building. But most of the unforeseen expense was probably just the result of the difficulties inherent in the task of estimating the cost of building operations at a period when the profession of architect and methods of costing were undeveloped. The shell of the house did not cost much more than Nottingham had expected; what inflated the cost was the expense incurred after the main fabric of the house was completed and the family in residence— the cost not so much of interior decoration, as of the finishing- off operations in the gardens and subsidiary buildings; and it may be that it was just in this field that the original estimate went most astray, or that Nottingham's plans became more elaborate.

II. THE FAMILY

Much more was involved in "establishing a landed family" than the purchase of an estate and the building of a house. Arrangements had to be made for securing their permanence in the family. On this point there was a constant conflict. It was the interest of the family to keep the estate intact, not merely because it was the material basis for the social standing of the family, but also for more strictly utilitarian reasons; if the owner for the time being had complete power over his estates he might injure it by extravagance, and thus endanger the provision made for his uncles and aunts, his brothers and sisters, and his own children. The interest of the family was, therefore, to limit the power of the owner for the time being. The interest of the owner for the time being, on the other hand, was to retain the maximum freedom, not simply that he might more easily indulge his own inclinations, but also that he might maintain control over his children, and particularly his eldest son. Family settlements were a compromise between these two interests, and the balance reflected the particular family cir- cumstances at the time when the settlement was made.

Daniel's father, the first Earl, put the arguments very well in the negotiations for Daniel's first marriage with Lady Essex Rich. The bride's mother, the Countess of Warwick, was pressing him to make Daniel only a life tenant. The first Earl agreed that this was a reasonable request and would give Lady Essex greater security; for 'no man knows what kind of husband he may prove, nor how he may use his children by the first wife if he lived to have a second; nor what dangers he may incur in troublesome times if his estate be unsettled'. As against this, the Earl argued, if Daniel was made a life tenant, his wife's jointure and the portions of his daughters would be limited by the settlement; whereas, if his ownership of the estate was unfettered, he would be free to increase jointure and portions as he pleased. This was a rather specious argument, and the real reason why Daniel's father wished to retain power over his estate was the desire to maintain parental authority.

> It is against nature to make the father subject to his child. . . . It is against experience, and a bitter one in my family; for I have known the son of such a settlement cast away himself in marriage and then often to disinherit his father by treating to sell the inheritance for a song while his father lived. It is against my practise who never demanded it for my daughter, and insisted to have it otherwise for my Lady Frances. Lastly, it is against my promise made many years since to my son, that I would never enthrall him when he married.[36]

The settlement that emerged from this discussion marked a clear victory for the bridegroom's father. The Buckinghamshire estate, which was worth about £1,200 p.a., was settled on Daniel and his wife immediately; some £400 p.a. was for the separate maintenance of the wife and if she outlived her husband she was to retain it all as jointure, and Daniel was empowered to charge the estate with £8,000 portions for daughters if the couple had no sons. This was a definite and firm commitment, beyond the power of either Daniel or his father to revoke, but the rest of the family estates, which were to come to him after his father's death, came to him on easier terms which gave him power to modify the settlement. On his second marriage, in 1685, Daniel settled Daventry as his bride's jointure, but retained power over the rest of his property.[37] In most of his estates therefore—in the London estate which he inherited from his father, in the estate at Milton, which he and his father purchased in 1677, in Burley, which was his own purchase, and in the Essex estates left him by his first wife—he had more or less complete power, and was thus very much less fettered than most landowners of comparable wealth. This freedom had important effects on the way he financed his various activities, for had he not been so free he could hardly have built his house, or at least would not have been able to finance it in the way he did.

Daniel seems to have had the same inclination as his father in favour of allowing freedom to the owner of the estate for the time being; he regarded the strict settlement as something undesirable in itself but which might be necessary to curb possible extravagance. When he made a will in 1695 his heir was his first-born Heneage, who was blind, and he left him the estate for life only. 'But', he writes to his executors, 'if he recovers his sight . . . and if you find him fit . . . I have left you power to make him tenant-in-tail.' In case Heneage should die, he writes in the same letter,

> I wish you could persuade my son, to whom my estate and title will come, to make himself upon his marriage but tenant for life, reserving a power (as I had) to make his son so too. This, if it had not been too nice and difficult, I would have done in my will, not so much out of a vain affectation of continuing a great estate in my family, as because he will thereby be under a necessity of observing some good economy that he may be able to provide for his younger children, and consequently will not run into that foolish or extravagant way of living which debauches and corrupts the manners of many families, as well as ruins their fortunes . . .[38]

As Nottingham himself observed, 'no estate can provide so fully for younger children, but that they must in great degree help themselves'. In his final will he provided annuities, charged on the estate, for all his younger sons, £300 for William and John, and £200 for Henry and Edward, the two youngest.[39] And all the younger sons did, in fact, procure independent sources of income. William and John were trained to the law. The former was secretary to Lord Carteret in 1719 and 1720, envoy to Sweden from 1720 to 1724 and afterwards to

Holland, and from 1742 to 1765 he was Vice-Chamberlain of the household. The latter was a successful practising lawyer. Henry had a grant of the office of surveyor of His Majesty's Works, and Edward, the most successful of Nottingham's younger sons, held a succession of diplomatic posts, as well as a number of sinecure offices. All four of them were Members of Parliament for almost all their adult life, and they illustrate the advantages enjoyed by a great political family in the eighteenth century in providing for its younger sons.[40] Even so, in wealth and social standing they were very far below their elder brother, who in due course inherited the entire family estate.

Daughters were more important than younger sons, for they were the means by which the great landed families made their alliances, and, like most landowners, Nottingham endowed his daughters more generously than their younger brothers. His eldest daughter, Mary, the only child of his first marriage, received £20,000, a large portion, but one appropriate to the only child of an heiress. The daughters of his second marriage were more moderately dowered, for Essex, the eldest, received £7,000 and the others £5,000 each; but these sums were substantially more than the annuities received by their brothers. Annuities for life were generally bought and sold at seven years' purchase, but sometimes family settlements provided for a more generous rate, and a younger son who preferred a capital sum to an annuity might be allowed the option of capitalizing his annuity at ten years' purchase. Even at this more generous rate, the capital value of the incomes which Nottingham provided for his younger sons amounted to only £3,000 and £2,000. Moreover, while £300 or £200 a year did no more than make the life of a younger son as a placeman a tolerable one, even such a modest portion as £5,000 might in favourable circumstances secure for his sister the hand of a peer. Nottingham's daughters, unlike his younger sons, remained in the social group in which they were born. Five of them married, and of these four made unusually advantageous marriages. The eldest daughter, Mary married twice, first the second Marquis of Halifax, and secondly John, Duke of Roxburgh. Essex married Sir Roger Mostyn; this was the least elevated of the marriages, and Nottingham's correspondence echoes with his son-in-law's financial misfortunes. Mary—to the confusion of genealogists Nottingham called two of his daughters by this name—married Thomas Wentworth, later Marquis of Rockingham; Charlotte married Charles, Duke of Somerset; and Henrietta, William, Duke of Cleveland.

It is not surprising that his eldest daughter with a portion of £20,000 should have made a splendid marriage. But £5,000 was quite a modest portion and none of the daughters were beauties. Most of them seem to have inherited the peculiarly swarthy complexion that earned for the family the nickname of the Black Finches. The fact that three of Nottingham's daughters, so dowered, were able to contract aristocratic marriages reflects the social connections and personal standing of their father. The marriages between landed families in the eighteenth century were more like treaties of alliance between sovereign states than love matches; they involved hard bargaining in which the size of the bride's fortune was carefully matched against the income which the bridegroom's father was prepared to settle on him. But it was not all a matter of money. The family friends and relations had a great deal to do with the conclusion of a marriage. They helped each other to find advantageous marriages as they helped each other to secure profitable appointments. They gave assurances about the character and standing of potential wives and husbands, persuaded reluctant fathers, established preliminary contacts and acted as go-betweens. Evading a possible suitor for the hand of his eldest daughter, Nottingham explained that 'a friend of mine, unknown to me, had very kindly made some steps in another affair before my coming to town' and that a marriage agreement had already been concluded with Lord Halifax, 'whose son has already been so good a husband (his first wife had been a niece of Nottingham's) and is in himself so very desirable that I have done more than ever yet I intended'.[41] When this daughter, now a widow, was sought in marriage by the Duke of Roxburgh, two of Nottingham's political and personal friends, Lord Dartmouth and the Earl of Jersey, acted as intermediaries and persuaded the reluctant father to accede to the Duke's proposal.[42]

The son of Halifax was "so very desirable" because he was

his father's son, and the general standing of a father had a powerful influence on the marriages of his children. 'I entreat you', wrote Nottingham to his executors on the question of his son's marriage, 'not to be tempted by any fortune to marry him to a person whom he does not entirely like ... nor to marry him into a foolish family ... despite great fortune.' 'God be thanked', he wrote of this son, 'he will have an estate which will give him greater liberty for choosing; and as he may pretend to the great and noble, so he will not be obliged to decline those of a lesser rank and fortune, since he will not need much addition.'[43] There is no reason to believe that such considerations were not present to other great families of the period, and the personal repute of Nottingham and his standing in the political life of his times made his daughters attractive brides despite the relative smallness of their fortunes. It is, perhaps, not a coincidence that of the three daughters unmarried at his death, two never married at all.

Nottingham had an exceptionally large family; besides the only daughter of his first marriage, he had five surviving sons and seven daughters by his second wife.[44] Their endowment was therefore a heavy burden. The portions of his daughters alone cost Nottingham £37,000 during his life, and £15,000 charged on his estate after his death, altogether £52,000, a larger sum than the cost of purchasing Burley or the building of the house.

IV. FINANCE

Between 1694 and his death in 1729 Nottingham spent about £50,000 on the purchase of the Burley property, and more than £30,000 on the building of the house, and he either spent or committed his estate to the spending of £52,000 on portions for his daughters. The period of greatest expenditure came between 1694 and 1702, which saw the purchase, most of the building, and the marriage of the most expensive daughter. Thereafter the only exceptional items of expenditure he had to meet were the portions of his other daughters; these fell to be paid at wide intervals, and therefore presented less difficult problems.

How did Nottingham finance this expenditure? Was it out of landed income or from the profits of office; out of savings, or by the sale of land or by borrowing?

Nottingham did not inherit from his father any significant personal estate; the money he received from his father had been received during his life and had been laid out in land, in the purchase of the estate at Milton. Indeed he inherited debts from his father, for the estate was charged with the portions of his sister and four of his brothers amounting in all to £15,000. The estates which he acquired from his father and his wife yielded an annual income of a little over £5,000 after paying taxes and the cost of administration. In most years almost all this income appears to have been absorbed by current expenditure and annuities. In 1687, for example, the family spent £4,976, the main items of expenditure being:[45]

	£
Housekeeping	1,651
Stables, coaches, dogs and liveries	792
Repairs and gardens	272
Children	246
Lady Nottingham	278
Lady Mary Finch⎱ Mr. Robert Finch⎰	290
Briefs (i.e. charities)	183
Physick	62
Accidents (i.e. incidentals including Lady Nottingham's lying-in)	446
Wages	525

His current income therefore did not allow much scope for saving. Nor did he make much while he was a Commissioner of the Navy from 1679 to 1684.

When he first started to look for an estate in 1686 he does not appear to have had any non-landed wealth, except for £10,000 due from his father-in-law, as his wife's marriage portion. At that time he intended to sell the property at Kensington and he was looking for a modest estate such as he might pay for with the proceeds of the sale and his £10,000 portion. From the sale of his house at Kensington he received £19,000; he was looking, that is, for an estate of a capital value of less than £30,000. The estate which he eventually bought cost about £50,000, and this more ambitious scale of purchase reflects the gains he made during his first period as Secretary of State.

Nottingham was Secretary of State from March 1689 to

Daniel Finch, second Earl of Nottingham

Burley-on-the-Hill from the north

November 1693: Secretary for the Northern Department from 3 March 1689 to 2 June 1690; sole Secretary from 2 June to 26 December 1690, and Secretary of the Southern Department to November 1693. As Secretary he received certain fixed payments. First of all an annual patent salary of £100 p.a. Then an allowance, or pension as it was called, of £1,850 a year. Finally, a sum of money in lieu of diet; the Secretary of the Northern Department received £242, and the Secretary for the South £730. In addition to these fixed annual sums the Secretary received a large sum in fees for obtaining the royal signature to various classes of document. As Professor Mark Thompson has observed, 'In the first year of a reign the amount of fees was especially large, since a demise of the Crown rendered all offices vacant and all commissions void. Years of war were also very lucrative, owing to the great number of military commissions then issued.'[46] Nottingham's first period as Secretary covered part of the first years of the reign of William and Mary which were also years of war. Nottingham also had his share of the profits of the official Gazette. But the largest single item were payments of secret-service money; at this period the Secretary of the Southern Department received £3,000 a year and the Secretary for the Northern £2,000. Even at this date these sums were regarded as additional salaries; for the cost of real secret service Nottingham received separate payments which are not usually recorded in his private accounts, and when his private accounts record payments for secret service—e.g. £50 to the person 'who apprehended De Foe'—they are generally covered by receipts of money granted specifically for the purpose.

From all these sources Nottingham received the following sums.

The Earl of Nottingham's Income as Secretary of State,
1689–1693:

Pension	£8,487	14	6
Diet	2,082	14	8
Gazette	4,376	19	3
Patent Fee	483	11	0
Fees	5,383	18	2½
Secret Service	16,000	0	0
	£36,814	17	7½

Against this has to be set the expenses of his office. Certain deductions were made from his emoluments for the fees of the issuing officers. Various bills had to be met for cleaning and heating the office. Both these payments were small. The heaviest costs of office were those involved in the style of life of the Secretary, and especially the expense of maintaining a substantial establishment in London for a large part of the year. The total household expenses during his years of office [1689–1693] amounted to £25,519; for the five years 1695–1699 they were £16,312. It would probably be reasonable on this account to deduct about £9,000 from his office emoluments, which would make his net gain between £26,000 and £27,000.

Nottingham invested the money he had received from the sale of Kensington House and some of his emoluments of office in mortgages. Like most other people, he was anxious not to let his money lie idle, and since, in the later seventeenth century, it was difficult for a lender to secure good mortgages at exactly the moment when he had the money to lend, he anticipated the proceeds of the sale of his Kensington House and, at least to some extent, the emoluments of office. Between November 1688 and December 1689, he acquired new mortgages to a value of about £34,500, and in order to tide him over the time between his lending the money and his being paid by the State he borrowed short-term money, from Thomas Fowle, a London goldsmith, and Anthony Keck, a scrivener; he also borrowed £2,000 short-term from Lord Halifax and £500 from a Mr. Franklin. After the end of 1689 there is no trace of Nottingham's acquiring further mortgages. By that time he had decided to acquire Burley and it is reasonable to suppose that he wanted to keep any further accumulated funds in a more liquid form. At any rate, after 1689 he put his surplus money into government tallies, i.e. Government promises to repay out of the proceeds of taxation. At one time in 1693 he was holding as much as £18,250 worth of tallies. It is not easy to say how much of this was obtained by actual purchase of tallies, for Nottingham received part of his emoluments in this form: £13,000 of his secret-service money was paid in this way. On the other hand, it is certain that in 1692 and 1693 Nottingham was buying tallies for cash—he specifically says so in one of his letters[47]—and it is probable that in 1692 and 1693 he invested £15,000 in this way. Tallies varied in their merits, according to the funds on which they were secured and the prior charges on these funds. They had the advantage of yielding a high return, from 6 to 8 per cent. in the case of those held by Nottingham. On the other hand, if the purchaser could not hold them until the fund on which they were secured was sufficient to pay them off, he might have to sell them at a substantial discount. Nottingham himself, when raising money to make his purchase of Burley sold one tally of £5,000 for £4,900, a 2 per cent. discount, and another of £3,000 for £2,820, a 6 per cent. discount. But presumably, on balance, they were preferable for Nottingham's purpose to loans on bond.

In 1694 and 1695 Nottingham sold his tallies, obtained the repayment of some of his mortgages and assigned others, and called for payment of his £10,000 marriage portion. Altogether, from these sources, he raised about £71,000. This was to within a fraction of what he had expended on the purchase of Burley and the portion of his eldest daughter. The implication, however, that he did not need to borrow for these purposes is not justified, for he had often to make payments before he could realize assets and had to borrow to tide over the interval. He also had to borrow a large part of the marriage portion of his eldest daughter and, in order to repay, sold his London property at Whitefriars for £7,770 and a farm in Buckinghamshire for £4,400. But it remains true that about half the price of Burley was paid for out of the emoluments of office.

It is a common impression that while great estates were purchased out of capital, great houses were paid for out of current income. Since the building of such houses extended over a number of years, this was, indeed, the most obvious method of financing the operation, and a number of cases are known of land-owners who specifically declared their intention of acting in this way. When, for example, the Earl of Newcastle started to rebuild Nottingham Castle in 1674, he set aside the income of several of his estates for this purpose.[48] George Doddington provided in his will for the building of Eastbury, which was 'to go on without any stop as fast as the revenue the Southsea left will allow of, which will be about £1,800 a year'.[49]

What exactly Nottingham's intentions were in this matter, we have to deduce from the instructions he drafted for his executors in case of his death.

> You will see among my papers [he wrote in 1695], my design of a house and gardens at Burley, which I reckon may cost about £15,000. I do not prefix or limit the sum, but I would have my intentions pursued by such degrees as the profits of my estate, not necessarily directed otherwise by my will, will enable you. For I would not have my eldest son under the temptation of living in town for want of an house nor of being too extravagant in building one. . . .[50]

He estimated that, after his death, there would be a surplus, after his family was provided for, of £2,800 p.a. and he directed that for three years this was to be devoted to the building of the house. But even in these circumstances he envisaged a sale of land, for he empowered his executors to sell certain of the Essex estates inherited from his wife and out of the proceeds pay the portion of one of his brothers (£2,000) and his sister's portion (£5,000) and use £8,000 to complete the building.[51] How Nottingham intended to provide for the finance of his building in the event of his death is imperfect evidence of the methods he intended to employ if he lived. But it seems clear that both annual income and the sale of land were intended to contribute.

In the event, since he did not die until 1729, the surplus of his annual income proved much smaller. At the time he made his calculations, Nottingham's income from estates had just been augmented by the purchase of Burley. The annual value of this property was £3,800, but Nottingham received much less than this. For one thing, a great park was as essential as a great house, and he created here a park of 1,360 acres, some 500 acres of it in wood, and the rest in pasture. Though he received a small income from the sheep and cattle who grazed in the park, he made some £600 a year less than he would have by letting the land to tenant farmers. Moreover, Burley at the time of his purchase, was burdened with the jointure of the Duchess of Buckingham, amounting to £1,240 a year, and an annuity to Lady Exeter of £200; the Duchess lived to 1704 and Lady Exeter to 1703. Altogether in 1695, Nottingham's total income from his estates, before deducting taxes and costs of maintenance, was about £8,400 a year. In that year he estimated that taxes came to £1,170 and the costs of administration and maintenance to £217; in fact, the costs of maintenance generally proved higher than this because Foulnesse was several times flooded. In the later 1690's, therefore, his net estate income normally came to about £7,000. At this time his expenditure was distributed in this way:[52]

	1699			1700		
Household Expenses	£3,026	14	11½	£3,096	6	7¼
Horses & Stables	134	18	0	38	13	7
Lord Nottingham	49	3	0	76	0	6
Lady ,,	359	8	4	241	11	0
Children	106	18	6	104	2	9
Sister & brothers	568	7	8	572	18	11½
Legal Expenses	56	19	2	90	0	0
Charities	194	0	0	189	12	9
Annuities	217	10	0	220	0	0
Incidentals	2	19	3	73	18	0
Allowances	42	16	2	37	10	0
Furniture & Utensils	284	17	0	35	2	0
Physick	1	1	6	3	4	6
Rent [of London house]	58	6	6	60	7	0
Spinners	10	0	0	—	—	—
Taxes [on the houses]	39	12	8	15	8	10
Interest	510	0	0	510	0	0
TOTAL:	£5,663	12	8½	£5,364	16	5¾

Despite the increase in his family his expenditure was not a great deal higher than it had been in 1687 and he had a surplus, one year with another, of about £1,500.

Moreover, as we have seen, the house cost more to build than Nottingham expected, and in the year where the main fabric was being built its cost far exceeded the surplus available out of annual income. During the years of most intensive building Nottingham was therefore compelled to borrow, which he did in amounts which were relatively small from friends like Sir George Rook, the admiral, from his brothers, from his steward and sometimes even from his own servants. To repay these debts he sold a considerable part of his Essex estates. From this sale he obtained some £18,000, and almost all this sum was absorbed in the discharge of debt; there was nothing over to fulfil his original intention of paying the portions of his brother and sister. Not all the debts so discharged had been incurred as a result of building operations—some were a relic of loans raised towards the £20,000 portion of his eldest daughter—but it would be safe to assume that not far short of half the building expenses incurred up to 1700 were ultimately met by the sale of property.

From 1702–4 Nottingham was Secretary of State for the second time and during this term he received the following sums[53]:—

Pension	£3,185	11	0½
Diet	1,102	3	10
Gazette	953	12	11
Patent Fee	200	0	0
Fees	2,260	16	11
Secret Service	5,807	0	0
	£13,509	4	8½

About £1,000 of this was absorbed in office expenses and taxes. The greater part of what remained contributed to the payment of a marriage portion of £7,000 with his daughter Essex, and there was a little over to settle the costs of building. By 1704 there were no debts upon the estate except for the portions for his sister and two of his brothers.

After 1704 his income improved slightly, for, though he had lost some £800 a year from the sale of the Essex property, he gained £1,440 when the jointure and annuity ceased to be paid out of Burley. For some six years or so, until his children came of age to be educated, his expenditure on household and family was well below his revenue, and he was able to meet the costs of the building that was done after 1704 out of income, with an occasional short-term borrowing. After 1710, however, the maintenance and education of his children began to cost him a large part of his income—for many years almost as much as his building operations had cost—and generally left no surplus. In 1703 the annual maintenance of his children had cost £103: in 1710 and 1711, when his eldest son was on the Grand Tour, and William and John were at Eton, the cost came to £1,694 and £2,097 respectively. The Grand Tour alone cost over £3,000. Nothing so expensive as the Grand Tour of the eldest son occurred again; the second son spent two years on the Continent, but at a total cost of only £415, and the remaining sons do not appear to have gone on tour. Nevertheless the cost of the children's maintenance was generally well over £1,000. In 1717, for example, the eldest daughter had an allowance of £120, the next two of £80 each and the two youngest £60 each; the second son was on the Continent with an allowance of £200 p.a., the next two had an allowance of £120 each and the youngest had £50; altogether the children in this year cost some £1,300. It may well be that it was the growing expense of his family which finally put an end to the adornment of his house and gardens. At any rate, after 1710 Nottingham had no surplus out of current income; in some years he was borrowing despite the lower level of taxation in the last decade of his life. And though he once again held office, as Lord President of the Council from 1714–16, his gains from this source were modest. He received a salary of £1,500 a year and a "pension" of £3,500 a year, but no fees, and his total emoluments, after deducting the incidental expenses of his office, came to only £6,730. His household expenses, while he held office, were over £3,000 more than usual, and his net gains were probably not more than £3,500, and almost all this appears to have been spent on the maintenance of his children.

The portions for the remaining daughters who married in his lifetime were therefore raised by borrowing; and at his death Nottingham owed, besides small debts, about £22,000:[54]

To Anne, Countess Dowager, as executrix for his sister Mary	£9,900
Edward Finch, his brother	5,800
William Finch, ,,	1,600
Henry Finch, ,,	1,000
Daniel, his son & successor	2,573
Daniel Armstrong	1,500

Except for the debt to Armstrong, who was the son of his steward, all these were debts to his family, and were either payments to his brother and sister charged upon the estate by his father, or borrowings by him to pay the portions of Mary and Charlotte. In addition there were also charged upon the estate £5,000 each for the three of his daughters remaining unmarried at his death. Shortly before his death, Nottingham directed that these debts should be paid off by the sale of Foulnesse. As it turned out this property was not sold; it was indeed an unattractive property to a purchaser since it was liable to inundation. And when the family finally sold property to pay debts—not Nottingham's debts but debts which might very well not have existed but for the charges he left upon the estate—it was not until 1786, and the estate they then parted with was not Foulnesse but Daventry.

In one of his letters Nottingham recommended his son never to 'accept any public employment from any King or Government'.[55] His dismissal in 1693 rankled. Yet the gains of office—amounting in all to between forty and forty-five thousand pounds—provided a large part of the finance for the creation of his estate and house. But for these gains, it is certain that he would not have bought so large an estate as Burley, and it is unlikely that but for the income of Burley he would have built so large a house. We cannot be categorical on this second point. For one thing he could have sold more of the property he had inherited. He could also—and this would have been a more probable alternative—have raised money by borrowing. In particular, instead of paying the marriage portions of his first two daughters out of his own resources he might have conformed to the common practice among landed families and mortgaged his estate. He might also have provided them with smaller portions; he was only obliged by settlement to give his eldest daughter £8,000, not the £20,000 he in fact gave her, and the portions of his other daughters were entirely at his discretion. Because of the nature of his marriage settlements, Nottingham had a degree of power over the disposal of his estate which was not common among landed families, and we do not know how his favours would have been distributed between his estates, his house and his family, had he not enjoyed gains from office. The most perhaps that can be said is that these gains enabled him to make a substantial net addition to the estates left him and to build a house, without sacrificing the interests of his children and without burdening the estate with intolerable debts. It was a substantial estate, though not one of the first magnitude. Its gross income in the 1720's was about £9,000 and it was well below the £20,000 a year enjoyed by many of the ducal families. What altered the financial position of the family in the eighteenth century was Nottingham's succession, in the last months of his life, to the estates of the elder branch of the Finch family, the Earls of Winchilsea.

From this single case we cannot draw large conclusions about the importance for English landowners of wealth made in politics. Indeed Nottingham's story must suggest doubts whether any simple generalization on this subject will ever be possible. We can tell very little from the gross gains until we know how much was absorbed in the temporary and necessary inflation of the recipient's standard of living. Even then, much depended on the precise time in a family's history at which the gains were made. Nottingham's most lucrative period of office occurred at a critical point in his life, soon after his marriage, and when he was already looking for a country estate to purchase; equal gains made by a man late in life might have been disposed of in quite different ways. Then again, much depended on how wealthy the recipient was to start with and on the size and character of the claims on his wealth by other members of his family. Nottingham was tolerably wealthy before he entered on office, he had an unusually large number of children, and some of his property consisted of scattered estates in a county distant from the region of his main interests, estates which had come into the family by marriage, and which could therefore be disposed of with much less reluctance than the family's ancestral domains. This combination of circumstances was distinctive. Perhaps most of all the reaction of a man to gains from office depended on his personal character. On his mother's side, Daniel Finch was one of the Harveys, a merchant and professional family of great ability which included among its members the discoverer of the circulation of the blood. Daniel acquired from them not only his christian name but probably a good deal of his ability—'the exterior airs of Business and application enough to make him very capable'—and his prudent attitude to money matters. In one of his letters he directed that his sons should have an allowance of £100 a year until they came of age, and added

> Perhaps if any of them should come to the Inns of Court and study the law the way of living even of sober men is so enhanced that some addition may be necessary, but I do not think it is so at the University, notwithstanding their foolish customs, and intreat you to suppress in my children the vanity and affectation of what they call there a Nobleman, of which kind scarce any ever came to be considerable men.[56]

Unlike most noble landowners, Nottingham liked to pay his capital charges out of income, and, when this was impossible, to raise the money by sale rather than by mortgage. The debts he left at his death amounted to about one-tenth of the capital value of his property, not a high proportion by the standards of the early eighteenth century. Had he had the temperament of the princely Duke of Chandos he might have yielded to the temptation to purchase more expensive estates.[57]

Nor can we generalize from this single instance about the effect of the building of a great house on the finances of landed families. It is sometimes supposed that a wave of housebuilding, such as took place among the English aristocracy and gentry between the Restoration and the middle of the eighteenth century, reflects the increasing prosperity of landed families. In Nottingham's case it is true that the scale, if not the existence of Burley was due to the gains of office; and other great houses of the period were built by "new men" out of money made in trade or law, for example the house which Sir Gilbert Heathcote built at Normanton not far from Burley. Of such men it may be true that they built because they could afford to build. But several old families, who depended entirely on their rents for income, built or enlarged their mansions and this was a period when, over most of England, rents were stationary. It cannot be the case with families such as these, that they built because their incomes were increasing. Rather they built because it had become fashionable to do so. Here perhaps it was that the wider significance of houses such as Burley really lay. They helped to spread the fashion. Both Nottingham's fondness for tapestries and the subjects chosen—The Triumphs of Julius Caesar, for example, and Hero and Leander—suggest the influence of Versailles, which was certainly present in explicit form in the building of Blenheim. In this sense Nottingham was following a fashion. But he was also the intermediary by which new fashions in building and decoration penetrated into the remoter manor houses of gentry who had not set foot abroad. The quality of country houses, of their furnishings and ornaments was, to judge from contemporary correspondence, a favourite topic of conversation. The new houses, with their larger rooms and ampler decorations, changed the assumptions of local landowners about the style of house that was appropriate to their dignity. And it is a reasonable guess that the country squire who dined for the first time at Burley went away discontented with his smaller and older manor house, in a mood to add a wing or a floor, or give it a more fashionable façade. It is in the account books of the families who in this way followed the fashion without the help of gains from office, trade or law that the most important effects of housebuilding are to be traced.

The age of the great houses is now so remote that it is natural for us to wonder why men should have wished to employ so much of their wealth in building them. It is not in the course of nature that moneyed men should buy great estates and build country mansions. Nineteenth-century America did not lack men of great wealth, yet they rarely employed it in this way. The aristocracy of the Italian towns remained primarily an urban class; their houses were the great palaces which still line the streets of Florence. The immediate reason why Nottingham wished to build was quite simple. While he still lived in Kensington, he had a large domestic staff, which in 1683 consisted of fifteen women and twenty-one men. The women included the housekeeper, an under-housekeeper, several lady's maids, two housemaids, one plate maid, one kitchen-maid, one dairymaid, one nursery maid and two laundry maids. The men included the bailiffs, a cook, a butler, a porter, and a coachman, four footmen and four grooms, a huntsman, a carter, a butcher, a groom chamber and a gardener.[58] This was a large staff for so modest a house. After his second marriage, in 1685, Nottingham could expect that his family and the necessary domestic staff would increase. By 1693, after he had decided to purchase but while he was still living at Exton, his female staff had increased to twenty and his male staff to twenty-nine; it looks as if he had already allowed for the increase in maids and helpers around the grounds which Burley would allow or need, for there was no further increase in staff after the family moved into their new house. The need to accommodate this large establishment certainly influenced Nottingham in his decision to move to the country, though it can scarcely have been the decisive factor since the needs of his growing household could have been met by enlarging the house at Kensington. And if overcrowding made Nottingham leave, why had it not moved his father in the same direction? It must have been a tight squeeze at Kensington even in Heneage's time, when Daniel and his first wife joined him there after their marriage.

Nottingham's own account of his motives for wanting an estate in the country are quite explicit. It was simply that he wanted to live in the country. He wishes to buy, he writes, 'that I may have the satisfaction of having some place to retire to'.[59] 'I am resolved to go into the country,' he says on another occasion, 'though I live in the stables at Burley.'[60] 'I much long to be in the country.'[61] In his draft instructions to his executors in 1705 he writes, 'I have appointed my gardens, cow-yards and a building opposite my stable to be finished. These things being done the habitation will be convenient and pleasant and may induce Daniel (his eldest son) to live in the country, which I hope he will love, and mind his own affairs and estate, which is part of a gentleman's calling.'[62] In the event, except for the years of office, the family did spend the greater part of their time at Burley. Normally they stayed in London only for January, February and March, occasionally for part of December and April, and even during these months the children seemed to have stayed in the country, at least when they were young. For most of the time the family did not even have a London house of their own. At some time in the 1680's Nottingham sold his father's house in Queen Street and thereafter generally rented a house for the season. In 1705, for example, Nottingham rented a house in Soho Square; later he took lodgings in York Buildings, in 1710 for ten weeks and in 1711 for twenty-one weeks. In 1712 he took lodgings in Blooms-bury Square, and in 1714 in St. James Street, and it was not until 1715 that he took a long lease, a twenty-two-year lease from Lady Russell of a house in Bloomsbury Square.[63]

It would be foolish to ignore these explicit declarations that Nottingham liked life in the country simply for the amenities it afforded. These lush and undulating Midlands, still at this time mainly unenclosed, afforded some of the pleasantest landscape in Europe. It would be perverse to seek out obscure reasons why men should want to go and live among them. Yet it is likely that there were other reasons, so widely influential that they were taken for granted and thus escape from the explicit expression of motives by any individual landowner. But not from the explicit expressions of the individual architect. 'I believe that if your Grace will please to consider of the intrinsique value of titles and blue garters, and jewels and great tables and numbers of servants etc. in a word all those things that distinguish Great Men from small ones, you will confess to me that a good house is at least upon the level with the best of 'em.'[64] Thus Vanbrugh wrote to the Duke of Newcastle in 1703 in an attempt to persuade him to rebuild Welbeck. A good house was not only one distinguishing feature of a Great Man, of no more import-ance than several others; it provided the necessary setting for great tables and numbers of servants. The country mansion was formed, as Mr. Whistler has put it, 'to express a particular way of living' which could not have been so aptly expressed in any other milieu. Daniel's father, to the end of his life, retained something of the character of the indispensable legal expert; Daniel on the other hand was a leading political figure, and in building his house he was completing the picture of himself as the equal of such as Halifax and Danby.

A great house was more than the expression of a certain style of living. It was a monument to the achievement of the builder. The absence of an existing house when Nottingham bought the estate at Burley was from his point of view an advantage not a defect, for it gave him a free hand to raise his own creation. When a new house cost so much to build it is at first sight curious that houses already built should have sold for so little.

The existence of a house, even one that was ample and well-conditioned, added little to the market value of an estate, and sometimes added nothing at all. When Bubb Doddington's house at Eastbury, completed at great cost less than twenty-five years before, was put up for sale in 1762 it failed to find a purchaser, and had to be pulled down.[65] The same fate befell Lord Montfort's house at Horseheath.[66] The cases could be multiplied, and the explanation is that men who were buying an estate did not want a house simply to live in, nor even in order to give scope for their crotchets about domestic architecture. They wished to provide posterity with tangible and enduring evidence of their achievements. The motives which inspired Sarah and John Churchill at Blenheim were reflected in a less intense form in the building of Burley.

Nottingham thought of himself not only as an individual with personal achievements to commemorate, but as the representative of his family, responsible for the preservation of its repute and its fortunes for succeeding generations. When in the closing months of his life he inherited the estates and title of the elder branch of the Finches he vigorously resisted the extinction of the title which his father had acquired in that of the senior title of Winchilsea.

> I know very well [he wrote to his son in September 1729] that I cannot refuse the title of Winchilsea and all that you say of it is very right, but I am not debarred from using the addition of Nottingham in all deeds and papers I shall sign, nor even in the House of Lords in my subscribing the oaths and tests and any protestations, for this I will certainly do to distinguish my branch of the family from the former—[67]

This sense of family was not confined to Nottingham, but was widely diffused among his uncles and his brothers and sisters. Primogeniture would not have survived so long among English landed families had it not corresponded to a sense among the younger children themselves that the standing of the family and its maintenance from generation to generation was of more importance than their own individual interests. They did not regard themselves as deprived of their rights by settlements which secured the family estates to their elder brother. The younger members assisted the principal representative of the family with occasional loans, and when they died without children of their own they bequeathed their property to the main line. In the case of the Finches at least, the annuities paid to younger children were not an entire loss to the estate. The brother who became a clergyman and remained a bachelor, the spinster sister, had thriftier habits than a great landowner, and some of their income was accumulated and in due course returned to enrich the main stream. Thus a great house was more than a pleasant place to live in, more than a memorial to its builder. It was the capital of the family and the repository of its traditions.

NOTES

[1] Information on Nottingham's estate and house is to be found in the Finch papers, now temporarily deposited with the Historical Manuscripts Commission. These contain (a) his correspondence, which is at present being calendered—this is referred to in this essay as Finch MSS. Correspondence; (b) miscellaneous deeds, surveys and accounts, which are referred to here as Finch MSS. Miscellaneous. The main volumes of Nottingham's accounts, covering the period 1681–1724 are numbers 131, 122, and 123. Number 119 contains details of the expenses of building for the period 1696–1707. There are also volumes of household accounts. I wish to express my gratitude to Lt.-Col. James Hanbury, the owner of these manuscripts, for making them available, and to Mr. R. L. Atkinson for providing facilities for work on them.

The earlier documents belonging to this collection have been calendered and published by the Historical Manuscripts Commission, Report on the Manuscripts of the late Allen George Finch, Esq., 2 vols. 1913–1922. These are referred to here as H.M.C. Finch MSS.

The Hatton Finch papers at the British Museum, which contain a large amount of Nottingham's official correspondence, include also many of his private letters. The most useful for the present study have been his letters to his father-in-law, Lord Hatton (Add. MSS. 29594–5), and his wife's letters (Add. MS. 29596).

The Finch-Hatton collection at the Northamptonshire Record Office contains, besides some of Nottingham's official correspondence, the commonplace book of one of his daughters. (N.R.O., F.H. 281.)

The family papers were used by Miss Pearl Finch for her valuable History of Burley-on-the-Hill, 2 vols. (London 1901, privately printed). There is an article on the house by Mr. Christopher Hussey in *Country Life*, February 10 and 17, 1923. For this reference, and for much other guidance in the architectural literature of the period, I am greatly indebted to Mr. H. M. Colvin.

² Daniel Defoe, *A Tour through England* (1927), ed. G. D. H. Cole, ii, 502–3.

³ *The Diary and Correspondence of Charles Abbot, Lord Colchester*, ed. Charles Lord Colchester (1861), ii, 634.

⁴ H.M.C. Finch MSS., ii, f. 19; *Victoria County History of Buckinghamshire* (1905–28), iv, 441; J. Bridges, *History of Northamptonshire* (1791), i, 45; G. Baker, *History of Northamptonshire* (1822–41), i, 307.

⁵ W. J. Loftie, *Kensington* (1888), p. 138. *Diary of Samuel Pepys*, ed. Lord Braybrooke, ii, 336.

⁶ P. Faulkener, 'Nottingham House', *Archæological Journal*, cvii (1950), pp. 69–71; G. H. Chettle, 'Kensington Palace', *Journal of the British Archæological Society*, xvi (1953).

⁷ The marriage settlement is in Finch MSS., Misc., nos. 31–5.

⁸ It is a curious side-light on the reliability of contemporary gossip about the size of marriage portions that Bridget Noel should have written of Anne Hatton, 'Her portion was but £1,000' (quoted in *Complete Peerage* under Winchilsea), whereas in the marriage settlement and in Nottingham's accounts the sum is quite clearly £10,000.

⁹ Add. MS. 29594, f. 101.

¹⁰ *Ibid.*, f. 89.

¹¹ *Ibid.*, f. 23.

¹² *Ibid.*, f. 170.

¹³ *Ibid.*, f. 180.

¹⁴ H.M.C. 11th Report, app. 11, p. 305 ; 12th Report, app. part VI ; *House of Lords MSS.*, 1689–90, pp. 218–19; C.J x, p. 382.

¹⁵ Add. MS. 29595, f. 33.

¹⁶ *Ibid.*, f. 44.

¹⁷ He wrote to Sir John Lowther, to enquire who had made the model for Lowther Castle (Pearl Finch, *op. cit.*, i, 63).

¹⁸ Add. MS. 29595, f. 44, 1 May 1694.

¹⁹ B.M. Sloane MS. 3828, ff. 176–80. 'Some Directions for my Lord Nottingham's Building by Sir Henry Shere. 5 July 1695.'

²⁰ For Poulteney, see Publications of the Wren Society, xx, p. 167.

²¹ For Dormer, see H. M. Colvin, *A Biographical Dictionary of English Architects* (1954), and for Lumley, see Rupert Gunnis, *A Dictionary of British Sculptors* (1953).

²² Add. MS. 29595, f. 52

²³ H. J. Massingham, *Where Man Belongs* (1946), pp. 92–3.

²⁴ Add. MS. 29595, f. 112.

²⁵ Wren Society, v, 31, 49.

²⁶ *Ibid.*, xv, xxi.

²⁷ *Ibid.*, xvii, 55.

²⁸ These stages in the building are reconstructed from the payments in Nottingham's accounts. Mr. Hussy suggests that 'Probably from motives of economy, for the Earl seems to have been building out of income only, the roof was not put on till 1704–5, by which time the masons and builders would have been paid off and the money be free with which to engage the carpenters and lead workers'. But the correspondence about a roof on which this

view was based refers more probably to the roof of the stables which had
to be repaired after fire in 1705.

[29] Add. MS. 29596, f. 9.

[30] Defoe, *op. cit.*, I, 502.

[31] Finch MSS., Correspondence: box V, bundle 22.

[32] Pearl Finch, *op. cit.*, i, 26.

[33] Except for the years 1699–1702 inclusive, the costs have been calculated from the individual items in Nottingham's account. For 1699–1702
the totals are those calculated by Nottingham's steward.

[34] Lawrence Whistler, *The Imagination of Vanbrugh and his Fellow Artists*
(1954), p. 161.

[35] Pearl Finch, *op cit.*, i, 381.

[36] H.M.C. Finch MSS., ii, ff. 18–19.

[37] Finch MSS., Miscellaneous, nos. 31–5, contains Daniel Finch's marriage
settlements.

[38] Finch MSS., Correspondence, nos. 515 and 515a.

[39] Private Act: 10 Geo. 2, c. 14.

[40] See their biographies in the *D.N.B.*

[41] Add. MS. 29595, f. 69. He means that he has given a larger portion
than he intended.

[42] H.M.C. 11th Report, App. Pt. V, MSS. of Earl of Dartmouth, p. 294.

[43] Finch MSS., Correspondence, nos. 515 and 515a.

[44] Besides ten other children who died young and seven still-born.

[45] Finch MSS., Miscellaneous, no. 131. Lady Mary and Mr. Robert Finch
were sister and brother of Daniel Finch. It is difficult to give a representative
figure for Nottingham's landed income at this time for some of his Essex
property was let on beneficial leases.

[46] M. A. Thomson, *The Secretaries of State, 1681–1782* (Oxford 1932),
p. 147.

[47] Add. MS. 29595, f. 48, 24 May 1694.

[48] A. S. Turberville, *Welbeck Abbey and its Owners* (1939), II, 147–8.

[49] Vanbrugh to Lord Carlisle, 19 July 1722, quoted by Whistler, *op cit.*,
p. 156.

[50] Finch MSS., Correspondence, nos. 515 and 515a.

[51] This calculation is contained in Finch MSS., Miscellaneous, no. 35. In
this document, written almost certainly in 1695, Nottingham declares that
'probably taxes on land will not last above three years for the war cannot last
so long'. The same expectation is to be found in Gregory King, "Natural
Observations" [in *Two Tracts*, Ed. Barnett (Baltimore, 1936), pp. 48–9].

[52] Finch MSS., Miscellaneous, p. 129. The expenditure on furniture and
utensils in 1699 probably includes an abnormal element, since he was
preparing to move into Burley.

[53] These are calculated from the detailed receipts recorded in Nottingham's private accounts. Miss Pearl Finch quotes a document, '*Thomas
Armstrong's Account of the Profits of the Office from 22nd May 1702 to 22nd April
1704*', which gives the receipts of office as £16,279 14s. 8d. and expenditure
as £4,191 0s. 0d. I have not been able to trace this document. The most

12

likely explanation of the discrepancy with the figure in the text is that this account included money received and spent on real secret-service purposes.

[54] Private Act, 10 Geo. 2, c. 14.

[55] Finch MSS., Correspondence, nos. 515 and 515a.

[56] *Ibid.*

[57] For the acquisitions of the Duke of Chandos, see C. H. Collins Baker and M. I. Baker, *The Life and Circumstances of James Brydges, first Duke of Chandos* (1949).

[58] Finch MSS., Miscellaneous, no. 125.

[59] Add. MS., 29595, f. 23.

[60] *Ibid.*, f. 44.

[61] *Ibid.*, f. 60.

[62] Finch MSS., Correspondence, letter of 21 June 1705.

[63] Finch MSS., Miscellaneous, no. 123.

[64] Whistler, *op. cit.*, p. 36.

[65] *Ibid.*, p. 176.

[66] Catherine E. Parsons, 'Horseheath Hall and its Owners', *Proceedings of the Cambridge Antiquarian Society*, xli, 45.

[67] Add. MS. 29549, f. 127.

VI

The Walpoles:
Father and Son

J. H. PLUMB

VI

THE Walpole manuscripts from Houghton Hall consist mostly of foreign despatches, cabinet papers, parliamentary speeches and Treasury memoranda—the expected relics of a long ministerial career. But there was found amongst these papers a number of bundles of a more personal nature —private family letters, account books and household bills— documents which Archdeacon Coxe ignored when he came to write his official life of Sir Robert Walpole.[1] Unfortunately they are sadly incomplete. There are very few private letters after 1707; the accounts illuminate only an occasional decade; the bills relate to a year here or there. Yet these documents are very precious for they are the only source we have which throws any light on the way Sir Robert Walpole lived or on his family background and early education. Also some of his father's accounts survive, and it is possible to compare the daily life of a simple country gentleman of the seventeenth century with that of a great statesman of the eighteenth, a contrast which illuminates the class structure of the Augustan age, and reveals some of the causes of the political bitterness of that time.

The Walpoles had lived for many generations in North-West Norfolk. They had emerged, like so many gentle families, in the late thirteenth century, taking advantage of the great expansion in agrarian prosperity. Possibly their success was due to their enterprise in taking into cultivation the arid and desolate heathland of this corner of Norfolk. Thereafter generation had followed generation at Houghton; their lands increased little; their social position remained what it had been for centuries. They belonged to the ruling class of families, providing Justices of the Peace, Deputy Lieutenants, Colonels of Militia—and on rare occasions, a Member of Parliament. They were akin to scores of families which spread like a net across the counties of England, giving them coherence and form and government.[2] The Walpoles lived and died and were buried at Houghton, the little village which nestled by the side of their rambling house and which provided so many generations of its servants. The pattern of life there scarcely changed as century followed century—the great fields were tilled and cropped as they had been time out of mind; the vast flocks of sheep grazed on the brekes as they had done since Doomsday; the tenants paid their rents in cash, in produce, and by boon work according to the ancient manorial custom. More often than not they were in debt to their lord. It mattered hardly at all, for little was needed which the manors themselves did not provide.

Nathan Solden, the steward of Sir Robert Walpole's great-grandfather, kept a careful account of his household expenditure in a neat but angular hand—one book from 1647–9 survives. The purchases which it records are of the simplest. Food is the most important item—'a cupple of ducks'; teal occasionally; and a regular purchase of two hundred oysters for two shillings every week. Meat was entered in large quantities but this can only have been a question of book-keeping between home and farm for no Walpole can ever have needed to purchase mutton. 'Oringes and lymoms' were a different matter and these and a peck of turnips were most probably bought at Lynn. But such fancy foods were rare. The family diet was plain; the routine of meat and game was only occasionally relieved by a 'dishe of udders'. Lumped in with the food are other purchases—nails, matting, wire, new tiles, calico for shirts, the mending of doublets, but even so the household expenditure was very small. Robert, an elderly widower, lived with his son, Edward, and his wife who had five children, and a flock of indoor servants, but only on occasion did the weekly bill, including the meat, rise above £10, usually it was about six or seven. There are no signs of any extravagance. Robert Walpole's income was about £750 a year. During the Civil War he behaved himself with great circumspection, thereby evading the compoundings and sequestrations which bore so heavily on many Norfolk families. And as Walpoles were wont to do he had married well, the daughter of a Lord Mayor of London, and so had his son whose wife, Susan Crane, the daughter of a

Suffolk gentleman, brought a jointure of £132 a year. They were a prosperous family and Robert's son a rising man who had helped Townshend seize Lynn for Charles II in 1660. He became its Member of Parliament in the Cavalier Parliament— a tribute to his own as well as his family's standing in the county for he did not possess a settled interest in the borough. To add to his glory, Charles II made him Knight of the Bath, and in 1661 life must have seemed sweet to Sir Edward Walpole. He could look forward to a distinguished career, excellent marriages for his children, and a steady accumulation of wealth in land. But rich or poor in seventeenth-century England lived constantly in the shadow of death. Within a few years his father, his wife and himself were all buried. Sir Edward's bright hopes were gone, and Houghton was left to the care of his son, Robert; a boy of seventeen who had been born in 1650.

Robert inherited a good estate but many obligations. There were his aunts, his brothers, his young sisters, all had to be provided for, and soon there would be children of his own. We know very little of this Robert Walpole. Only a few of his letters remain and there is but one reference to him in contemporary memoirs. But his account books are extensive and they disclose the man. Later in life Robert Walpole became known as Colonel Walpole—his rank in the Norfolk militia— and it is simpler to call him by this title in order to distinguish him from his more famous son.

Colonel Walpole was a solid, well-integrated character. The steps which he took were those of a man who had measured carefully his opportunities. They were never hurried yet he was not an over-cautious man for he was quite capable of taking risks with the money which he garnered so carefully. He had temper and made it felt opportunely when his interests were endangered, but it was never wanton nor rash like his brother Horatio's. He was also a highly intelligent man; very well read in the classics, with an abiding passion for his library. Whenever he went off to the Norfolk fairs, he rarely came back to Houghton without a parcel of books strapped behind his servant's saddle. They still remain at Houghton—histories of Sweden, the Netherlands, Bohemia, in large folio: bound volumes of sermons including those of his old Trinity tutor, Dr.

Barrow, for which he paid £1 14s. 6d. on 26 January 1684. He was interested in the new learning and Francis Bacon's works found a place on his shelves. This passion after knowledge gave him a reputation, according to Francis North, 'for study and learning extraordinary'.[3] He provides another illustration, if another were needed, of the falsity of Macaulay's picture of the illiterate rural squire of seventeenth-century England. Colonel Walpole was well read in history, geography, theology, law and the classics. Much of his time was to be spent in farming, in hunting, in drinking, in those rural pursuits which were natural to a country gentleman, but his love of books remained with him to the day of his death.

Perhaps his intelligence can best be seen at work in the way he managed the farming of his own estates. In the early seventeenth century the Dutch had developed new agricultural methods on dry sandy soils similar to those at Houghton. The contacts between King's Lynn and Holland were very close, and the new husbandry must have been discussed by the gentlemen farmers and merchants when they met together at the fairs and markets, for there were very few of the great merchants of Lynn who were not almost as interested in land as in merchandise. By 1660 a certain publicity had been given to the improvements of the Dutch by pamphleteers, but there is no evidence that Colonel Walpole had read their books. During his early years as a farmer he never once visited London, and his knowledge was most probably derived from the talk that he heard in Lynn or what he saw about him in Norfolk. He was certainly convinced of the wisdom of Dutch techniques and he became one of the pioneers of a new school of agriculture in which root crops and grasses played an important part. By 1673 turnips were being grown at Houghton in very considerable quantities; they were weeded regularly and double-hoed—payments for both processes occur regularly year after year in the account books. Colonel Walpole was interested in the new grass crops as well as turnips. On 25 April 1677, he paid 'Godfrey for 4 days sewing my clover seed, beside his board . . . 04s. 0d'. He had bought the two hundred pounds of seed a fortnight before for £4. The next year he grew some of his own seed, but it was insufficient for his spring sowing in 1679, so he bought another three combs. The accounts also refer to "The Great Clover Close". Clover, along with turnips, had become a part of the established Houghton practice. He was also experimenting with wheat, a difficult crop on these dry sandy soils, on a modest but not insignificant scale, for he bought seven bushels of seed wheat in October 1679, at thirteen shillings and sixpence. Marling and enclosing were long established processes which Colonel Walpole not only maintained but also extended. A hundred years later Arthur Young regarded these features of Norfolk husbandry as new and progressive: later centuries, following his lead, hailed their introduction into England as a part of the eighteenth-century agrarian revolution.

It is time that revolution was antedated by a century, for Colonel Walpole was not a lonely pioneer. He bought clover seed from his cousin, Ruding, a yeoman farmer of Rougham; from Mrs. Arminger, another small landowner at Burnham Thorpe; from Allen of Ingoldisthorpe, one of the lesser gentry, and from Kent, the steward of Lord Townshend. So it would seem that landowners great and small were busily experimenting with Dutch methods in this corner of Norfolk. Nor was it only Dutch methods which Colonel Walpole adopted. The demands for food of the growing population of London had influenced the husbandry of southern and eastern England for many generations; the influence gradually spread in ever widening circles until it reached Scotland. In London Scotch beef became a luxury food, and it occurred to Colonel Walpole and probably to others that Scotch cattle could be fattened in Norfolk after their long trek south for the London market. In August 1676 he bought half a dozen steers, possibly as an experiment; they cost him £17 2s. od. Another famous point of Norfolk husbandry established long before the days of "Turnip Townshend" or Coke of Holkham! There can be no doubt that Colonel Walpole was an intelligent, adventurous man, quick to seize his opportunities, and free from many of the prejudices of tradition and custom.

And of course, he prospered, but this prosperity, derived purely from his farming, was not dissipated; few young men of seventeen with a large patrimony can have been so cautious or so level-headed. It was some seventeen years after his inheritance of Houghton before he ventured to London. Until then his journeys were confined to visits to the Norfolk fairs and Norwich assizes or to his Suffolk property where his father-in-law, Sir Jeffery Burwell, lived hard by at Rougham. A similar prudence can be discerned in his expenditure; there is no extravagance, not even at election times—a guinea and a half was all that he laid out at Norwich in 1679. There is no sign of self-indulgence, save perhaps for eight barrels of Colchester oysters for nineteen shillings (but surely a bargain at that price!), and even then he had the excuse that doctors thought oysters essential for health. The accounts illustrate a life of utmost simplicity. The reason was not only the need for Colonel Walpole to accumulate capital to buy land, although that doubtless was important, but the extent of his family obligations also constrained him to a plain way of living, unless he were to risk burdening his estate with debt, for at seventeen he had inherited not only an estate but a nursery full of children. On 22 February 1671 he had married Mary Burwell, only a girl of sixteen, and their own children arrived with the regularity of the harvest.[5] During the early years of his marriage his sisters were boarded out, rather expensively, with Lady Crane; his brothers, Horatio and Edward, had to be maintained at school. This was costly enough, but the time would soon come when he would have to find his sisters' portions, together with the interest which had accumulated over the years. He could and did charge them for their maintenance, but even so he had difficulty in raising the money. In the end he persuaded his father-in-law to sell his estate to Sir Robert Davers who had made a fortune in the Barbados. Colonel Walpole, whose wife was to inherit his property in any case on her father's death, then paid Sir Jeffery Burwell an annuity, equivalent to five per cent. interest on the capital raised by the sale, and so by this ingenious method he avoided mortgaging his own property. This, at least, was the kind of business transaction of which his own son might well have been proud. This deal, and the marriage of his sisters, eased considerably Colonel Walpole's circumstances and allowed him and his wife to live a little more expensively. At the end of June 1678 he made a brief trip to London, visiting his Suffolk property on the way. It is very probable that the preliminary negotiations for the sale of Rougham to Sir Robert Davers made a visit necessary. He left his wife with her father and stayed with his cousin, Edward Mann the linen-draper, in the Strand. He bought himself a watch 'of Jones make' for six pounds, a couple of wigs for £3 14s. 6d. and exchanged his sword for a better one, paying a guinea for the difference. He did not forget his wife, her modest present was a gown for £3, and he found a few trinkets for the children. He also took the opportunity to have his coach entirely refurbished—an expensive item, costing him £32. But even so his expenses for the whole trip did did not amount to £50.

It was not until 1681 that Colonel Walpole permitted himself a long stay in London with his wife. They remained there for the whole of June and July. They spent £290 12s. 6d., a quite considerable sum and a clear indication of Colonel Walpole's growing prosperity. Most of this money went on the purchase of a new "chariot" and Mrs. Walpole, in London for the first time since her marriage, seized her opportunities with both hands and ran through nearly a hundred pounds. The trip was not purely for pleasure; the long negotiations for the sale of Sir Jeffery Burwell's estate had at last been concluded and Colonel Walpole spent many days with his lawyers going over the final settlements. The sale of land was always a very protracted business at this time, for estates were rarely free from a multitude of obligations which had to be resolved before a sale could take place. The lawyers thrived on this complexity and Colonel Walpole had to pay out £69 8s. 0d. to Messrs. Cracherode and Mosier for their pains. It was four years before Mrs. Walpole saw London again, but her husband seems to have made a short visit every year until he became a Member of Parliament in 1689. In the early summer he would set off for Loughborough in Leicestershire where his favourite sister, Susan, was living with her husband, John Wilson. From there he made his way to London, spent a few days with his cousin Mann, then returned to Houghton via Suffolk, where he viewed his property and collected his rents. It was done with great frugality: the whole trip cost only £16 in 1684. Apart from her pregnancies which did not always fall conveniently for a summer jaunt to London, there was a good reason for Colonel Walpole keeping his wife in Norfolk, for we know that she was an extravagant woman. The entire correspondence with her son consists of demands for money, and whenever she did get to London, the entries in Colonel Walpole's account book increase rapidly. In 1685, she went with her husband for three weeks, taking her eldest girl with her, who was immediately placed with a writing master. She bought clothes for herself and the younger children and persuaded Colonel Walpole to spend quite extensively on the house—for the first time in her fourteen years of married life. In all this time nothing had been bought for Houghton except a few tin dishes at Lynn fair and a coffee-pot for a shilling. Now his wife persuaded him to buy six Dutch chairs and three dozen cane ones and to spend £32 18s. 6d. upon their upholstery. They were packed and sent to Houghton by sea. But Mrs. Walpole probably took the pendulum clock back with her in the coach, along with her picture which she had had painted— not by an artist of repute for the picture and its frame only came to £6 14s. 6d. It is probably the one which still hangs at Houghton—a dull, wooden-faced picture which betrays nothing of the sitter's character.

Such trips were rare, and in the main, Mrs. Walpole and her daughters had to rely for their finery on what they could pick up at the Norfolk fairs. She seems to have been a poor needle-woman. Her children's clothes and her husband's cravats were made up for her by local gentlewomen—Lady Barkham of Southacre made the girls' coats and the father's cravats; and a Mrs. Cremer was called in to do the shirts. Payments for stockings, shirts, neckerchiefs, even an Indian gown and a screw of black buttons are carefully listed in these meticulous accounts by Colonel Walpole, but they may be searched in vain for payments to a tailor for himself, or even for broadcloth for a suit. From 1671–89, Colonel Walpole probably made do either with the clothes that he had as a young man or those which he inherited from his father. He only bought one hat, and even then he sold his old one in part exchange.

Such a model of prudence did not waste his substance in riotous living. Until the eighties there is very little mention of wine, and it is not until the nineties that he began to buy in any quantity. Until then half a hogshead of claret, a small barrel of rum, or a couple of bottles of Rhenish sufficed to meet his needs. The same is true of food—a cag of sturgeon, a barrel of oysters, oranges and lemons, a few luxuries such as these make an occasional appearance in the accounts but in general the household at Houghton lived entirely on its own produce. The same economy was exercised in relation to his children. Sir Robert Walpole's pocket money as a boy was two shillings a year, paid half-yearly; his and his brothers' only toys, unless made at home, were the 'Shittle Cocks and Battledores' which cost their father half a crown. Their neckerchiefs were bought from the 'tinker woman'; and their hats, in bulk—ten at a time—at Lynn fair. What a contrast this makes with the way Sir Robert Walpole's youngest son, Horace, was treated forty year later. That pampered little boy received expensive toys, made by Edward Beach, every few months. His French tailor, Nicolas Olivier, charged as much for one small satin suit as his grandfather spent in his lifetime on clothes; before he was ten he had a footman of his own. His childhood was elegant, cushioned, metropolitan, and when he left his private tutor for Eton—he took with him his fine furniture and smart chintz curtains.

His father had a ruder childhood. At six he was packed off to school with his two brothers. His master was Richard Ransome, the parson at Great Dunham, which lay some twenty miles from Houghton towards Swaffham. There he stayed most of the year, coming back home only for two short holidays. When he was thirteen, he rode with his father to Eton where he was entered in College, prudently under a false age (twelve instead of thirteen) so that he would be eligible for a scholarship. During this austere and isolated boyhood he learned to love the simple pleasures of the countryside, particularly hunting, in which his father had indulged as soon as he felt that his wealth was capable of supporting a huntsman and hounds.

The picture which emerges from Colonel Walpole's account book is one of prudence and careful husbandry; of growing riches wisely invested in yet more land, that solid basis of his wealth. But with Colonel Walpole prudence was allied with ambition. He rode regularly to elections at Norwich; and he became a freeman of Lynn, no doubt in order to acquire a parliamentary vote there. He was appointed a Justice of the Peace; he was active in the Norfolk militia. He managed his political career with that same wise patience with which he conducted his private affairs, and it was not until 1689 that he stood for Parliament for the pocket borough of Castle Rising which belonged to the Howard family, partly to the Duke of Norfolk and partly to Thomas Howard of Ashted, the son of Sir Robert Howard, the dramatist. On whose interest Colonel Walpole first entered Parliament may only be guessed; his cousin, Cufaude, was the Receiver-General of the Duke of Norfolk's rents, and Robert Walpole's election bill of £20 was paid to him, so most probably he was brought in by the Norfolks. Once elected he began to create rapidly his own interest. With the help of his brother, Horatio, and his brother-in-law, James Hoste of Sandringham, he bought up enough cottages, which carried a vote, to secure the control of one seat, and this control was so firm that it lasted in his family until the Reform Bill. In this struggle Colonel Walpole was reckless of expense, spending as much as £300 for houses which had sold at £30.[6] For the next ten years he played the part of one of the leading men of his county, going up to London for the parliamentary session, sitting on the back bench, voting no doubt as his conscience dictated, but keeping, if his friendships are a guide to his views, to a whiggish attitude. And when he died in 1700, at the early age of fifty, his life could be taken as typical of the most enterprising and effective members of his class—the country gentlemen.

He remained rustic. Rustic in his tastes, in his clothes, in his old house: rustic in his pleasures, in his devotion to the land. His life was simple in all its aspects but it was not uncultured. His farming was a model of efficiency and enterprise: his library was well stocked and well read: the wandering fiddlers from Thetford, Swaffham or Lynn were always sure of a warm welcome and a modest tip at Houghton. But it was a plain hard life that had its dark places. His children came and went like the swallows. 'Paid for digging my little girl's grave . . .2s. 6d.'; so the accounts run, and the register at Houghton records their frequent funerals. Usually they lived long enough—two, three, four or more years—for their deaths to be a deep sadness; on one occasion an epidemic with tragic suddenness emptied the nursery. At Houghton few years passed without dying or suffering, and Mrs. Walpole bought her powders to excite labour, vomits, electuaries, and "hysterical cordeall water"; Colonel Walpole, never after 1690 a healthy man, needed his night pills and purges. 'Little miss' was given 'a Julap against the Rickets', and Master Charles, who did not last long, "Hydropick Syrup". The apothecaries and the doctors with their violent and repulsive cures were never absent for long. And this aspect of life, at least, did not change from father to son. Sir Robert Walpole's life was threaded with sickness, from his boyhood a recurrent fever, possibly malaria, and the stone attacked him year after year. His wife's bills tell the same story of sickness and misery. His children were bled and purged and vomited with the same gruesome regularity of his own childhood. But in every other way his daily life makes a remarkable and violent contrast to that of his father.

Unlike his father, Sir Robert Walpole rejoiced in spending money whether he had it or not, and at the beginning of his career he certainly lacked it, for his father died at a most inopportune moment for the family fortunes. The creation of his parliamentary interest at Castle Rising had been very costly, and in 1697 Colonel Walpole raised a considerable sum of money to buy his Cousin Pell's estates at Dersingham and West Winch, worth £450 p.a., but this property carried two considerable life interests. These were burdens which the prudent Colonel could have borne, but his son was faced with paying off a number of his father's loans immediately. Furthermore, the payment of his mother's jointure and his sisters' annuities cut sharply into his income, for true to the tradition of the time they immediately left Houghton and became the paying guests of Lady Turner, Sir Robert's eldest sister, at Warham near Wells-on-Sea. His brother Horace was at King's; his brother Galfridus at school. He himself had recently married Catherine Shorter, a woman of small fortune and extravagant tastes. Bad harvests or low prices dogged his early years and his tenants fell badly behind with their rents. Nevertheless he was determined to cut a figure. He touched everyone he could for a loan—shopkeepers at Lynn, his father's old friends, his uncles, his cousins—and all that he could lay hands on he spent. For the next forty years he went on spending all that he could get and, fortunately for Robert Walpole, he was destined to get hundreds of thousands. Yet extravagant as he was, there was a certain prudence, a sense of direction in his spending which prevented it from being merely wanton or reckless. Robert Walpole lived and spent as the great men of his day lived and spent, because from the very first he intended to live and die a great man.

As soon as he succeeded his father he was in a hurry. Even before the funeral he wrote to Thomas Howard of Ashtead telling him of his intention to stand for Castle Rising and, as soon as it was over, he set out for London without bothering to wait for his election. Yet before he left Houghton he had given extensive orders for the reconstruction of the old house—new sash windows, new fireplaces, new wainscotting. He never lived again permanently in Norfolk. He might parade the country gentleman, and after his enforced retirement he was prepared to extol the virtues of country life, but London, the Court, the Palace of Westminster—there was the atmosphere which he really loved to breathe. And when he quitted Norfolk in December 1700, he was never to return except for short periods, often reduced to two or three weeks in a year.

In London he had no intention of living like his father. He set up house with his wife's grandmother in Berkeley Street— modish and grand. A room over a linen-draper's in the Strand, at a pound a week board, had been good enough for Colonel Walpole, nor had he ever considered it desirable that his wife should keep him company. Her place had been at Houghton with her children and women. But Catherine Walpole had been born and bred in London, bred on the fringe of fashionable life, yet lacking either birth or sufficient wealth to give her a secure social position. Both her mother and her grandmother had used their husbands harshly, spending on extravagant living every penny that they could extort from them. Unfortunately it became a family habit, and Catherine Walpole was as determined as her husband to lead a gay life in London. She was a difficult wife, moody, hysterical, given to acts of cruelty, but

Colonel Robert Walpole by Mary Beale

Sir Robert Walpole by John Wootton

Walpole's love for her can be judged by this one letter of his which survives:

'May I measure your heart by my own. O there I find that love that tendernesse for you that are there any failings in you they are still perfections to me and doth my Dearest doe or omit any thing that might seem better otherwise, I am blind, cannot, would not, see any thing in my deare self but what is most agreable.'[8]

She disliked Norfolk intensely and frequently stayed in London when Walpole had to go there for elections or the business of his estates. So from the very first he was compelled to maintain two households—an expense which bore very heavily on his already burdened estate.

Houghton was made to contribute all that it could. A wagon service had recently been started from Lynn via Swaffham, Brandon and Newmarket—a slow lumbering affair but a most necessary artery in Walpole's household economy in these years. Geese, turkeys, collars of bacon, barrels of oysters, jars of mushrooms, apples, hampers of home-brewed 'hogan' ale, flowed along it, for a wagon rarely left Lynn without two or three boxes for the Walpoles in Berkeley Street. And the steward, fat John Wrott, who was always so anxiety-ridden by his master's debts and the tenants' inability to pay, used to secrete the rents inside the geese—a simple countryman's dodge for avoiding the depredations of the highwaymen. Bulkier goods, particularly hay, went by sea by the regular coasting service from Wells to London. Without these supports from Norfolk, Walpole's debts would have been far greater. But within a few years Norfolk was full of gossip of the extravagant way the young Walpoles lived; a great stir was caused by a ball which they gave at Christmas in 1706 at which the Duke of Grafton was present. Uncle James Hoste of Sandringham disapproved and said so sharply to the Turners, Walpole's relatives, who lived at Lynn. Old Charles Turner wrote off to him in great distress, begging Walpole to send him some money to stop the mouths of his creditors who were making bitter remarks and doing his reputation great harm. Naturally the simple Lynn shopkeepers, who had lent him twenty or fifty pounds, could not realize that a young and ambitious politician had to cut a figure in the world.

But the Walpoles succeeded in cutting a figure and their social success may be measured, not only by the dukes who attended their ball, but also by the election of Walpole himself to the Kit-Cat Club—the most exclusive and fashionable of all the Whig clubs. In rotation each member acted as host, vying with other members in the production of exotic food and magnificent wines. When Walpole's turn came round he bewildered Wrott by his request for ruffs and reeves. These were netted for him by his cousin, Thomas Turner, in the marsh-lands of the Wash and sent to Houghton to be fattened. They reduced Wrott to a jelly of anxiety; his letters are full of concern about them and he longed to get them despatched to London. 'I think the Ruffs and Reefes', he wrote 'are now fat and I feel there will be danger of their dying if they be kept too long, therefore the sooner you have them up the better, and I know no safer way than to kill them and send them up by the Lyn coach.' And then with a touch of sly humour, he added: 'John Cornwall brought here a couple of young Shelducks which I shall send by the wagon'. Shelduck is said to be so rank that the bird is quite inedible even when skinned. It seems unlikely that these were served to the Kit-Cats.[9]

Houghton was a great support to the household living in Berkeley Street, and Walpole also relied upon Norfolk for the bulk of his wine and beer. His Turner cousins were wine-merchants and with them he could run up big bills for hogs-heads of port, white Lisbon and claret. But he was able to supplement this, when he became a member of Prince George's Council, with a little smuggling. The Prince was Lord High Admiral, so Walpole's first job brought him in touch with Josiah Burchett, the Secretary of the Admiralty. Walpole and Burchett, by adroit use of an Admiralty barge to fox the Customs officers, managed to smuggle in a fair quantity of champagne and old burgundy, a welcome addition to the rather commonplace wines which he got from the Turners.[10] Smuggling, of course, was widespread. James Swanton, the Wells smuggler, called regularly at Houghton with his Dutch linens and Walpole's old mother at Warham recounts with glee how she had baffled the Customs officers and got a load in through the back door.[11] But, even so, for two highly placed officials in the Admiralty to engage in large-scale smuggling is, perhaps, somewhat brazen. No doubt it made a good joke at the Kit-Cat and led to many toasts.

His creditors remained unpaid; some of his lands were sold or mortgaged, yet Walpole prospered. He had his reversals, even a taste of the Tower, nevertheless office came his way, first Secretary of War, then Treasurer of the Navy. During these years of modest affluence he took a house in Dover Street and began to invest seriously in the funds. Then he lost office and hard times followed—his wife had to borrow half a crown from her maid to hire a hackney coach when visiting him in the Tower. (It was eighteen months before the maid got her money back.) But when Queen Anne died, Walpole came safely home to port. At first he enjoyed the extremely lucrative office of Paymaster-General which he left in 1716 to become Chancellor of the Exchequer. His career was interrupted by three years of opposition in which he and Townshend struggled with Sunderland and Stanhope for supreme power. This he captured in 1720. For a time he took the office of Paymaster again. 'He was lean', he is reported to have said, 'and needed to get some fat on his bones.' But he fattened quickly and in the reshuffle of offices which followed the South Sea Bubble he became First Lord of the Treasury and Chancellor of the Exchequer, posts which he held until he was forced from office in 1742.

He made an enormous fortune. It cannot be calculated. He banked with so many bankers; involved with his own money were the government surpluses with which he was allowed to speculate; at times, especially in the boom months before the bursting of the South Sea Bubble, he was investing money for his relatives and friends in Norfolk. His salary was handsome: the fees which his offices brought him, princely. And yet none of these sources seems quite sufficient for the river of gold which flowed in and out of his coffers. Such bank-books of his which remain throw little light on the sources of his wealth. The entries are brief and laconic:

Reced of y^r Hon^r in Bank	500	0	0
Reced of D^o　　　　D^o	500	0	0
Reced of y^r Hon^r	4000	0	0
Reced more	500	0	0

And so on and so on, with here and there the receipt of money from the sale of tallies or the interest from investments. Where the bank notes came from in such profusion no one will ever know and it is idle to speculate. The standards of Augustan morality were not ours, and Walpole never claimed to be a saint. He loaded offices on his brothers and children; no Norfolk friend went without reward. The 'Robinocracy' became the butt of the Grub Street hacks but it was no myth. Having arrived at the summit of political power, Walpole was determined to make his family so rich that it would be immune to the natural disasters of time. He built for eternity. This ambition was not peculiar to Walpole; but his attitude was becoming a little old-fashioned, and he was one of the last of the King's servants to make a great fortune from politics. But in his day, apart from Charles II's bastards and their descendants, there was scarcely a noble family whose fortune had not been founded or augmented by the loot of office. And Walpole saw that, no matter how many centuries had elapsed since their ancestors had served the state, these families had remained great and powerful in the land.

We may not know how Walpole acquired his wealth, and we can only surmise the causes of his voracity, but we know exactly how he spent his money—two important accounts survive—one with his banker, Robert Mann, from 1714–18, and more importantly the accounts of his London steward, Edward Jenkins, from 1714–26. In addition to these valuable sources there are several cubic yards of bills, perhaps almost complete for 1733. Finally, there is Houghton itself; apart from the pictures sold by his grandson to Catherine of Russia, it is as he left it. From this evidence it is possible to build up a detailed picture of the way 'The Great Man' lived. And what a contrast it makes with the simple homespun life of his father!

Let us begin with Houghton. The old house, medieval in origin, patched and added to by the succeeding generations, had been good enough for his father. At his inheritance, Walpole had spent a lot of money on its modernization; in 1716 he reconstructed it again, but by 1721 he had decided it was hopeless to attempt to turn it into a great house. So he razed it to the ground and from 1722 to 1735 the masons and carpenters and plasterers were at work. At the same time Bridgeman began to change the landscape for miles around. In 1729, the village which for centuries had clustered about the house was moved a mile away. The furnishing of the rooms went on for years; France and Italy were combed for pictures to adorn their walls, for Walpole was an avid collector who paid the highest price then known for a Poussin. Even amidst the anxieties of the political crises which preceded his fall, he could find time to negotiate for a Domenichino. Artari did the plaster work; Rysbrack the chimney-pieces and statuary; Kent the furniture and decorations. Genoa velvet, the best silks and damasks from France adorned its walls. The state bed, a magnificent creation by Kent, blazed with gold thread. Everything that was used was of the finest; the craftsmanship the best which money and discerning taste could buy. The house was built to outlast time. Those of Walpole's contemporaries who did not hate him regarded Houghton as the finest house of its kind in England, and that remains true today. Architecture, furniture, landscape, harmonize like notes in music, for Walpole who exercised complete control over every detail was a man of superb taste.[12] No one will ever know what it cost Walpole to transform Houghton from a country-gentleman's house to a nobleman's palace. But with the furniture and pictures it must have run into tens upon tens of thousands.

Yet he rarely lived there. During the twenty-one years while he was the King's first servant he visited Norfolk only twice a year—for about a fortnight at the end of parliamentary session, which normally ended in May or early June, and for about a month in November when he held what the satirists called his 'Norfolk Congress'. Then Houghton was filled with the most important men of affairs. They hunted; they ate gargantuan meals and drank ferociously, but hunting, drinking or eating, they talked politics. In the charming library which Walpole built for himself (lined with his father's and grandfather's books, for his own editions were confined to his College books and the Statutes of the Realm), he settled the business of the next session with his most intimate advisers—Newcastle, his brother Horace, Henry Pelham and Hardwicke.

There was an extravagance, a grandeur about his hospitality, a wantonness in its profusion which argues that it was the expression of a deep-seated need of Walpole's nature. Had he resented bitterly his confined and parsimonious childhood; a younger son with no prospect but the Church and Bircham parsonage? Or had he hated the plain homespun and the cheap neckerchiefs bought from the tinker's wife? Or did his ostentation spring from a lack of security that went deeper than the insecurity of class or family origins? Was there in this great man of whom the world went in awe the need to please, the need to compel both admiration and gratitude? Whatever the cause the hospitality was unique of its kind and became the gossip of society and the butt of satirists.[13]

The same profusion, the same reckless expenditure, marked the whole of Walpole's life. Houghton was not the only house on which he allowed his imagination full play; in many ways he was more devoted to his Chelsea home—Orford House—from which he was to take his title. He went to live there when he was Paymaster-General and later he managed to secure a long lease from the Crown. It was a part of Chelsea Hospital, but Walpole spent large sums adapting it to his needs. Sir John Vanbrugh was responsible for the alterations but Walpole was, it seems, keenly critical of his plans.

'I have conceiv'd about your Room', Vanbrugh wrote to him in 1716, 'and will bring it to you (I think) on Tuesday morning. 'Tis an expedient between the two so perhaps you'll like it.'[14]

One of the major additions to the house was the orangery which Walpole intended to use as a picture-gallery, for his pictures at Chelsea were as fine as those at Houghton. He bought adjacent land for enlarging his garden; built a river-wall by the Thames, creating a large terrace walk adorned at one end with an elegant octagonal summer-house; there was also a 'vollery' or aviary where Mrs. Walpole kept her exotic birds. The hospitality at Chelsea was as prodigious as that at Houghton but, as Walpole lived there most of the year, more constant and more expensive; the most sumptuous banquet ever given by the Walpoles was at Chelsea in August 1729 when they entertained the Queen and the Royal children:

some idea of the splendour of this entertainment can be derived from the description in the *London Journal*:

The Dinner was in Sir Robert's Green House. A kitchen was built on purpose in the stable yards near as big as that erected for the Dinner of the Knights of the Bath, with above 20 places for Fires, etc. The fruit for the Dessert was collected a week preceding from all quarters of the Town.

After Dinner Her Majesty and the Royal Family retired to the [*Octagon*] Banqueting House on the River to drink Tea; where were several Barges of fine Musick playing all the Time. After which they returned to the Green House, where the illustrious company were entertained with a ball, and afterwards supped in the same place.[15]

In 1727 the King made Walpole Ranger of Richmond Park and gave him the lease of the Old Lodge there: at once the carpenters, plasterers and upholsterers got to work and within a few months Walpole had created a charming villa for his week-end retreats.[16] There at Richmond with his hounds and his mistress, Molly Skerrett, he could find a few hours' untroubled repose. A Mrs. Burton seems to have been his housekeeper there and every few months she was paid five or eight hundred pounds, but out of this, the household expenses both of Molly and her baby daughter had to be paid. Molly, of course, had her own income derived from the considerable sums which Walpole invested for her in the annuities. One way or the other Richmond proved an expensive addition to Walpole's burdens, but it brought him more private happiness than his other homes. His delight in it may be judged from the fact that in many of his unofficial portraits, he is dressed as Ranger of Richmond Park.

Both Chelsea and Richmond were too far from St. James's for a leading minister and during the parliamentary session, or when the Court was in London, Walpole lived first at Arlington Street and then at 10 Downing Street, when the King made it over to him. Walpole refused the house in Downing Street for himself but accepted it for the First Lord of the Treasury, who has lived there by right ever since. Both the houses in Arlington Street and Downing Street were small town houses by wealthy aristocratic standards but they were an additional burden on

Walpole's finances. He had to pay a high rent—£300 per annum—as well as rates and taxes on Arlington Street. He had to furnish and adorn both, for Walpole inherited nothing from his father which he felt that he could use in his homes, except a few family portraits and the splendid set of Mortlake tapestries, which still hang at Houghton, acquired no one knows when or how by his father. And finally, to complete the account of Walpole's hospitality, each year in the summer he spent a number of weeks with the Court either at Windsor Castle or Hampton Court. He took with him his cook, Solomon Sollis, and his servants and kept an open table there for all who wished to dine at his expense, and usually the four or five weeks cost him about three hundred pounds.

By wealthy standards of the nineteenth century, or even the early twentieth, such a number of houses as Walpole possessed and lived in, was not exceptional. After all, the Buccleuchs rejoiced at one time in Dalkeith, Bowhill, Branxholm, Drumlanrig, Richmond, Boughton, Beaulieu and two town houses; the Devonshires in Hardwick, Chatsworth, Bolton, Lismore, Compton Place and Devonshire House. But almost all of these possessions were the accumulations of centuries, the result of judicious marriages and the happy accidents of fate by which one large estate became amalgamated with another. And behind these ducal palaces stretched the vast landed estates which alone could give them stability. Of this Walpole was well aware. The estate which his father left, worth a mere two thousand a year, would have been totally inadequate to support the new Houghton; so Walpole was faced with the necessity, not only of living and spending like a great man, but also of accumulating sufficient wealth to enable his descendants to continue to do so. To this end he bought considerable property in Norfolk even before land prices fell at the bursting of the South Sea Bubble, and he went on buying land whenever he had the chance of a bargain or the opportunity of acquiring an adjacent estate.

He more than doubled the extent and value of the Walpole property in Norfolk. In addition he married his eldest son well, if not wisely. He found for him Margaret Rolle, the heiress of considerable estates in Devonshire and Cornwall and, equally important, the owner of two parliamentary boroughs —Ashburton and Callington. The marriage proved even unhappier than his own and the couple quickly gave up all pretence of living together, but the fortune which strengthened immensely the Walpole family was secure. Certainly this marriage was a most important factor in the growth of the estate, but it should not detract from Walpole's own achievement, for the transformation which he himself brought about in the wealth and standing of his family was remarkable.

By the time Walpole had become the King's first servant Houghton ceased to be a support to his London households. Apart from a little venison, the Lynn wagons brought nothing; indeed the traffic now was the other way. When Walpole set out for his yearly visit he was preceded by his servants. Solomon Sollis took with him the luxurious foods and wines that his master was accustomed to see at his table. The simple Norfolk fare, plainly cooked, no longer sufficed. Nor was the bulk of his wine bought at Lynn as it used to be. Walpole had developed an excellent taste in claret which was, with burgundy, the really fashionable drink in spite of the high duty on French wines. He himself preferred the very best—Lafite, Latour, Margaux, Haut Brion; these great wines occur over and over again in his bills. Apart from fine claret, Walpole had a taste for hock. In 1714 he was paying high prices for the vintage of 1706 which was being imported in bottle. Old burgundy and champagne were lesser favourites but frequently drunk. His cellar always contained a large number of hogsheads of port and white Lisbon for use at his public tables or for those of his friends who preferred it. In one year he spent more on wine than the income of a prosperous country gentleman. In 1733 he bought wines worth £1,118 12s. 10d. from James Bennett, his principal, but not sole, wine merchant. Five hundred and forty dozen empty bottles were returned to Bennett within the twelvemonth— a consumption of over eleven dozen a week. Only the French wines were bottled, the rest was drawn from the barrel as required, so to get any idea of what his household consumed this five hundred and fifty-two dozen must be at least doubled.

As with wine, so with food. James Mill made chocolates for Walpole; in his bills each item—the chocolate, the nuts and sugar are all carefully specified and then he gives the weight of the chocolates made. The order which he received was usually for a hundred pounds (weight) at a time, which cost Walpole £17 2s. 3d., more in fact than he paid in wages to three footmen for a year. The same prodigality is to be found in all the bills and household accounts which survive—the bills for oysters in 1733 are as fabulous as those for his wine.

One cannot begin to guess at his total expenditure on food and drink but it must have run into thousands of pounds a year, and to this must be added the wages of the army of servants who helped Solomon Sollis prepare and serve it. Not that servants were expensive. Even the prudent Colonel Walpole had allowed himself and his wife a fair bevy of them, although they were an insignificant number by his son's standards, who at one point had twenty-seven men and fifty women working as weeders in his plantations. But Walpole's regiment of household servants put little strain on his resources. They were paid very little, and that not very often. Edward Jenkins, the steward, received ten pounds a year and by 1726 this salary was twelve years in arrears. But Jenkins did not suffer; as Walpole's steward he received a large income in tips. Walpole's porter at Arlington Street is said to have received more in gratuities than many a country gentleman derived from his estates. No wonder then that the names of the same servants appear year after year in the Walpoles' accounts!

As with wine and food, so with clothes. Old Mrs. Walpole had to be content with the clothes which either she or her friends made at home or with an occasional gown from London bought cheaply from Cousin Mann. Lady Walpole lived in different style. Mr. Joseph Windham, Linen Draper, was paid £209 11s. od. on 3 September 1715, Mr. Turner, Laceman, £76 10s. od., Mrs. West & Co., Mercers, £26 10s. od. on the same day— £10 os. od. was a frequent sum paid to Mr. Downs for "my ladys stockens" and Mrs. Foster, the Mantua Maker, is always in and out of the accounts for anything from five to twenty-five pounds. Walpole's own clothes were as expensive as his wife's. On 4 December 1716, £543 os. od. was paid for 'cloth, lineings etc' for Walpole. Lace for a neckcloth and two pairs of ruffles cost £17 10s. od.; but his purchases were not always so very expensive, once he bought Indian neckerchiefs at six shillings each (did he remember the ones he wore as a boy, bought by his father from the tinker woman at half-a-crown?). His father had been content to buy his wigs very cheaply (two cost him £3 14s. 6d.) and he made them last for years. Walpole's wigmaker was Monsieur de Guignicour whose charges varied from eight to eleven pounds—and a wig lasted Walpole about twelve months. There must be added to this steady drain of guineas on clothes the jewelry—watches from the French maker, De Charmes, a diamond ring for himself, necklaces for his wife; the chairmen; the coaches; the portraits which never ceased to be painted; Mrs. Walpole's more than generous support of Heidegger and the Opera; and her children's education, no longer undertaken by a village person or old Dr. Short. The two elder boys were at Eton under the care of Dr. Bland—furnishing their rooms cost Walpole £70; their board cost £200 a year and they expected a regular supply of the best 'Bohea' tea and Lisbon sugar. The two girls went to a fashionable school run by Madame Nezerauw, at Chelsea, fashionable but expensive at £60 a year.

Walpole was open-hearted, lavish, almost absurdly generous to his friends. Walpole's father, when his brother Horatio came of age, sent him a token worth five shillings. By contrast Sir Robert paid £68 for a gold repeating watch by Quare which he gave to his own brother Horace to celebrate their success in 1715. As soon as he was in the money his relatives knew it— parcels rattled off to Norfolk, a wig for young Mrs. Turner, a riding habit complete with hat and feather for his sister, Mrs. Hamond. His old friends often touched him for a loan: Sir Richard Steele borrowed £500 in September 1716; Charles Dartequenave, a fellow Kit-Cat, took £100 from time to time.

What did all of this amount to? We shall never know, for Walpole had several bankers and none of his accounts survive with any continuity. Between August 1714 and May 1718, £152,251 17s. 8d. passed through his account with Robert Mann; of this £61,778 14s. 9d. was spent on investments, the rest went in personal expenditure. His Norfolk expenses play no part in this. Nor does it account for all his personal expenditure. Edward Jenkins did not always draw on Mann. Walpole often paid him in cash and Walpole rarely drew money for himself from Mann; Jenkins also received money from time to time for the Houghton sheep sold at Smithfield. And it is also known that at this time Walpole had another account with the bankers Gibson and Jacombe; in August 1718, whilst at Houghton, he drew £3,400 from his account with this firm for his expenses in Norfolk. Walpole had become, and remained, colossally rich.

Much has been made of the fact that at his death he left debts approaching £40,000: and this has been used to prove that he made little out of his career and that his extravagance was far beyond his means. In fact a debt of £40,000 was of no great significance in relation to Walpole's total estate—and in any case a considerable part of that debt consisted of legacies, left by Walpole, for which ready cash had to be raised. From the evidence which remains there can be no doubt that Walpole spent and created an immense fortune. Furthermore, he was able to provide magnificently for his brothers and children. Horatio, his brother, built the fine house at Wolterton from the profits of office conferred on him by his brother. His son, Horace, thanks to the sinecures given to him as a child, was able to live a long life in luxurious and whimsical elegance. The rest of the Walpole family, in their own ways, did equally well.

Walpole created for himself and his family the splendour of aristocratic life. His houses, his furniture, his pictures, horses, hounds and coaches were equal to any in the land, and in many ways he lived more extravagantly than the richest dukes. His style of life makes a vivid contrast with his father's; it requires an effort of imagination to savour it to the full, but it is worth the effort, for this contrast provides a key to some of the bitterness of political life in Walpole's day. There was at least one common feature to their lives—both were members of parliament, both were members of the governing class. The generation which separated them did not witness any revolution in the wealth of the governing class comparable to that which took place between father and son. In 1720, in 1730, in 1740 there were country gentlemen and members of parliament, living lives of simplicity equal to Colonel Walpole's. It is true that such men were far more numerous in 1700 than 1740 but they were numerous enough even in 1740 to be an important factor in politics. Many of these independent country gentlemen were not able or successful men, and unlike Colonel Walpole they saw their slender estates contract rather than expand. It was natural enough for many of them to develop a passionate hatred of courtiers, placemen and pensioners, and an intense loathing for Sir Robert Walpole himself. This hatred, which sprang partly from envy had made them Whiggish in Charles II's and James II's reigns and Toryish or, at least, independent after the Revolution. These squires made up the country, anti-Court, party. Their bitterness, their sense of being excluded from wealth and power, gave a keen edge to the political rancour of Walpole's time, for, like his father, Walpole was not alone. Perhaps no one made quite so much as he, but there were other ministers of the Crown who acquired a very tidy fortune—Sir Thomas Osborne, Duke of Leeds; Henry Brydges, Duke of Chandos, Sir Stephen Fox and his son, the first Lord Holland—all created great and enduring wealth from the opportunities given to them by service to the King.

In some, such careers aroused envy, in others emulation. For centuries royal service had brought affluence to many gentle families and with affluence the prospect of fine marriages. It was the way in which the aristocracy had been recruited. That political success brought enduring wealth was well known. This knowledge naturally added to the competition for office and the King's favour; it increased intrigue and the formation of rival factions; it sapped loyalty and corrupted political principle. The facts of Walpole's career, when seen in terms of his personal affluence and power, provide a key to the nature of much of English political life in the seventeenth and eighteenth centuries which was personal and factional rather than ideological.

Yet in many ways Walpole's career illustrates earlier centuries than his own. The great ministers of the Crown, after Walpole, used their power to further the interests of their families, to find safe and lucrative sinecures for their brothers and children, but they refrained from taking great wealth for themselves. The Duke of Newcastle and the Marquess of Rockingham lost wealth through their political activities; Chatham and his son, William Pitt, both died poor men. North gained nothing from his long period of office. The great legal officers still did very handsomely and so did many placemen below the highest level, but the contrast between the two halves of the century is very marked. There seems to be no easy answer to explain this change. Possibly it was due to the increased control of all aspects of political life by the *established* aristocracy, and the nobility's own growing consciousness of itself. It would have been far more difficult for country gentlemen such as Sir Thomas Osborne or Sir Robert Walpole, born outside the circle of any aristocratic group, to achieve supreme power in the state in the late eighteenth century. And also with each passing generation nobility became more a question of birth than of either wealth or power. It is probable that behind this change lies buried a more important social revolution of which this is but a small facet. The middle years of the eighteenth century witnessed a decay in the influence of the country gentry; for centuries they had been a factor of immense importance in politics; their aspiration for wealth and power, and their envy of those who had achieved it, had helped to create that constitutional struggle with the monarchy which stretched from the reign of Elizabeth I to that of George I. By 1760 their influence had dwindled almost to insignificance and the aristocracy was supreme, and Cecils and Walpoles were as much out of fashion as Rockefellers and Carnegies today.

In many ways Walpole was the last royal favourite rather than the first prime minister, more akin to Tudor or Stuart statesmen than to Victorian party leaders.

The two Walpoles, father and son, illustrate some of the more interesting aspects of English social and political life from 1660–1760; the prudent, intelligent, but essentially homespun father, with his ambition adjusted to those ends that were well within his reach—an increased estate and the leadership of his county—was so typical of all that was best in the gentry of his day; whereas the brilliant son, greedy for power, greedy for riches, yet creative in all that he did, was limitless in his ambition; in the brilliance of his taste and the grandeur of his opulence, he outshone the aristocratic world in which his talents had won for him and his family a distinguished and enduring place.

NOTES

[1] This chapter is based on the Cholmondeley (Houghton) MSS., deposited at the University Library, Cambridge, by the Marquess of Cholmondeley, to whom I am deeply indebted for the permission to quote from them. The following account books are the major sources:—Nos. 9, 15/1, 20a, 22, 24; the bills too have been used, principally those for 1733, and detailed references to these sources have not been given. Anyone requiring them can find them in my Life of Walpole.

[2] J. H. Round, *Family Origins and other Studies* (1930): 'The Origin of the Walpoles'.

[3] *Lives of the Norths* (1826), III, p. 304.

[4] Naomi Riches, *The Agricultural Revolution in Norfolk* (Chapel Hill, 1937); J. H. Plumb, 'Sir Robert Walpole and Norfolk husbandry', *Ec. Hist. Rev.* (1952), pp. 86–9.

[5] J. Foster, *London Marriage Licenses* (1887), p. 1406.

[6] H. L. Bradfer-Lawrence, 'Castle Rising and the Walpoles', *Supplemen to Blomefield's Norfolk* (1926–9), ed. C. Hussey.

[7] *Cholmondeley (Houghton) MSS.*, Letters from 1700–1.

[8] *Walpole MSS.*, Yale University, quoted by kind permission of Mr. W. S. Lewis.

[9] Pages 21–3 are based on *Cholmondeley (Houghton) MSS.*, Letters, 1703–6.

[10] *Ibid.*, 1706.

[11] *Walpole MSS.*, University of Chicago.

[12] For anyone who doubts Walpole's detailed interest in his building there is Harvey's testimony that he alone was responsible, against all advice, for the stone cupolas (Ilchester, *Lord Harvey and his Friends* (1950), p. 71). The second Earl of Oxford, it is true, said that Gibbs was responsible for them (*H. M. C. Portland*, vi, p. 160), but Harvey was Walpole's friend, Oxford a casual visitor to the house. There is also a rather bawdy joke in the plasterwork of the ceiling of the Stone Hall which can only have been Walpole's idea. The dado is festooned with *putti* but one, hidden in a corner, is quite blatantly a little girl. Artari is most unlikely to have done this on his own initiative. Walpole liked a coarse joke and I suspect this gave rise to a great deal of fun at the Norfolk Congresses and to many wagers. But it does show how closely he was in touch with the work.

[13] *The Norfolk Congress* (1728) is a good example of such satires.

[14] For Orford House, cf. C. G. T. Dean, *The Royal Chelsea Hospital* (1950). Vanbrugh's letter, unpublished, is in *Cholmondeley (Houghton) MSS.*, Correspondence, 1716.

[15] Quoted in Dean, *op. cit.*, p. 205.

[16] The alterations to the Old Lodge are said to have cost Walpole £14,000. E. Beresford Chancellor, *The History and Antiquities of Richmond, Kew and Ham* (Richmond, 1894), p. 218.

VII

The Romantic Element—1830 to 1850

G. S. R. KITSON CLARK

VII

IN the minds of the intelligent, but uninstructed, the history
of England in the first half of the nineteenth century seems
to be divided into two periods, rather sharply contrasted in
style and morals, "Regency" and "Early Victorian". In fact,
if precisely defined by dates those two periods would leave un-
distributed between them rather more than a quarter of a
century. But they are not often precisely defined. Many would
use but the one date, 1837, when the Queen came to the throne
and, presumably, early Victorian England began. And to be
quite frank it would have been better if they had forgotten
that date also, for the first fifteen or so years of the Queen's
reign were years of nervous strain and difficulty not to be
separated too sharply from the period which preceded them,
nor confounded too absolutely with what came later. Nor did
the accession to the throne in 1837 of a respectable young
woman, nor even her marriage in 1840 to an even more respectable young German, have as much effect on society as is sometimes loyally believed.

In fact, though convenient, these period names are a
nuisance. Between 1837 and 1852 much exists that is Victorian,
much survives that is Regency, if these terms mean anything.
In the late thirties and early forties the Dandies still existed,
they were hairier than before and their dress often flashier and
uglier, but they were still there. Duelling was still an accepted
English custom, although it seems to have gone out generally in
the forties, possibly after the outcry that followed the fatal duel
in 1843 between Lieutenant Munro and his brother-in-law
Lieutenant Colonel Fawcett. Aristocratic insolence and profligacy still continued; while the Earl of Cardigan survived,
the insolence retained a peculiarly ripe example and not a

little profligacy lingered on too, even if his Countess' stories must be taken with many reservations; and in the country in general there remained much else that was quite frankly and unconcernedly of the eighteenth century.[1] On the other hand respectability and piety were already common among the middle classes and were spreading rather rapidly upwards. Victorian prudery had a long history before the Queen was born, there are signs of it in the diary of Mrs. Arbuthnot and the novels of Jane Austen, and for that matter in the eighteenth century itself. The decay of taste in the visual arts had already begun, as some of the silverware or furniture designed even before 1830 will show; and, most important of all, very many of the typical problems of Victorian England had already come into rather clamorous existence before 1837.

The truth of the matter is of course that in history there are no clear beginnings and endings. Origins are often unexpectedly early, survivals almost always stubborn and long dated, and anything that suggests that history can be cut into exclusive watertight compartments must be a falsification. Yet periods are a necessary convenience, and there is one fact which must remain true of any period however arbitrarily chosen; the men who lived through it did, at the least, all live at the same time, and they all lived in a mental atmosphere which is not that of the world of today.

Certainly the atmosphere, or perhaps it would be more correct to say the atmospheres, of any period are difficult to isolate and still harder to describe. Too often the only evidence available is that of impression, also they seem to change subtly and continuously, to differ for different sections of society but to modify one into another by indefinable degrees. Yet it is very bad history to ignore them. It is bad history to assemble the relevant facts, depict them with an unmitigated sharpness of outline and uncompromising minuteness of detail and then to suggest that contemporaries would base their actions on the way those facts appear to us. They could not have done so. They could not possibly have seen things like that. There would be unexpected blind spots and differences of perspective, and there would be a variety of tones and values contributed by the observer himself. In order to understand why dead men acted you must look with dead men's eyes and that means thinking with dead men's brains.

This, as every historian knows, is no easy task. It may be reasonably possible where a man's letters survive and there are fairly full memorials of what he did or was like as an individual; but for the bulk of humanity there are at best few records of individual actions, such letters as there were have long since gone into the dustbin and the last memories perished with the grandchildren. The desire to fill this blank leads to two temptations; one to fill the back of the stage with types, crudely painted lath and canvas figures which run easily in grooves, the other to believe rather trustfully that where no individual motive is known it is relatively easy to supply a simple economic one. Any knowledge of the complexity of contemporary human beings or of their banking accounts for that matter, or any detailed research into any part of the past will suggest that each of these methods is naïve and unsatisfactory, and it may well be that all that can be done is to put aside preconceptions, find out as much as is possible about as many people as possible and correlate it with their actions; and then to confess our ignorance.

There may, however, be another supplementary method of approach. It may be possible to recover something of the atmosphere in which men lived, and for this purpose there may exist evidence which reveals something even about those who have left no trace. For instance if what men wrote has perished, what they read, or men like them read, may not have perished with them. If what they said is lost, the speeches to which they listened with applause may still be on record. The pictures they saw and liked, their newspapers, their music, their architecture, their furniture, even their crockery, all these things may have their story to tell about the people themselves if we can only understand the language. These things formed the background against which they lived and expressed their preferences. To grasp this kind of evidence the political and social historian must make greater use of the assistance of the historians of art and literature than he has been wont to do. He must, however, use them with this proviso. The historians of art and literature have a natural preference for good art and valuable literature and those who produced them, the general historian cannot allow himself any such prejudice, he must jettison his own taste and remember that the most important evidence may by its very nature be supplied by what he personally most deplores.

Now the word which is most often used about the art and literature of the period between 1830 and 1850 is the word "romantic". It is what may be called "romantic" as an element in the thought and feeling of that time that I wish to investigate, not because it is the only element present—clearly it is not— but partly because it may well be the element which separates the minds of that period most markedly from our own. To do this it is necessary to come to terms with the word itself, and it is not a satisfactory word, since it sprawls uncomfortably over the late eighteenth and early nineteenth century, applied pretty gene- rously to a good many obviously different things. An eminent scholar has in fact suggested that we ought not to talk about romanticism, but rather about romanticisms;[2] and certainly romanticism describes alike what is consciously simple and "natural", and what is very heavily ornamented and histrionic to the last contortion of which the human mind is capable; it is variously attached to the influences of Rousseau, of Herder, of Schiller, of Wordsworth, of Byron or of Walter Scott; it is the description of an important tendency in serious philosophy, the reaction of the Germans and of Coleridge against the philosophy of the eighteenth century, according to A. N. Whitehead 'the romantic reaction was a protest on behalf of value',[3] yet the word is quite rightly used about the frothiest novel which the silliest miss got from a circulating library. However, the word does mean something, there are important common factors and basic connections to be discovered in most of the things which are called romantic, and possibly the best thing to do for present purposes is to suggest one or two common characteris- tics which may not unfairly be ascribed to romanticism in its later or nineteenth-century phase.

Perhaps the primary characteristic is the importance romanticism accords to emotion and imagination. The mo- tions of the heart are apt to be considered to be of greater validity and interest than what may be called the motions of the head, that is than cold calculation, or that intellectual exercise which the eighteenth century had called "reason", or even those restricting influences which any age might call common sense. Emotion and imagination have the right of way. Art must be freed from convention, or from the classical tradition of balance and restraint, so that they may find free expression; conduct must be guided by emotion rather than by strict rule. As the importance of emotion is enhanced so necessarily is the importance of the human being who entertains the emotion. If feeling is to be the test, then the history of the man who feels is peculiarly interesting and significant, and so is the moment at which he experiences the emotion at its strongest. There is, therefore, an emphasis on the moment of intense feeling rather than on the long duller days and months that may follow, on action, on decisive choice, even on gesture rather than on results, on the profoundly experienced part rather than on the reasoned and organized whole. But it must be remembered that to the romantic the true nature of the whole is more likely to be revealed by experience and vision rather than by the dry comprehensive processes of analysis and calculation.

All this may be the grounds of a perfectly defensible philosophy, in fact does probably convey something important about the way reality should be approached or a scale of values discovered. Inevitably, however, it has its weaker side. If classicism and rationalism deteriorate into dullness, superficiality and intolerable complacency, romanticism turns into silliness. The pleasures of emotion for the sake of emotion become dangerously attractive, and they are catered for by the extravagances of imagination. In literature forced situations are produced in which probability, ethics and all delineation of character have been sacrificed for the sake of emotion. Strange creatures are called into being, the exile from humanity, the mysterious wanderer with obscure but violent feelings, the improbable hero or the maniac lover, simply to be the vehicles of interesting if uncontrollable emotion. The romantic tourist, spiritual or physical, will frequent places or periods where habits are likely to be strange, motives passionate and unusual or the scenery suitable, places such as the Apennines or Switzerland or the Middle East, or periods such as what men chose to believe had been the middle ages.

As a matter of fact the pot had boiled over earlier. The most excited period of romanticism was possibly before 1830. By 1830 Shelley was dead, Blake was dead, Byron was dead, and the heyday of the Minerva Press, which had produced so many novels of horror, was over. But the models remained and were copied; moreover this choice of scene and character touches on another, and abiding, characteristic of romanticism, or of one form of romanticism, its love of what lay outside the experience of the ordinary man. This may indeed explain the novels of high life of the "silver fork school" of the '20's and '30's, but the most obvious reservoir for the exotic was the past, or what could be presented as the past. Of course in the Gothic novels and the novels of horror the fiction that any imaginable historic conditions had been reproduced was extremely thin, this was fairyland or goblin land and pretty silly at that. But the romantic impetus had driven men beyond the gates of the castle of Otranto into something more real, and more important. The loosening of imagination, the interest in what was different because it was different had sometimes led men to an emotional appreciation of the values and conditions of a past period which was profounder and more realistic than the old projection of fixed attitudes and common motives into any period that might be named. What romanticism could do for history can be seen in the great French historian Michelet, but the change was preeminently the work of that very sane man, Walter Scott. There had, however, been an earlier influence of profound importance both for Scott and for Herder and the Germans. One of the most important dates in the eighteenth century was probably the publication in 1765 of Percy's *Reliques*. After Percy the discovery, popularization and invention of ballads, or what could pass for ballads, went on apace. The ballad supplied for romantic ears what seemed to be, what sometimes was, the voice of the past speaking in thrilling terms of exciting things. They powerfully assisted the romantic conception of history; and, since ballads were of the folk and therefore essentially national, they as powerfully assisted what was perhaps the most important product of romantic history, the vision of nationalism, the deepened imaginative conception of the significant past and peculiar identity of a particular nation.

That conception was pregnant with future consequences. However, the past so realized was not the past of the scientific historian. It was the past with too much poetry put in, too much prose left out; that was after all what men wanted, for they had no desire to exchange the commonplace of their own day for the commonplace of another. This, however, emphasizes the third characteristic of romanticism. It is in general a literature of dissatisfaction, of escape or revolt and the last two terms can easily merge into each other. At its lowest this leads to a mere craving for the sensational and the macabre. At its highest it is the revolt of men profoundly dissatisfied with a shallow intellectualism which disdained emotion, or the intolerable complacency of a society which was at the same time artificial, self-satisfied and unjust. Of course revolt inspired by the attraction of the past might take the form of reaction, the contrast of a supposedly glorious yesterday with an undeniably sordid today. Yet it was still revolt, and two books by Lamennais *Les affaires de Rome* and *Les Paroles d'un croyant* show clearly the road that led even through Ultramontanism to the revolution. Some such road was taken by other great French romantics like Victor Hugo and Lamartine. But there was no need to go round that way, other romantics had never felt the pull of the past at all. It did not much matter, by the thirties the lesson for many men was the same. If romanticism had taught men to contrast, to imagine or to feel, then the feelings which the world of the nineteenth century was most likely to excite were disgust, pity and anger.

The vision was stabilized and solidified by the fact that in the nineteenth century a favourite instrument of literature was the novel. The novels of Victor Hugo, George Sand, even Eugène Sue and certainly Charles Dickens taught men to see and feel what the world was like and to protest against it; as the stories of William Carleton and the brothers Banim might have taught Englishmen something of what they sadly needed to know about Ireland. In fact in the forties in England a deeply valuable service was performed for Englishmen by the social novelists, such as Disraeli, Charles Kingsley, Mrs. Gaskell and the humbler 'Charlotte Elizabeth', who taught men much that they needed to know about industrialism.[4]

But it is necessary to be careful here. Romanticism had liberated two powers in men, one the power to present the world with renewed clarity and insight, and the other to dramatize it. These powers are not necessarily opposed, they can easily exist in the same person, but their results may be different. In poetry there is a contrast between Wordsworth and Byron, in painting between the Norwich school or Constable on the one hand and on the other Turner in his sensational phase, or Fuseli, or Blake. In the thirties the dramatic approach appealed powerfully to contemporaries and in painting inspired men who seemed more important then than they do today. There were the historical painters like the unfortunate Haydon, and the biblical and apocalyptical painters like Martin who painted vast over-dramatized scriptural scenes such as the end of the world or Belshazzar's feast, using the hysterical and horrific element which Fuseli had used. This was clearly what a large public wanted and both Etty, a painter whose temperament one would have thought would not have led him in this direction, and Danby, who was excellent at country landscapes and seems to have preferred them, yet went in for these things. Martin did it for money, and when about 1830 discriminating critics at the Academy got tired of him he exploited a much wider public by means of travelling exhibitions. In some quarters he retained a considerable reputation, in 1833 Bulwer Lytton singled him out for special praise in his survey of British Art, he called him 'the greatest, the most lofty, the most permanent, the most original genius of his age'.[5] It is probably an opinion which would not be widely held nowadays, but it may disclose something of the temper of the time.

*　　*　　*

The period 1830 to 1850 runs roughly from the first Reform Bill to the eve of the Great Exhibition. It was a period of great expectations and of as great and as reasonable fears. Until the repeal of the Corn Laws in 1846, or possibly till the Chartist fiasco in 1848, the weather was stormy. Party strife was very bitter, elections corrupt and tumultuous, and both in England and Ireland there was intermittent but noisy popular agitation. This was not unnatural in a country hard pressed by the problems created by an enormously increased population, by new, and often harsh, methods in industry, by hope and suffering and by new ideas. As a result there was a feeling of strain. The situation engaged the anxious attention of some because they were painfully and personally involved, of others as ring-side spectators a little too near a rather indeterminate ring.

But it was not only the urgency of politics or of the economic situation that served to fill and excite men's minds in the thirties and forties. A main point in the case is that there was probably a larger reading public than ever before. The improvements in the printing press, particularly the introduction by Koenig between 1810 and 1814 of the impression cylinder and flat-bed driven by steam had enormously increased the amount of printed matter which could be produced, and the eagerness with which such inventions were taken up suggests a great hunger for things to read which probably grew by what it fed upon.[6] The newspapers had increased in number and importance, and would certainly have increased still further if it had not been for the stamp duties. But it was not only newspapers that were being printed. The development of circulating libraries in the eighteenth century had created a taste for novels.[7] The great popularity of Scott and Byron and in due course of Dickens showed that there was a large public to be gained. There seem to have been a great many publishers, with a wide range of publications, while the activities of men like Colburn and Bentley showed what enterprise could do in extending, and in due course cheapening, what men and women had to read.[8] There were novels, there were books of travel, many works on religion, and by the 1830's a great many periodical reviews to cater for different sections of opinion. And from about 1825 there were the annuals which varied from the frivolous and fashionable to those suited for people of a more serious cast of mind, from the *Books of Beauty* or the *Keepsake* which had among its contributors 'one countess, three ladies of birth, two lords, two M.P.s, one honourable Mrs. and an Archdeacon' to the *Iris*, 'a literary and religious offering', and *The Christian Keepsake and Missionary Annual*.[9]

Who all these readers were it would be difficult to say, or, with any exactness, what their numbers were, since the habit of borrowing from libraries probably vitiates circulation figures. The problem of literacy is a difficult one, and possibly the working class reader was a class apart.[10] One thing, however, is likely, the reading public was probably more sharply divided up into sections than it is now. The development which began in the eighteenth century of literary and philosophical societies and the development of a local press suggests a vigorous provincial intellectual life which seems to have honoured their local celebrities. Literary criticism followed to some extent the political and denominational divisions of the country, the *Edinburgh* was a Whig review, the *Quarterly Blackwood's* and possibly *Fraser's* were Tory reviews, the *Eclectic* and the *Monthly Repository* catered for Dissenters, the *Westminster* and Tait's *Edinburgh Magazine* for Radicals and so on; while the stricter Evangelicals seem to have constituted a class by themselves with publishers and publications to match.[11]

Yet though men and women were reading greedily this was a world in which the eloquent speaker still played a much greater part than he does today, for the speeches over the wireless would seldom by earlier standards be considered eloquence at all. In Parliament, on the hustings, in the pulpit, or even on a cart in the open air, the orator was very much master of the occasion. It is true that Tom Moore suggests that by 1825 the dampening pressure of public business and of political economy was already squeezing him out of the House of Commons, but with Canning and Brougham at large obviously at that moment that process had only just started, and Moore allows that eloquence was still practised in the law courts.[12] Sergeant Buzfuz, who is fictitious, comes most easily to the mind, but in real life orations not entirely unlike his can be found in the speeches of Curran at the Irish bar just before the eighteenth century closed.[13] There was a great deal of preaching, indeed, among Dissenters, a minister largely lived by his voice. There were also a great many moral or political movements which depended on oratory, the Temperance movement, the Anti-slavery movement, the Anti-Corn Law movement, while at Exeter Hall and elsewhere the dangers of popery were regularly and profusely demonstrated.[14] And, as if all this was not enough, the public was extraordinarily ready to hear lectures on almost any subject, and even recitations from Shakespeare.[15]

All this produced some very considerable rhetoricians such as, to go outside the strict politicians, George Thompson, the Anti-slavery orator, or W. J. Fox, the Unitarian minister who was one of the most eloquent opponents of the Corn Laws. But our age is possibly unique in its neglect of rhetoric. It was honoured and studied in Classical times and such authors as Cicero, Quintilian and Longinus have played an important part in the history of European thought. A good many books on rhetoric and elocution were published in England in the late eighteenth and early nineteenth centuries, such as those by Thomas Sheridan, Blair, Walker and Sheridan Knowles, which well repay study. There were speeches at Eton to prepare the young patrician for his duties and like exercises at say Rugby before Arnold, or at Stonyhurst or elsewhere. The style developed was on the whole the old style of public speaking, a British style grafted on a Roman stem. It is believed that this can still be heard in remote parts of Ireland or of the United States, but it would be difficult to find it in use in Britain today notwithstanding its tried effectiveness in expressing manly defiance, withering scorn, enthusiasm for liberty and other appropriate emotions. It is possible that the tempo of speaking both in public and on the stage quickened in the late eighteenth and early nineteenth centuries, and probably the extemporary speaking of the religious revivalists worked a change in those who derived from them. The sentences became shorter and less elaborate and the massed repetitions more numerous. There is a decadent sample of this in Dickens' Chadband, but in real life there are better examples even of his own peculiarity, the reiterated question, as in the temperance orator, J. B. Gough, on 'What is a drunkard?' or elsewhere.[16] These repetitions could make the right audience mad, and would also enable an extemporary speaker to think what he would say next or go on without thought. Perhaps the most extreme examples can be drawn from the sermons of Joseph Rayner Stephens, the minister who was expelled from the Wesleyans for his attacks on the Church of England, and in 1838 was moved by the situation in the North to make violent attacks on the New Poor Law.

He is in this passage urging violent opposition to it on his congregation.

> Oh yes My Lord Russell [said he] it is too late, it is too late, it is too late, thank God, it is too late! Put me where you like, and keep me there as long as you like, as long as God and my poor body will allow you. You may do just what you like with me, it is too late, it is too late, it is too late; the blood is up, aye! it tingles in your fingers, it is ready to spurt out at your finger ends, and to blow the skull cap off. Your father's blood is up; your mother's milk is flowing round, and round, and round; you are beginning to be men; you are beginning to be women.; you are beginning to be the offspring of men and women; thank God for it! He has poured a new language upon the people, it is too late, it is too late.[17]

Contemporary oratory ought, however, to be compared with what was going on the stage at that time. As is well known in the thirties British drama was artistically at a level below which it has seldom if ever sunk. The comedies were feeble and stagey, often poor translations from the French, the tradition of blank-verse tragedy continued in decadent imitation of sixteenth- and seventeenth-century plays not much improved by the influence of Kotzebue. Often enough they are only machines for the wordy display of violent emotions in improbable circumstances, influenced perhaps by the old view that a "passion" was an entity which could exist apart from the complexities of personality,[18] while the blank verse resembles what Thackeray in *The Rose and the Ring* puts into the mouth of King Valoroso in his more excited moments. It was, however, a period of great actors and actresses: Edmund Kean died in 1833, Macready, Dickens' friend, left the stage in 1851. But it may be doubted whether a modern public, or at least modern critics, would much approve of their style, for they were in the great romantic tradition, passionate, sometimes very noisy, with a great deal of violent gesture and action.

But they acted with power, and in these matters our taste is not germane. In those days they were rated high, notably when they appeared in Shakespeare, or for that matter in contemporary tragedies, and, however we may estimate it, the contemporary stage had its influence on contemporary thought and speech. Fuseli had been greatly influenced by the Shakespearian revival, Byron tried his hand with drama with little success, echoes of the stage creep into the language of the characters of Dickens. But it probably affected the style of more important people on more important occasions than that of Mrs. Wilfer in her more majestic, or of Dick Swiveller in his more exuberant moments. R. L. Sheil was in the thirties probably, after O'Connell, the greatest orator among the Irish, and earlier in life he had produced tragedies at Drury Lane, two of which at least, *Evadne* and *The Apostate* were successful. They are certainly bloody, bold and resolute, and it is not surprising that his style of speaking when he went into politics was histrionic.[19] Dissenters, and the stricter religious, were apt to consider that the stage was to a peculiar degree under the dominion of Satan and it might be thought that Dissenting preachers were immune from this influence. But this was not always true, they might have enjoyed the stage when unregenerate or even covertly when regenerate. Sheridan Knowles, possibly the best of the tragic dramatists, became a Baptist minister. W. J. Fox has described how when he was at the orthodox seminary at Homerton he with other lads stole out to see a Shakespeare play and how they discovered that next door to them in the gallery was a party from the even more orthodox seminary at Hoxton.[20] Even J. R. Stephens acted in boyhood in a play written by his contemporary at school, Harrison Ainsworth, the novelist. He played the part of a bandit.[21]

Clearly none of this can be neglected in considering the influences acting on men's minds at the time. If men like to be harangued in this way, and their taste is frequently and amply gratified, it displays something of the way in which their minds work, in fact it will determine how on certain subjects their minds shall work, particularly if they are harangued with sufficient fervour in this style on morals or politics.

Something of this mentality may have been encouraged by the literature that was proliferated for them to read. The drama had in fact perhaps prepared the way. Sentiments not unlike those heard from the stage and the platform were repeated with flashing eye and curling lip by the heroes of novels. 'Fiction', said Bulwer, ' . . . is the oratory of literature.'[22] He was talking of the sensationalism of the lesser novelists. The great imaginative literature of the day, Carlyle, Dickens and the Brontës is of course, with lapses, in general of an infinitely higher intellectual calibre, yet the same upthrust of emotion is there and the same appeal to the passions. It can be found in lesser but quite respectable writers who were popular. Harrison Ainsworth is, at his best, a better novelist than any of the Gothic writers. But his first great success *Rookwood* was written explicitly in a spirit of admiration for Mrs. Radcliffe, and her influence remains with him in the overcharged phrase and melodramatic situation, reflected in the terrific energy, usually of sinister import, of the Cruikshank illustrations. Bulwer Lytton is a more varied and intelligent writer than is sometimes believed, but he is at times most inflated and stagey, particularly perhaps in his historical novels such as *Harold*. Behind these is the large chorus of lesser men and women of varying merit many of whom also make their violent assaults on the emotions, sometimes by way of melodrama, sometimes through the sentimental, often by both combined.[23]

An equally significant factor is the great company of poets. Tennyson was only beginning to make his mark and there were complaints that no great poet had arisen to interpret the age, but if so it was not for want of trying, for the number of people writing poetry is beyond count. The names of some of the lesser ones may awaken memory, Thomas Hood, James Montgomery, Bailey, the author of *Festus*, Sir Henry Taylor, Mrs. Norton, Mrs. Hemans, Aubrey de Vere, Ebenezer Elliott and Letitia Landon; most of them would not. Yet even some of those who are almost forgotten seemed to be important people in their day. The fact that Mrs. Norton applied to be Poet Laureate on the death of Southey should probably be dismissed as the desperate gesture of a desperate woman.[24] But for a time Bailey's confused and violent metaphysics were taken seriously.[25] The *Edinburgh Review* had declared of Mrs. Hemans that she was 'the most touching and perhaps the most accomplished writer of occasional verses that our literature has yet to boast of'.[26] The *Eclectic Review* placed James Montgomery among the chief living poets, Byron and Wordsworth accepted him, Southey wrote to him as an equal.

THE
SPIRIT
OF THE
NATION

*Romantic Politics: the title page of the volume of national ballads
produced by Young Ireland*

Romantic Acting : Charles Kean as Sir Giles Overreach

No doubt there were a variety of reasons for this outpouring. It was very easy to publish. Publishers, particularly local publishers, seem to have been ready to produce single volumes by unknown poets at only a trifling cost to the author, and there were a great many magazines which printed poetry. There was also by now a large number of models. There were Byron and Scott and Burns and Wordsworth to copy, and the whole apparatus of romanticism to use, chieftains, bards, lovers, wanderers, shipwrecks, spirits and the Swiss. There was much suitable literature in other languages to assist, and Mrs. Hemans was in particular obviously a person of considerable erudition. There was also, most unfortunately, Milton, who probably suggested the poems on large-scale religious subjects very like what the public demanded from the apocalyptic painters, as when Thomas Ragg, a working man, wrote an epic in twelve books on *The Deity*, or William Ellis Wall, an M.A. of Trinity College, Oxford, another, also in twelve books, on *Christ Crucified*. But the whole range English literature inspired; James Montgomery was marked out for poetry by hearing his schoolmaster read Blair's *Grave*; some still essayed the heroic couplet of Pope. More than this the course of English poetry, the discipline of the eighteenth century, the chastening of language and imagery that succeeded Cowper, had produced a prosody which was ductile, various, melodious and easy to command, matched with a natural serviceable and not too ponderous vocabulary.[27] Consequently in the first half of the nineteenth century an extraordinary number of people seem to have been able to write correct, easy and reasonably effective verse.

The most important cause, however, remains behind. A great many people wrote because a great many people wanted to write, and what is more surprising a great many people wanted to read what they, or some of them, had written. They wanted the cloudy enthusiastic metaphysics, the sensational religiosity, the medievalism and the appeals to the heart. Some things they wanted because they fitted in with the fashion of the time, and others because they were what a large part of the public has always wanted and still asks for. One reason for the force of the romantic movement was its ability to find forms to gratify instincts which have always existed, and to destroy inhibitions which prevented their free play. This tendency may also have been assisted by the size and nature of the reading public which new facilities in publishing and printing called into being. In our own day the taste for the lachrymose and the taste for excitement even when conveyed by unbelievable characters in impossible situations has been well catered for by the cinema and is being taken over by television. It was then gratified by the sensational novel and the poet who specialized in the luxury of tears and the thought of death. Consider for instance the titles of some of Mrs. Hemans' poems, printed almost successively in her works, 'On a leaf from the tomb of Vergil', 'For a design of a butterfly resting on a skull', 'The Dying Bard's prophecy', 'The graves of a household', 'The last wish', 'A Monarch's death bed', 'The hour of death'. They are skilfully written, and she was very popular.

In most ages these instincts are held in check by countervailing forces, the power of ridicule and the power of criticism. Both existed in the early nineteenth century and were often used with peculiar brutality, but they were possibly less effective than they are today, and the area left for the unchecked range of sentiment was correspondingly greater. One reason for this was not only the size but the sharp divisions of the reading public. The reviews which commented most savagely could often be rightly suspected of pursuing party or personal feuds, this was particularly true of *Fraser's* under the editorship of Maginn, and it vitiated their effect even when they had reason on their side.[28] For instance Jeffrey in the *Edinburgh* tried to kill James Montgomery's poem 'The Wanderer in Switzerland', but Montgomery was supported by the *Eclectic Review* and by the forces of Dissent, and twenty years later the poem had reached its 9th edition, having sold 12,000 copies earning him £800, while there had been a score of editions in the United States.[29] His namesake Robert Montgomery's bombast on the 'Omnipresence of the Deity' was more notoriously savaged by Macaulay, but he retained his supporters, who had probably never heard of Macaulay and would have dismissed him as a worldling if they had, and it went on to achieve its 28th edition.

There was therefore probably an unusually large section of the public beyond the reach of scholarship or criticism, it even stretched beyond the Atlantic. But there is again a more profound reason. The tide of sentiment was at the flood, it had poured not only into the weakest literature but into the best, even into the work of some of the major critics. Thackeray spent a good deal of time laughing at the weaknesses of the literature of the day. He wrote his mock novels in *Punch*, he laughed at the flamboyance of young Ireland in the 'Ballad of Limerick', he satirized the sentiment of the time in his description of Blanche Amory's poems in *Pendennis* and possibly more subtly in his estimation of Amelia and Dobbin in *Vanity Fair*. Behind all this there was a genuine distaste, as he says of Bulwer Lytton, 'there are sentiments in his writing which always anger me, big words which make me furious and a premeditated fine writing against which I can't help rebelling.' [30] Yet in his own writings, Thackeray was himself a sentimentalist, nor was he impregnable to sentiment in other people's. His praise of the description of the death of Paul Dombey still excites wonder and terror, when it is remembered what that passage is like; it should be compared with the tears shed by Jeffrey, the scourge of poets, over the death of little Nell. Of course Dickens himself wanted, sometimes outrageously, to make people cry, he wanted to teach the superiority of those who feel over the cold-hearted like Scrooge, Mr. Dombey or Mr. Gradgrind who could only calculate. It is an important lesson, one that an age that had inherited a great deal of gross callousness and brutality needed rather badly to learn, but it was not at that time an unpopular one, for it was much the same as was taught by many writers in the Christmas annuals.

It would be as well here to say something of music, particularly of the significance, possibly of the popularity, of Mendelssohn, and certainly of that of Spohr. Space, however, does not suffice, and there is an important problem to be faced. What significant results derive from this exuberance? Much of this literature—the minor poetry, the sensational novelists, much even of Dickens himself—is of the dregs of romanticism, the sentiment shallow and mawkish, the "big words" and heavy emphasis bombastic and unconvincing. Probably these efforts were popular, the playthings of the day for those who liked that sort of thing, but they seem to be as little likely to excite deep or lasting emotion as they were high art. If so is their popularity of any importance? What is there here which a serious historian should take into account as one of the important operative factors of the period?

The question is not easy. It raises the difficult question whether what is admittedly trivial, produced to fill an idle moment with facile emotion or excitement, does not yet reveal something of the mind that likes to be amused in that way. But the phrase 'admittedly trivial' begs a still harder question. It is difficult to know what it is permissible to dismiss as trivial and superficial; the touchstone of what we hold to be good taste may be in such matters the worst of guides. What began as a plaything may very easily come to symbolize something much more important. The passion for medievalism was probably in the eighteenth century mainly a whim, and in the 1830's was producing such things as the novels of G. P. R. James, which are but readable fustian, and many 'a tale of olden time', which is undoubted rubbish. It was also filling the country with a great deal of very mediocre architecture and many objects of quite disastrous design. Yet to Pugin it was the symbol of important values, it probably profoundly affected the religious history of the country. It was the source of political idealism to men like the enthusiasts of 'Young England', and encouraged an attitude to the past which instructed the ideas of others who have made a much deeper mark than they upon the history of Europe.

Moreover, what seems to be unquestionably trivial and superficial to us is of precisely the same nature as what touched on matters of unquestionable importance. The sentimentalism which was gratified by the fate of little Nell or by the various songs and poems about orphans is not easily distinguishable from the sentiment that instructed men and women what to think about the negro slave, the factory child or the boy chimney sweep. It was indeed stimulated by much the same techniques. As has been suggested the bombast in the novels and on the stage bears a close family resemblance to the over-vehemence of public speakers in the various agitations, moral or political, of the twenty years after the Reform Bill. So violent was the language used at these meetings, political or religious, that they inspired a travelling American, who might have been expected to be familiar with reasonably lively performances in his own country, with very serious doubts about the future stability of Great Britain. He talks of 'the morbid excitability of the British public, amounting almost to a mental disease'.[31]

The diagnosis is surprising, but the reports of contemporary public meetings suggest that it was not absurd. Nor is this suggested by the reports of public meetings alone. The tone of much contemporary journalism, the methods and vehemence of much contemporary controversy, the style of much contemporary religion—all these things combine to suggest that in his dealings with this period a historian must take into account an emotionalism which was more general and more easily excited than anything he knows today. If that is so he must learn to recognize the words, the ideas, the associations, the literary forms, which were then likely to stimulate strong emotions and would not do so today.

He must at the same time realize that the same stimulants did not have the same effect on all sections of the community. Certain types of systematic thought would reject them, the necessary realism of many occupations would deaden them, aristocratic traditions make them seem nauseating or absurd. In their place men might be controlled by the most rational arguments, logically even harshly applied, by the most earthy common-sense, or by the demands of office or party in a system of politics which had long been founded squarely on the practical. Indeed, there were many men in Great Britain who were not noticeably the victims of any unusual emotionalism. The Duke of Wellington seems to have been immune, and so too were probably not a few of the nobility and gentry to be found on the benches of either house of parliament, so too to an exemplary extent were the Benthamites, so too were many manufacturers or farmers in matters that strictly concerned their business.

These men were important since in their hands lay many of the keys of power. Yet there were many not affected by these counterbalances, or to whom the literary fashions of the day seemed to give profound utterance to what was most important in life. For instance in the lower ranges of literature and art religious motifs were prominent. There were the painters, the writers of religious epics; nor was Mrs. Hemans alone among the poets in writing from time to time religious verse of a meditative nature. This is not surprising and does not necessarily go very deep. Christianity supplied much of the furniture of the minds of a good many English people, particularly of the middle class. It supplied the literature they knew best, their cosmogony, their ethics, their ancient history and their most interesting experiences. Naturally, when they wished for a sensational subject they turned to the most sensational, if least sentimental, book they knew, which was of course the Bible; as naturally they turned to Christianity for their literature of feeling. But here a change sometimes occurred. Religion could, it by no means always did, give to their verse a deeper sincerity and a more permanent significance than was supplied by the ordinary objects that inspired it. This is the great age of the extension of hymn singing; before this hymns, except paraphrases, had seemed to many unscriptural and in the services of the Established Church probably illegal. Not a few of the myriad poets were writers of hymns. James Montgomery wrote many important ones, they are indeed his best poetry, the most notable being in all probability 'Hail to the Lord's Anointed'. Sarah Flower Adams, who was the author of a dramatic epic called *Vivia Perpetua*, a ballad poem about Edward the First and other poems mainly unpublished, wrote also, 'Nearer my God to Thee'. One writer in the thirties, of blameless, if unremarkable secular verse, was the Reverend H. F. Lyte; he also wrote 'Abide with me'. And whatever rank these efforts may achieve as literature, they are certainly not trivial, for some of them have come very close to the hearts of men.[32]

There is, however, a matter of deeper significance here. In the eighteenth century there had been the great Evangelical revival, and though by 1830 the tide was ebbing, it had not ebbed very far. Now Evangelical Christianity seems to satisfy all the categories of romanticism, except the love of fancy dress. It, too, was an appeal to vital emotion. For the Evangelical the inner history of the individual is of supreme importance, his literature is subjective and his hymns, the hymns of Toplady or

Charles Wesley and still more of Newton and Cowper, speak from heart to heart. He also emphasizes the supreme moment of dramatic choice with, as his background, the vast and terrifying perspectives, not of Switzerland, but of eternity. The parallel is not accidental. The social complacency of the earlier eighteenth century and its rationalism, itself a reaction, had not given permanent satisfaction to men. Each in his own way, men like Rousseau and men like John Wesley had taught men to look into their own hearts to find truths and values that an overcivilized, over-intellectualized, society had never known or had forgotten. To look within is always exciting, and the results may be explosive.

The Evangelical revival had spread into every class and corner of England, from the lowest to the highest. It had revivified the older Dissenting sects, it had poured new life into the Church of England. It, too, had had its period of prophets and visionaries, the age of Joanna Southcote and of Richard Brothers, which was also that of Blake; and there had been a recrudescence of this in the late twenties and early thirties with the Rowites, the Irvingites—the followers of Carlyle's friend, Edward Irving, among whom there was speaking with tongues, and the Millenarians. After 1833 this outburst seemed to die down. In 1834 Edward Irving died, and in 1834 the *Eclectic Review* reported that 'the mania of the Millenarians appears to have subsided into a mild chronic imbecility'.[33] Yet at about that time the Evangelical impulse, acting on very different men, helped to produce the Oxford Movement, which came to much closer terms with the ordinary incidents of secular romanticism. The history of John Henry Newman is significant. As a boy he had been powerfully attracted by the Waverley novels as they came out; as a youth he was an Evangelical; as a young man in the thirties with the pressure of politics upon him, he had brought the thought of the early fathers to rebuke the liberalism and infidelity of the age; in middle age he entered that institution which profoundly attracted some romantics, as it was the despair of others, the Church of Rome.[34]

But the main stream of the Evangelical movement continued to run strongly in its more normal channels. Its moral force remained effective and widely diffused, so also was its power of well-savoured moral denunciation. It provided for much of the nation an ethical code, strongly enforced by emotion, for general reference; more than this of all forms of romanticism it was the best organized. The first really effective nation-wide organization to secure one particular political object was the agitation against slavery and the slave trade organized by the Clapham Saints. They canvassed the whole country, and gave to many what was possibly their first taste in romanticism, a stirring emotional experience and an interest in unhappy far-off things. It was the forerunner of many moral agitations which supplied a spice to the lives of many who thought the drama was sinful. But it was not only religious agitations that it inspired; when Cobden was meditating his attack on the Corn Laws he came explicitly to the conclusion that success would be his if he turned it into a great moral movement like the agitation against slavery. So he attracted Sturge and George Thompson from the anti-slavery crusade, and in 1841 Thompson organized for him a large meeting of ministers of religion to denounce the Corn Laws as 'opposed to the law of God ... Anti-Scriptural and Anti-Christian'. Of course Cobden founded his case on carefully developed economic argument, but he knew very well on what nerve he must play if he wanted to rouse the country.

But the emotional stimuli available for politics were by no means all of them religious. Romantic literature was full of the struggles of the heroes of liberty, such as Rienzi or William Tell; it abounded in such poetry as Byron addressed to the Greeks, or Burns to the Scots who had bled with Wallace, and, as has been said before, it gave force and reality to a resurgent nation's vision of itself. Scotland was rediscovered, almost re-invented round the eccentric nucleus of the Highlander; but possibly the classical example of the application of literary romanticism to emergent nationalism was in Ireland, in the forties. From almost the beginning of the century until 1843 Daniel O'Connell had dominated the agitation in Ireland. He was a tremendous orator with a style probably formed in the Irish Courts of Law which he knew well how to fit to his audience. He could be moving, he could be vulgar, or very violent; he could conciliate or defy the House of Commons. But a life-time of bitter struggle had left him honourably cautious. He would do all in his power to secure an independent Irish government but he was determined not to risk the great and useless suffering which would be the result of armed rebellion. Very different was the group which began to come into politics in the early forties, Thomas Davis, Gavan Duffy, Mitchell, Thomas Meagher and Smith O'Brien. The history of Smith O'Brien was rather different, but the rest were mainly young journalists and lawyers whose approach to politics was not through long hard experience, but was largely literary.[35] Their organ was that remarkable paper the *Nation*, and the approach of Davis, its first editor, is essentially that of the romantic of this period. He had the romantic's view of history, he turned to it both to escape from sordid reality and for a creed. History, he felt, was a much needed refuge from the degrading utilitarianism of his day, as the rewriting of Irish history was also necessary to vindicate the wrongs of Ireland and to revivify her. ' 'Tis a glorious world historic memory', said he. 'From the grave the sage warns; from the mound the hero, from the temple the orator-patriot inspire; and the poet sings in his shroud'[36]; and he and his friends were anxious to renew Irish history, to recover Irish antiquities and to inspire Irish novelists and tragedians. They also collected or wrote Irish ballads. 'National poetry', wrote Davis, and the ideas are familiar, 'presents the most dramatic events, the largest characters, the most impressive scenes, and the deepest passions in the language most familiar to us.'[37] That language was not for most of them Irish, and the ballads were of necessity at some removes from the originals. Nor are they all very good poetry. In fact many of them were not much better than, or very different from, the verses and ballads which were being poured out in profusion in magazines on the other side of St. George's Channel. But they served their purpose. No less than three editions of Gavan Duffy's book of Irish ballads were exhausted in a little less than a month. Indeed there seems to be little doubt that, whatever their limitations, they performed an essential service to the full emotional realization of Irish nationality.

It was such a service as men of like nature, using the same

means, were performing by the use of the same instruments for other nations in Europe, but perhaps the clearest and most interesting parallel is the development at the same time of national self-consciousness among the whites of the Southern States of America, with their tremendous set orations often on historical themes, their ballads, their tournaments and chivalry, and their admiration for Walter Scott.[38] Indeed their achievement is the more remarkable for the nation they created was artificial and its traditions imaginary, whereas in Ireland the background was very real. The results were likely to be violent. The idea of force has a strong literary and dramatic attraction and, as in America so in Ireland, literary romanticism was bellicose. In due course there came a clash between Young Ireland and O'Connell and the climax came when John O'Connell proposed to the repeal association that they should forgo all thought of armed resistance. He was answered by Meagher in one of the most notable of romantic speeches, in praise of 'the sword', of which he said if 'it has sometimes reddened the shroud of the oppressor, like the anointed rod of the high priest, it has, at other times, blossomed into flowers to deck the freeman's brow. Abhor the sword and stigmatize the sword? No my Lord for in the cragged passes of the Tyrol it cut in pieces the banner of the Bavarian, and won an immortality for the peasant of Innspruck. Abhor the sword and stigmatize the sword? No my Lord—.'[39] and so on, but the whole should be read. Nowadays such words might not carry conviction, then quite certainly Meagher meant them, every word.

In England with Chartism the literary background is different, for romantic nationalism would not have been relevant, but the same issue emerged there between those Chartists who advocated moral and those who advocated physical force; and the speeches of the physical force men—Stephens, Feargus O'Connor, McDouall and Harney—provide interesting examples of romantic oratory. They also draw attention to an interesting problem which is also present in Ireland, the relation of what is mere literary form to what is a not unreasonable appreciation of the real situation. On the one hand many orators are using language in which appeals to dread alternatives, just vengeance, or liberty or death, are almost a literary convention, but on the other hand the misery of sections of the working class in England and the peasantry in Ireland was so great and the obduracy with which redress seemed to be refused was so impregnable that without that stimulus men might understandably come to believe that violence was the only resort.[40] But the romantic element with its encouragement to vehemence and self-dramatization was certainly present in England as well as in Ireland. Perhaps an example may be given where the nature of the audience might, one would have thought, have enforced sobriety. It is Harney speaking at his trial at Lancaster in 1843.

> But if [says he], the verdict should be guilty—though the cold prison cell, though my consignment to the living tomb of crime and misery should be the consequence—yet believe me, gentlemen, I speak not the language of idle rant or bombastic folly, when I declare to you that I would not change my present situation for that of my accusers to escape all that torture could inflict upon me. Though my march from this court was to the scaffold, there to exchange the embraces of love for the executioner's red reeking hand, there to yield up life with its heart-correcting sorrows its hopes and joys, alas, too few for that unfathomable futurity beyond the grave—I would not—I speak the language of calm reflection— exchange my lot for that of my accusers.[41]

It is a relief after all this to remember that he was in no great danger, and was not in fact even called up for judgment. It is also important to remember that he was certainly sincere.

Yet if both in England and Ireland the realities of the situation justified the romantic approach, there were some realities that the romantic approach did not normally reveal. It did not encourage a cool appraisal of chances, or the careful preparations which are necessary for the use of force, or even a very clear appreciation of what words about force really implied. As with most forms of emotionalism the eloquent moment overshadowed the problem of what might follow. The Chartists flirted with violence, they talked about it, they never adequately prepared for it, and many of those who threatened it never consistently or realistically intended it; when challenged by the law both Feargus O'Connor and Joseph Stephens explained that they had not really meant what they appeared to have said, which was probably true. It was the same elsewhere. Even the Anti-Corn Law League, coolly led as it was towards a practicable objective, had its moment of folly when in 1841–2 it talked wildly about revolution, nearly considered an impossible general cessation of industry, and then shrank back.[42] In 1848 the miseries of Ireland and the magniloquence of young Irishmen led to a half revolt, ill-considered, unplanned and ending in complete fiasco, pitiable, but not ignoble, since those who involved themselves were prepared to give their all. Perhaps in each case it was better so, even if that meant that real wrongs were left really unredressed; for the keys of power were strongly held and the eloquent gesture was probably less expensive in human suffering than any more determined pursuit of that elusive impostor, practical success.

*   *   *

If this diagnosis is correct there was then in these twenty years an atmosphere more heavily charged with emotion than anything we know. That emotion was potent, it had revived religion and was forming morals, it could enliven politics, it could revivify nationalism, it taught men to feel and to understand the lot of the less fortunate and to stand up for their own wrongs, if not to understand what was meant by armed revolt. It is also seeped into poor drama and not very good painting, into death-bed literature, or silly novels, or into religion at the level of the oleogaph and of those hymns which present no real personal experience, no statement of dogma, but are mere collections of well-tried stimuli for the easier feelings. Whence it came might be a difficult question. Some part of the answer has been suggested; it came partly from the exciting, often distressing, situation of the moment, partly from the unchanging appetites of the human mind gratified and excited by the prevailing passion for oratory, and by the fact that the ingenuity of inventors, the enterprise of publishers, the fertility of authors had given so many of them so much that was so suitable for them to read.

But behind all this, through all this, sweeps that mysterious tidal wave which passed through Europe, which men have called romanticism. Only, to be properly understood, romanticism must be considered not only as something which affected some of the leading minds of the day, it must be considered as a popular movement, even a vulgar movement; with the expressions of exalted politics and important thought must be read much that was ephemeral and seems to us absurd. But the case is that, when all these things are considered, they present an element in the public mind which cannot be disregarded by those who desire to understand how men thought or why they acted.

NOTES

[1] E.g. in electoral matters, see N. Gash, *Politics of the Age of Peel* (1952), G. Kitson Clark 'The Electorate and the Repeal of the Corn Law', *Transactions of the Royal Historical Society*, 5th Series, i. (1951.)

[2] Arthur O. Lovejoy, *Essays in the History of Ideas*, Essay XII. (Baltimore, 1948); Irving Babbitt, *Rousseau and Romanticism*. (Boston, 1928, *passim*); Maurice Souriau, *Histoire du Romantisme en France*. Introduction 'Qu'est-ce que le Romantisme?' (Paris, 1927.)

[3] A. N. Whitehead, *Science in the Modern World*, Chapter V. (Boston, 1926.)

[4] Louis Cazamian, *Le Roman Social en Angleterre 1830–50*. (Paris, 1904.)

[5] The Right Hon. Lord Lytton, *England and the English*, p. 304. (1874.)

[6] Before 1811 'Common,' 'Blaew' and 'Stanhope' presses could possibly produce about 300 impressions an hour; after 1814 Koenig's 'Times' machines could produce about 1,100 and in 1816 his "improved machines" about 2,000. In 1827 Cowper and Applegarth's machines could produce about 6,000. Speeds claimed by manufacturers are not the same as output, but these figures show the general rate of increase. Koenig's 'Perfector' which claimed 1,600 to 2,000 on both sides was not suitable for newspapers.

[7] Dorothy Blakey, *The Minerva Press, 1790–1820*. (1939.)

[8] M. Sadleir, *XIXth Century Fiction; a bibliographical record, based on his own collection*. (1951.)

[9] On the Annuals see Michael Sadleir, *Blessington-D'Orsay—A Masquerade*, pp. 197–203. (1947.) The number of Annuals and their contents can be studied in the yearly review of them in the *Eclectic Review*.

[10] R. K. Webb, *The British Working-class Reader, 1790–1848: Literary and Social Tension*. (1955.)

[11] E.g. See *Quarterly Review*, vol. lxxii, pp. 25 to 53. Article on 'The Lady of the Manor—Evangelical Novels'.

[12] Thomas Moore, *Memoirs of the life of the Right Honourable Richard Brinsley Sheridan*, ii, 463–5. (1825.)

[13] *Speeches of the Right Hon. John Philpot Curran, Master of the Rolls in Ireland in the late very interesting State trials embellished with a striking likeness of that gentleman*. (Dublin 1808.) See the speech for the Rev. Charles Massey asking for damages against the Marquis of Headfort in a case of Crim. Con.

[14] See the remarks in the *Quarterly Review*, vol. lxx, pp. 387-90.

[15] On lectures and recitations see G. J. Holyoake, *Sixty years of an Agitator's Life*, vol. i, ch. ix. (1892.)

[16] E.g. John B. Gough, *Orations*, p. 17 (London, 1855); cf. R. S. Gregg, *Memorials of John Gregg, D.D.*, p. 164. (Dublin, 1879.)

[17] R. G. Gammage, *History of the Chartist Movement, 1837-54*, p. 58. (1894.) For other speeches and sermons see G. J. Holyoake, *Life of Joseph Rayner Stephens, Preacher and Political Orator*. (1881.)

[18] E.g. Joanna Baillie tried to write plays each of which would exemplify one passion. See Joanna Baillie, *A series of plays in which its attempted to delineate the stronger passions of the mind. Each passion being the subject of a tragedy and a comedy*. (1798.)

[19] On Sheil: see R. McCullagh Torrens, *Memoirs of the Right Honourable R. L. Sheil*. (1855.)

[20] Richard Garnett, *The Life of W. J. Fox*, p. 27. (1910.)

[21] S. M. Ellis, *William Harrison Ainsworth and his friends*, i, 54. (1911.)

[22] Lord Lytton, *op. cit.* 261.

[23] See Michael Sadleir. *Bulwer: a Panorama, Edward and Rosina, 1803-1836* (1931.); also Amy Cruse, *The Englishman and his books in the early XIXth Century* (1930.); K. Tillotson, *Novels of the Eighteen-forties*. (1954.)

[24] British Museum. Add. MS. 40526, f. 312. The Hon. Mrs. Caroline Norton to Sir Robert Peel, 25 March 1843.

[25] On Bailey and others like him, see J. H. Buckley: *The Victorian Temper: a Study in Literary Culture*, chapter III. 'The Spasmodic School'. (1952.)

[26] *Edinburgh Review*, vol. l, 34-47.

[27] On this see George Saintsbury, *The Peace of the Augustans*, pp. 100-104. (1916.)

[28] On Fraser's see Miriam M. H. Thrall, *Rebellious Fraser's*. (New York, 1934.)

[29] John Holland and James Everett, *Memoirs of James Montgomery*, ii, 136. (1855.)

[30] *The Letters and Private Papers of William Makepeace Thackeray*, ii, 485, collected and edited by Gordon H. Ray. (Harvard University Press, 1945.)

[31] Wilbur Fisk, *Travels on the Continent of Europe; viz. in England, Ireland, Scotland, France, Italy, Switzerland, Germany and the Netherlands*, p. 529. (New York, 1838.)

[32] See C. S. Phillips, *Hymnody past and present* (1937); *Hymns Ancient and Modern*, Historical Edition 1909, Historical introduction by the Rev. W. H. Frere. It should be noted that the important developments in hymn tunes took place largely after 1850.

[33] *Eclectic Review*, 3rd Series, No. 11, 86.

[34] See Rev. Y. Brillioth, *The Anglican Revival—Studies in the Oxford Movement*, chapter V. (1925.)

[35] On Young Ireland see Sir Charles Gavan Duffy, *Young Ireland* (1896); *Four years of Irish History, 1845-1849* (1883); and Denis Gwynn, *Young Ireland and 1848*. (Cork, 1949.)

[36] Sir Charles Gavan Duffy, *Thomas Davis, the memoirs of an Irish Patriot, 1840–46*, p. 33. (1890.)

[37] *Ibid.*, pp. 95–6.

[38] See R. G. Osterweis, 'Romanticism and Nationalism in the Old South', *Yale Historical Publications*, vol. xlix (1949); W. J. Cash, *The Mind of the South*. (New York, 1941.)

[39] Gavan Duffy, *Four years . . . op cit.*, pp. 235–6.

[40] Probably the best account of these debates is in Edouard Dolléans, *Le Chartisme*. Deuxième Partie, Chapitre Premier, 'Du Réformisme à la violence'. (Paris, 1949.)

[41] *The Trial of Feargus O'Connor, Esq. (Barrister-at-Law) and Fifty-eight others, at Lancaster on a charge of sedition, conspiracy, tumult, and riot*, p. 238. (1843.)

[42] See G. Kitson Clark, 'Hunger and Politics in 1842', *Journal of Modern History*. (Chicago, vol. xxv, No. 4.)

VIII

The Intellectual Aristocracy

N. G. ANNAN

VIII

F AMILY connexions are part of the poetry of history. They call to mind the generations of men and women who were born, married and died, and perhaps bequeathed to their descendants some trait of their personality, some tradition of behaviour, which did not perish with the passing of the years but persisted in their grandchildren and their grandchildren's children, and so made the past immortal. But family connexions are most important to the social historian when they reveal some caucus of power or influence, such as the Whig cousinhood, which moulds the country's culture. Such an influence was exerted by an aristocracy of intellect which began to form at the beginning of the nineteenth century. A particular type of middle-class family then started to intermarry and produced children who became scholars and teachers. They joined those who at Oriel and Balliol in Oxford, or at Trinity and St. John's in Cambridge, were setting new standards in electing to fellowships; they led the movement for academic reform within the universities and sent representatives to the new civic academies; and their achievements as headmasters at Shrewsbury or Harrow or Rugby were watched by the professional classes eager to educate their sons well at schools where they mixed with those of the lesser aristocracy or gentry. When these sons in turn came to marry what was more natural than to choose a wife from the families of their fathers' friends whose fortune and upbringing matched their own? Thus the same names recurred as professors and tutors and schoolmasters; and by virtue of their affiliations their views on academic preferment carried weight.

But they were not a narrow professoriate. They could not be when most fellowships had to be vacated on marriage or the holder required to take Holy Orders. True to the traditional rôle of Oxford and Cambridge, which was to educate men for service in Church and State, they overflowed into the new professions. The days when Addison could define the professions as divinity, law and physic were past. Not only were the old professions expanding to include solicitors and apothecaries, but the establishment in 1828 of the Institution of Civil Engineers to further 'the art of directing the Great Sources of Power in Nature for the use and convenience of mankind' marked the rise of a new kind of professional man. Members of these intellectual families became the new professional civil servants at a time when government had become too complicated and technical to be handled by the ruling class and their dependents. They joined the Indian and Colonial services; or they became school inspectors or took posts in the museums or were appointed secretaries of philanthropic societies; or they edited or wrote for the periodicals or entered publishing houses; or, as journalists ceased to be hacks scribbling in Grub Street, they joined the staff of *The Times*. Thus they gradually spread over the length and breadth of English intellectual life criticising the assumptions of the ruling class above them and forming the opinions of the upper middle class to which they belonged. They were the leaders of the new intelligentsia. Stability is not a quality usually associated with an intelligentsia, a term which, Russian in origin, suggests the shifting, shiftless members of revolutionary or literary cliques who have cut themselves adrift from the moorings of family. Yet the English intelligentsia, wedded to gradual reform of accepted institutions and able to move between the worlds of speculation and government, was stable. That it was so—that it was unexcitable and to European minds unexciting—was in part due to the influence of these academic families.

Philanthropy was the magnet which drew them together. The agitation against slavery led to the alliance first in work and then in marriage of those leaders of the evangelical movement known as the Clapham Sect, from whom so many members of this class descended. Gisborne married Babington's sister, and Babington married a sister of Zachary Macaulay ; Charles Elliott married Venn's sister and Venn's daughter married Stephen's son; an Elliott grandson married a Babington granddaughter; and the Thorntons were distant cousins of the Wilberforces.[1] Evangelicalism, indeed, was the strongest ingredient in the spirit of this class and though the faith in its purest form might fade, the intellectual aristocracy were imbued with the principles which flowed from that faith. There was the sense of dedication, of living with purpose, or working under the eye, if not of the great Taskmaster, of their own conscience—that organ which evangelicalism magnified so greatly. There was the sense of mission to improve the shining hour and the profession to which they had been called. There was the sense of accounting for the talents with which Providence had endowed them. There was also the duty to hold themselves apart from a world given over to vanities which men of integrity rejected because they were content to labour in the vineyard where things of eternal significance grew—in the field of scholarship where results were solid not transient.

Philanthropy linked the Clapham families with others professing similar principles. The Quaker families, the Gurneys, Frys, Gaskells, Hoares, Hodgkins, Foxes and Barclays had intermarried in the eighteenth century. But as they became prosperous and began to play a larger part in the affairs of the world; as they turned from small traders into bankers and brewers; and as they began to own country houses and mixed with evangelical philanthropists or enlightened business men, many of them felt constrained by the narrow bounds of the Society of Friends. The children of John Gurney of Earlham, a banker and country gentleman, whose wife like many others could trace her descent back to Robert Barclay of Urie, the great Quaker apologist of the seventeenth century, had outgrown the simple narrow piety of their elders. They were a lively, gay household and referred to the Meeting-house in Goat's Lane, Norwich, as "that disgusting Goat's".[2] One of the gayest, Elizabeth Fry, suddenly experienced conversion and returned to the ways of the Society, but of her seven brothers and sisters who married, four knelt before the altar of a church. They were not alone in seceding. Mary Ann Galton left the Quakers for the Moravian Brothers, William Rathbone went over in 1805 to Unitarianism and James Wilson, the father-in-law of Walter Bagehot, ceased to attend Meeting in 1832 after marrying an

Anglican. Small wonder that an appeal was made not to ex-communicate members who married those of other religions.[3]

The influence of evangelicalism which gave nonconformist philanthropists allies within the Church of England had something to do with the change in their beliefs; the doctrine of following the inner light, which corresponded closely to Mill's injunction to follow the argument whithersoever it led, had even more. The effect of the secessions was to permit many of the descendants of these families, such as the Pryors or Gurneys, to go to Cambridge where no dissenter could take a degree until 1871. But whether or not they seceded these families reinforced the new intelligentsia.

They also linked the evangelicals to the third group of philanthropists, the Unitarian or philosophic radical families. For although many of these intellectuals descended from clergymen or business men who embraced the evangelical faith, some owed nothing to this tradition. The Wedgwoods, for instance, neither stemmed from a line of parsons nor did they breed them. Josiah Wedgwood of Maer, the son of the founder of the pottery, told his wife not to be uneasy about playing cards on Sunday, since she knew in her heart that it was not wrong. 'I am rather afraid', he wrote, 'of Evangelicalism spreading amongst us though I have some confidence in the good sense of the Maerites for keeping it out, or if it must come for having the disease in a very mild form.'[4] His first cousins, the Darwins, a singularly unreligious family, were equally untouched. They both belonged to the upper-middle-class world of Brougham and Mackintosh and the *Edinburgh Review*, a world which had ties with the cultivated French bourgeoisie. Their children made the Grand Tour and went to balls and race-meetings. Yet if their manners were freer they were not by the thirties very far removed from some of the children of Clapham who had abandoned not only their fathers' toryism but the rigidity of their religious principles; and Charles Darwin's description of his uncle Josiah as 'the very type of an upright man with the clearest judgment. I do not believe that any power on earth could have made him swerve an inch from what he considered the right course', does not suggest that in temperament these families differed greatly.[5]

Thus the separate roots grew into a trunk most massive in the sixties and seventies when the new liberalism of franchise reform, women's education, and university extension drew them together. Irish Home Rule, which they nearly all opposed, cleft this generation of intellectuals: thereafter they split into branches, some becoming Liberal Imperialists, others pro-Boer, others Conservative reformers, others Fabians. But in the sixties two objectives vital to their class and, as they rightly thought, vital to their country, united them. They worked tirelessly for intellectual freedom within the universities which, they thought, should admit anyone irrespective of his religious beliefs, and for the creation of a public service open to talent. If they can be said to have had a Bill of Rights it was the Trevelyan-Northcote report of 1853 on reform of the civil service and their Glorious Revolution was achieved in 1870–1 when entry to public service by privilege, purchase of army commissions and the religious tests were finally abolished. Then it was ordained that men of good intellect should prosper through open competitive examination; and that the examination, as Macaulay had recommended for the Indian Civil Service, should be designed for those who had taken high honours at the university.[6] No formal obstacle then remained to prevent the man of brains from becoming a gentleman.

They all regarded themselves as gentlemen. Some of them indisputably were—even by the standards of Cranford or Barchester. Babington was a squire who could appoint to a living and was considered by his relations to have married beneath him by making the daughter of a Scots minister his wife. The Trevelyans and Stracheys were old West Country families with baronetcies created in the seventeenth and eighteenth centuries. Even so the intellectual Trevelyans were a cadet branch of the family; and the Stracheys were nearly ruined in the eighteenth century so that the younger sons had to seek their fortune through service in India. Other families sprang from the sons of poor country parsons or dissenting ministers or of civil engineers or of nurserymen and artisans who had flourished. But the word, gentleman, in Victorian times became a subject of dialectical enquiry and nerve-racking embarrassment as readers of Charlotte Yonge and Trollope know. Newman and Huxley both re-defined it to meet the needs of their class and the realities of a new age. To have been to a public school was not a necessary qualification; but to have been to a university, or by some means to have acquired higher education or professional status, was. However the word was defined, the intellectual aristocracy never confused themselves with the real nobility and ruling class. Henry Thornton smiled satirically at his brother's breakfast party in his exquisitely embellished Clapham villa for Queen Charlotte and her daughters. "We are all City people and connected with merchants and nothing but merchants on every side" he would say, and the subsequent failure of his brother in business, who died under an assumed name in New York, may have seemed like a judgment on such luxurious display.[7] The only action of his father which Thornton regretted was allowing his sister to marry Lord Leven; and certainly those children of the intellectual families who married above their station rarely returned to the fold but followed the upper-class pursuits of politics or the army.

It is indeed the mark of most of these families to remain almost exactly where they were placed in society. Josiah Wedgwood had a country house and had married a squire's daughter, but the Wedgwoods were not a county family and they knew it. Their fortune rested on the pottery and not on land and during the past century and a half they have neither risen nor fallen in the social scale. The families which rose by business, especially the Quaker connexions, were affluent enough to enable some of their children to pursue their scholarly studies in leisure; but they had neither the wealth nor the inclination to become magnates and were always liable to have to save a brother whose affairs had failed to prosper. In any event a fortune divided among forty grandchildren did not give the cadet branches the chance to live extravagantly. The Anglican families tended to be less well-to-do. In the case of both, sound commercial principles were allied to ascetic habits. Even on their meagre stipends the poorer dons thrived and, as few of them were permitted to marry, they saved. Sidgwick wrote to his mother at the age of twenty-six from Trinity, 'I find that I have saved £1,700 and hope to save £400 a year as long as I stay here: in spite of all my travelling, books and the extremely luxurious life that I can hardly help leading'. A fortnight later he told her that he had opposed a College ball being held because 'I consider it a most unseemly proceeding on the part of a charitable foundation for the purposes of education and of which the majority are clergymen and . . . especially as it will be a great expense, and you know my miserly tendencies'.[8] His luxurious life was evidently restrained.

Restrained because for Sidgwick as for all of them the purpose of life was to distinguish in conduct as well as in concept the sham from the genuine, appearance from reality. Appearances were to be exposed and these men were splendidly eccentric in Victorian society in not keeping them up. They groaned at the thought of formal receptions and preferred to wear rough clothes. Even the gentlemanly Arthur Benson, Sidgwick's nephew, opined that a don should be well dressed in the style-before-last and obeyed this precept by wearing shapeless flannels.[9] Their self-confidence forbade them to ape the manners of their superiors in rank and their clothes, like their pursuits, were a protest against the pastimes of the upper classes which became increasingly more gaudy and expensive. They neither hunted nor had the money for vast *battues* of pheasants. Most of them had lost their roots in their soil and, cut off from country sports, had become town-dwellers. But they had not lost touch with Nature whom they sought mountaineering in the Alps or on forty-mile tramps or with their botanical satchel and geologist's hammer. Their manners lacked polish. Indeed they despised it as much as they despised the art of pleasing—that imperative accomplishment for those who enter politics or London society. But they did not become parochial or cut themselves off from London. Many of them lived there, and those who did not kept up with public affairs through dining clubs where they met their cousins and brothers-in-law in the professions or sometimes by themselves participating in politics.

Their good manners appeared in their prose. At its worst it was lucid and free from scholarly jargon; and time and again they produced works of surpassing literary merit. They wrote with a sense of form, of drama, of the possibilities of language; and they wrote not for a scholarly clique but for the intelligent public at large whom they addressed confident that they would be understood. Moreover their scholarly manners had an ease seldom evident in a parochial professoriate. With some notable exceptions they refused to follow the pulverizing polemical style of German scholars. The gentle Darwin and the sprightly Maitland each showed that it was possible to argue without breaking heads, and even such controversialists as Huxley were untainted by the *odium clericum* and distinguished between the charlatan and the wrong-headed. They valued independence and recognized it in others. Because they judged people by an exterior standard of moral and intellectual merit, they never became an exclusive clique and welcomed the penniless son of a dissenting minister as a son-in-law if they believed in his integrity and ability. Because their own proud standards were assured they tolerated a wide variety of belief. They might be Comtists, they were often followers of Mill, they might be agnostics, or they might continue to adhere to the church of their fathers; but they all respected each other's beliefs, however deeply convinced that the beliefs were wrong. They were agreed on one characteristic doctrine; that the world could be improved by analysing the needs of society and calculating the possible course of its development.

They could be intimidating to meet. Intellectuals often are. Their sense of responsibility to reason was too great for them to appreciate spontaneous behaviour. Spontaneity is attractive but its lack of rational consideration irritated them. They were bored by the superficiality of drawing-room gossip, and preferred to have their talk out rather than converse. As infants they had learnt by listening to their parents to extend their vocabulary and talk in grammatical sentences—of which the most famous was the four-year-old Macaulay's 'Thank you, madam, the agony is abated'. When older they subconsciously apprehended from hearing discussions between their elders how to reason logically. They lived in houses in which books were part of existence and the intellect was prized. They developed inner resources for entertaining themselves which did not depend on the ordinary social accomplishments. Competitive examinations at the schools and universities sharpened their minds, and if those children who did not inherit their parents' intellectual talents suffered unjustly by feeling that they had failed, the successful children gained by acquiring the habit of thinking accurately in concepts at an early age. Nor was childhood dull: they were freer to read and play as they liked than most middle-class children. Moreover, the daughters were educated as well as the sons: and if they remained spinsters they had the ability to teach or do social work at which the girls of the upper classes were so often ineffectual.

They had their limitations as every close-knit class must have. Their response to art was at best uncertain. Literature of course was in their bones. The poetry and prose of Greece and Rome had been their discipline and that of their own country filled their leisure hours. They were the first to admire Meredith and Browning and to dethrone Byron for Wordsworth. Goethe and the German poets were admired primarily for the moral precepts which their works embodied. French culture was another matter. Lady Strachey, her children gathered about her, might rise from her seat in the railway carriage as the train steamed into the Gare du Nord and bow to the great city, the mistress of European civilization, but such a gesture was rare. Matthew Arnold went as far as most were prepared to go in admiring French culture and he made strong reservations. The Parisian *haute bourgeoisie* combined a passion for general ideas with an interest in the arts, the theatre and opera, in a way which was impossible for them. Their experience of the visual arts was meagre. Beautiful objects and elegant rooms were not to them necessities: their comfortable ugly houses, in Kensington, Bayswater and North Oxford, rambling, untidy, full of glory-holes and massive furnishings and staffed by two or three despairing servants, were dedicated to utility, not beauty. Some may have bought some good pieces of furniture, a very few of the more prosperous may have invested in Italian primitives, others were affected by the pre-Raphaelites, but in the main they groped after artistic fashion in a manner inconsistent with their natural self-confidence. They worshipped beauty in Nature—in mountain scenery or in plants—but the old evangelical distrust of beauty as a temptress, which they tried to control by inadequate theories and which was unsusceptible to the kind of analysis of which they were masters, inhibited them in their dealings with art. A fashionably-dressed wife would not only have been an extravagance but an act of submission to worldly vanity: and the pre-Raphaelite cloaks and dresses which had been donned as a homage to beauty and a protest against the world of upper-class fashion degenerated in some cases into thick woollen stockings and flannel petticoats which were proudly worn as a badge of financial and spiritual austerity. By the end of the century there was a slight staidness, a satisfaction, a lack of spontaneity and intellectual adventure, even a touch of philistinism in the face of new forms of art; and some of their descendants such as Samuel Butler or the Bloomsbury group satirized these failings.

The artist's vision was not theirs. Nor was his world for, critical of conventions as they might be, they emphatically did not live in Bohemia. Pleasure was identified with happiness, and happiness by both their favourite philosophers, Mill and Green, with self-realization. There could be family jollity, but exuberance, raciness and inconsequential high spirits escaped them. They were a little too far removed from the battle of finding a job and exercising the arts of getting a better, a little too severe on inconsequential behaviour, fully to understand human nature. Nor was this surprising; those who have clear ideas on what life ought to be always have difficulty in reconciling themselves to what it is. Considering that their heart was set on transforming the old universities into institutions of education and research their genial and tolerant regard for the older generation of dons was remarkable. Their goals nevertheless were so clear and their purpose so single-minded that they were apt to sacrifice other valuable things to achieve them. Self-realization was not always extended to those gifted and capital creatures their wives. Fortunately for their husbands they were trained to self-sacrifice.

Great as their influence was in politics and intellectual life in the middle of the century perhaps it was even more important at the end. For then the restraints of religion and thrift and accepted class distinctions started to crumble and English society to rock under the flood of money. The class war, not merely between labour and owners, but between all social strata of the middle and upper classes began in earnest. *The*

Awkward Age, The Way We Live Now, The Massarenes, and *Belchamber* are only four of the novels which deal with the corruption of society by money; Shaw, Wells, Kipling and Galsworthy only four of the authors who suggested that the old political slogans were irrelevant for their age. A new bitterness entered politics, a new rancour in foreign relations and a materialism of wealthy snobbery and aggressive philistinism arose far exceeding anything hitherto seen in England. The intellectual aristocracy were one of the few barriers which resisted these forces. In politics they preferred the manner of Balfour and Asquith to that of Lord Hugh Cecil or Lloyd George. They insisted that honesty and courtesy were valuable; and they continued to set before the young unworldly ideals. They suggested that if public life was inseparable from spiritual ignominy, another life devoted to unravelling the mysteries of mind, matter and heart was to be desired.

For them, too, it was a period of change. In the eighties the ban on married dons was removed and many who in the past would have been forced to vacate their fellowships and pursue their studies elsewhere or find a different source of income were able to remain at Oxford and Cambridge. As a result they tended to become more purely academic. They also became relatively poorer as taxation and the standard of living rose. A young don, such as A. L. Smith, who later became Master of Balliol, the son of an unsuccessful civil engineer and one of a family of nineteen surviving children, had a hard time in making both ends meet. Stipends which had been tolerable for a bachelor such as Sidgwick, were grossly inadequate for a married man when they were reduced by the agricultural depression which had hit all colleges hard at a time when they had just begun to pay university taxation. It was also the time when inter-marriage between these families greatly increased; and the moment has come to follow this in detail.

It is not an easy process to follow. There are first two projections to observe, the horizontal and the vertical. The horizontal shows how these families ally themselves by marriage and form a new class in society. The vertical has already been studied by Galton and Havelock Ellis; but whereas they drew conclusions about hereditary ability, here it illustrates how certain families gain position and influence through persistent endogamy. At the same time we must note how the members of these families spread over the breadth of intellectual and official life and how some maintained while others rebelled against the ethos of their fathers. The following survey does not claim to include every member of the families mentioned who became intellectually distinguished—still less to record every single birth or marriage: genealogical trees and tables are therefore diagrammatic and selective. Moreover, only the principal appointments and honours gained are shown and *no distinction is drawn between fellowships or appointments occupied for life and those vacated after a term of years.* Since my space is circumscribed, a limit must be set to this inquiry. Those who hunt may in their dreams have started a fox in the Pytchley country and been rewarded by a two-hundred-mile point straight across the Midlands which ended on the edge of the Beaufort. So in our pursuit of this class we will start from one family and move to another only if one of its members is related to the antecedent family. Some intellectual families—the Moberleys, Clarks or Headlams—will lie off the line we hit but it is astonishing how many we will ride through, particularly if we follow their fortunes to the present day when it will be seen how the tendency to intermarry still persists.[10]

We had better first draw a covert in the Macaulay country to see how Miss Rose Macaulay descends from the eldest son of the minister in the Hebrides. Her father was a scholar and her uncle, W. H. Macaulay, a magnificent and imposing figure of a don, her great-uncle a headmaster, and she also descends from the Conybeares and Babingtons. The Conybeares were for generations parsons and scholars descending from an Elizabethan schoolmaster. There was the Rev. John Conybeare, who defended revealed religion against Matthew Tindal, in a book which George Washington always liked to have by him; there were his two grandsons, both expert in geology, the one a professor of Anglo-Saxon and the other a palaeontologist; there was the Rev. J. W. E. Conybeare who wrote a life of Alfred the Great and another Conybeare who was a Fellow of University College, Oxford and an Armenian scholar; and in recent

William Wilberforce with the Thornton Family

Josiah Wedgwood and his Family by George Stubbs

times a Conybeare was a master at Eton for nearly fifty years. Miss Rose Macaulay's grandfather, W. J. Conybeare, the noted *Edinburgh* reviewer, married a daughter of Lydia Babington who was taught by her father to read each morning a chapter of the Old Testament in Hebrew and a chapter of the New Testament in Greek. Her first cousin 'Beetles' Babington was professor of botany at Cambridge at the same time as another cousin, Churchill Babington, was professor of archaeology. Churchill's range was wide: he was also expert in ornithology, and numismatics and won praise for 'his able defence of the English clergy in the seventeenth century against Macaulay's aspersions'. The achievements of the Macaulay-Babington connexion are displayed on the next page.

But we must turn to Zachary, the brother of the Rev. Aulay and Jean Macaulay if we are to get the run for which we were hoping. Everyone knows that his eldest son was the historian Lord Macaulay, but one tends to forget that his youngest son, Charles Zachary, married a daughter of "Radical Dick" Potter, a founder of the *Manchester Guardian*. Here the pace begins to quicken. Their daughter, Mary, married Charles Booth, the author of *Life and Labour in London*, one of the greatest sociological studies of Victorian times. With Charles Booth we move into a new country, the families of radical Liverpool, into the Rathbones and Cromptons. Henry Crompton, the Comtian Positivist, was Booth's cousin, as was another Positivist, E. S. Beesly, professor of history at University College, London, and a sponsor of the First International; and so were the chemist, Sir Henry Roscoe, F.R.S., and the economist, W. S. Jevons, F.R.S. One of Booth's uncles collaborated with Stephenson in building the *Rocket* and another was secretary to the Board of Trade. Charles Booth's third son married the daughter of Stephen Spring-Rice, Fellow of Trinity, one of whose granddaughters is the wife of Professor C. M. Robertson, the son of Mr. D. S. Robertson, vice-master of Trinity and professor of Greek at Cambridge. The main connexion, however, follows through Charles Booth's wife in that her cousins were the nine Potter sisters who spread their enveloping wings over radical and socialist society at the end of the last century. The most famous was the eighth, Beatrice Webb. The eldest, Laurencina,

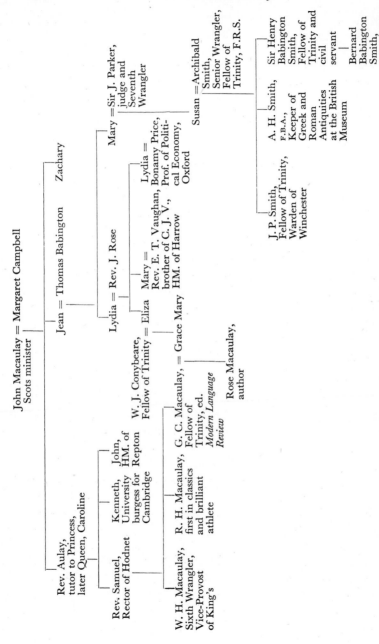

married Robert Holt, gazetted a baronet by Lord Rosebery who misread his humorous letter of refusal and was compelled by Holt to cancel the honour. The second, Catherine, married Leonard (later Lord) Courtney, Second Wrangler, Fellow of St. John's and Financial Secretary to the Treasury. The fifth, Theresa, married C. A. Cripps, later the first Lord Parmoor, whose eldest son was Bursar of Queen's, Oxford, whose younger son was Sir Stafford Cripps and whose daughter is married to Sir Jack Egerton, F.R.S., professor of chemistry, London. The seventh, Margaret, married a cousin of L. T. Hobhouse, professor of sociology, London, the Right Hon. Henry Hobhouse, local government reformer, who was the grandfather of Miss Theresa Clay, the zoologist. The youngest of the nine sisters, Rosalind, had a daughter who is married to Mr. Malcolm Muggeridge, editor of *Punch*. The link with the next family, however, is the fourth Potter sister, who married a banker, Daniel Meinertzhagen.

Meinertzhagen, too, was liberally supplied with daughters. The eldest married her second cousin, Mr. George Macaulay Booth, the son of Charles, and a director of the Bank of England. The second married Hubert Warre-Cornish, son of the Vice-Provost of Eton. She was thus sister-in-law to Sir Desmond MacCarthy whose daughter is married to Lord David Cecil—who can count a Fellow of All Souls and a Senior Wrangler among his ancestors. Her youngest sister married A. F. R. Wollaston, explorer, naturalist and Fellow of King's, of whom Keynes wrote that he 'could unlock hearts with a word and a look and break down everyone's reserve except his own'. The third Meinertzhagen girl married Robert John Grote Mayor.

Here the scent leads back to Cambridge, for the Mayors are a celebrated academic family. J. E. B. Mayor was professor of Latin, a man of vast learning and minute accuracy who, at the age of six, 'revelled in Rollin (in default of Plutarch)'. He was in the great tradition of dons. He wrote much but rarely the books on which he was working and ought to have written. He collected a library of over 18,000 volumes and during the long period in which he was University Librarian never left Cambridge for more than eight days together. He addressed Germans on 'Why I am a Vegetarian', never consulted a

17

doctor from the age of twelve to eighty-three, and boasted that he could dine every day off a penny halfpenny; he was also adamant in never taking exercise for its own sake. Lexicography and the deliberations of the Old Catholics were among his passions and at the age of eight-two he learnt Esperanto. One of his brothers was third Wrangler and a master at Rugby. Another, the third to be elected a Fellow of St. John's, became professor of classics at King's, London, and married a niece of John Grote.

Grote was professor of moral philosophy at Cambridge who founded a club at his vicarage in Trumpington at which animated and brilliant discussions took place. His brother, George, was the banker and philosophical radical who wrote the notable history of Greece. John Grote's great-nephew, Robin Mayor, was Senior Classic in 1890 and a Fellow of King's, who retired in middle age from the civil service to devote himself to philosophical speculation: his brother was a master at Clifton. His son, Mr. Andreas Mayor, entered the British Museum and his daughter became the second wife of Lord Rothschild, F.R.S., Fellow of Trinity and chairman of the Agricultural Research· Council.

But we must hark back to Zachary Macaulay to establish the well-known connexion between the Macaulays, Trevelyans, Arnolds and Huxleys.

From this we can see that Mrs. Humphry Ward, the novelist, was the niece not only of Matthew Arnold but of William Delafield Arnold of the Indian Civil Service and author of *Oakfield*, and of William Forster, minister for education in Gladstone's first administration. If her father was distinguished mainly for losing academic posts by his propensity to oscillate between the Anglican and Roman Catholic faiths, her grandfather was Dr. Arnold of Rugby. Her grandmother's family were also scholars. Mrs. Arnold's brother married 'Mrs. Markham', author of children's history books, otherwise Elizabeth Cartwright Penrose, daughter of the Doctor of Divinity who invented the power loom and niece of the agitator for parliamentary reform in the eighteenth century. Their son, Francis Cranmer Penrose, F.R.S.—the middle name indicated the descent from the great archbishop—was an art historian,

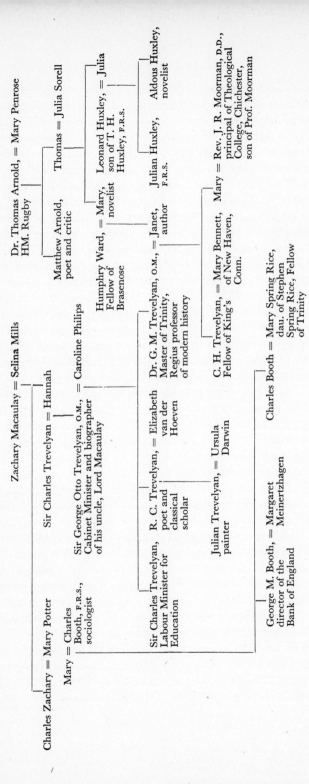

architect and surveyor of St. Paul's Cathedral. His daughter, Dame Emily Penrose, took a first in Greats and became principal in succession of Bedford, Holloway and Somerville Colleges. Dr. Julian Huxley, F.R.S., and Mr. Aldous Huxley are both grandsons of T. H. Huxley, "Darwin's bulldog". With this last name we ride out of the Macaulay country and over the Darwin-Wedgwood land. They are connected by two marriages. Mr. Andrew Huxley, F.R.S., physiologist, Fellow of Trinity and half-brother of the zoologist and the novelist, married the granddaughter of the first Lord Wedgwood, whose grandfather was Charles Darwin's brother-in-law. Mr. Julian Trevelyan, son of R. C., married (though the marriage was later dissolved) Ursula, a great-granddaughter of Charles Darwin.

Now we are in open fields and the pace is tremendous. The descendants of Josiah Wedgwood of Maer, son of the founder of the pottery, provide one of the most remarkable examples of the way in which a great intellectual connexion attracts to it in each generation distinguished brains from other families. Omitting the Master Potters among the Wedgwoods who carried on the craft, we find that in the first generation Josiah Wedgwood had the following brothers-in-law: Robert Darwin, F.R.S., son of Erasmus[11]; Sir James Mackintosh, the Whig philosopher who was attacked by James Mill in his *Fragment on Mackintosh* and who admitted that he could 'no more learn to play the game of life than that of whist'; and J. C. Sismondi, the Genevese economist who propounded the theory of over-production and the increasing poverty of the working classes. Josiah's own brother, Thomas Wedgwood, was the pioneer photographer. The second generation contains Charles Darwin himself; the etymologist Hensleigh Wedgwood, Fellow of Christ's, and Henry Allen Wedgwood, barrister and author. These generations found their chronicler in Darwin's daughter, Henrietta Litchfield,[12] and the third generation have been brought magnificently to life by Darwin's granddaughter Mrs. Raverat.[13] It contained the mathematician Sir George Darwin, F.R.S., Sir Horace Darwin, who made scientific instruments, the botanist Sir Francis Darwin, F.R.S., and Leonard Darwin, President of the Royal Geographical Society. Another Wedgwood became a

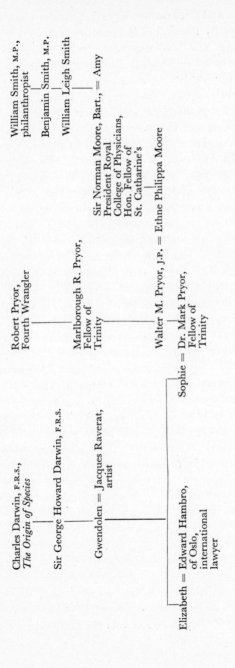

civil servant and yet another secretary to the Charity Organisation Society. By the end of the century a daughter of Sir James Rendel, f.r.s., the civil engineer, and a daughter of the civil servant, the first Lord Farrer, had married into the family. And late in life Farrer did the same.

The grandchildren and great-grandchildren of Charles Darwin have extended the intellectual affiliations of the family. Three of his second eldest son's children have played a part in this extension. The eldest, Sir Charles Darwin, f.r.s., Master of Christ's and Director of the National Physical Laboratory, married a daughter of F. W. Pember, Warden of All Souls. The second, Mrs. Gwen Raverat, who was the wife of the French artist, Jacques Raverat, has two daughters, one of whom married Dr. Mark Pryor, zoologist and Fellow of Trinity.

The Pryors are an example of a family, by origin Quaker, who conformed and sent their sons to Cambridge. On his mother's side Dr. Pryor descends from William Smith, M.P., adherent of the Clapham sect, who worked in Parliament to abolish slavery and religious disabilities. He was the son of the Clapham city merchant who sent a present of tea to Flora Macdonald when she was imprisoned in the Tower. We shall meet this family again, but for the present we can pause only to note that Amy Leigh Smith's marriage to Norman Moore was fostered by her aunt, Barbara Bodichon, who was the friend of George Eliot and the prime founder of Girton. Moore was a scholar as well as a brilliant doctor: he contributed 459 biographies to the *D.N.B.* and wrote a history of St. Bartholomew's Hospital. So poor as an undergraduate that he lived largely on bread and marmalade, he was unjustly deprived of his scholarship and sent down by his college for brawling— though he had in fact refused to brawl—but such was the outcry that he was reinstated and cheered on getting his degree.[14]

The third and youngest daughter of Sir George Darwin became the wife of the surgeon and bibliographer, Sir Geoffrey Keynes.

Lord Keynes claimed to be the first son of the marriage of a Fellow of a college with a graduate of Newnham, and the year 1882 in which they married was the date when the university

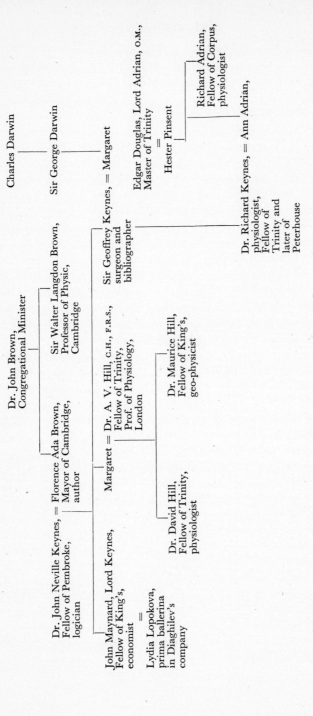

statutes were reformed to permit any Fellow of a college to marry. Their grandson, Dr. Richard Keynes, married the daughter of Lord Adrian, o.m., Nobel Prizeman and Master of Trinity.

Sir Horace Darwin's elder daughter, Ruth, became a civil servant and married a civil servant, Mr. Rees Thomas. His younger daughter married the Treasury official, Sir Alan Barlow, whose father was physician to three sovereigns and President of the Royal College of Physicians. Sir Alan's niece married Mr. Carl Winter, Fellow of Trinity and Director of the Fitzwilliam Museum. His son, Dr. Horace Barlow, Fellow of Trinity and then of King's, is related through his grandmother to the late Lord Farrer. Lord Farrer was brother-in-law to Sir Edward Bridges, the son of the Poet Laureate and Permanent Secretary to the Treasury, and to the historian, the Hon. Steven Runciman, Fellow of Trinity, whose mother obtained a first-class in the history Tripos of 1890.

Sir Francis Darwin was the father of Mr. Bernard Darwin, author and *The Times* correspondent, whose son, Mr. Robin Darwin, is principal of the Royal College of Art. Sir Francis was also the father, by his second wife, of the poet Frances Cornford, who married Professor Cornford, Fellow of Trinity. Their eldest son was John Cornford, the young Communist intellectual, who was killed in the Spanish civil war and whose son is a scholar of Trinity. Mrs. Cornford's mother was not only a Fellow of Newnham; she was also a cousin of Henry Sidgwick, the prototype of the new academic class. Sidgwick's grandfather was a Yorkshire cotton spinner, his father a clergyman and grammar school headmaster who was last Wrangler in 1829, and he himself was a Rugbeian who resigned his Fellowship of Trinity in 1869 on the grounds that he could no longer conscientiously sign the thirty-nine articles. Later, when professor of moral philosophy, he took the lead in promoting university reform and women's education. He married the sister of A. J. Balfour and thus became related to the physicist, Lord Rayleigh, f.r.s., who had married another sister, and to Professor F. M. and Gerald Balfour, Fellows of Trinity. Mrs. Sidgwick became principal of Newnham. Sidgwick's brother Arthur was Second Classic, became a Fellow of Corpus, Oxford, and was the father of the partner in the publishing house of Sidgwick and Jackson. His cousin Alfred was a philosopher, his nephew Professor Arthur Carr Sidgwick a scientist. Sidgwick's youngest sister married her first cousin once-removed. This was E. W., later Archbishop, Benson who taught Sidgwick at Rugby and thus the trio of Benson brothers, A. C., E. F. and Father Hugh Benson were all Sidgwick's nephews.

The following Wedgwoods are cousins of the Darwins. Dr. Ralph Vaughan-Williams, o.m., whose maternal grandparents were a Wedgwood and a Darwin ; the novelist Arthur Wedgwood; Sir Ralph Wedgwood, railway director, and his daughter, the historian and literary editor of *Time and Tide*, Miss Veronica Wedgwood; Mrs Irene Gosse, a Wedgwood through her mother and second wife (though the marriage was later dissolved) of Mr. Philip Gosse, son of Sir Edmund Gosse, critic and author of the brilliant description of a nonconformist childhood, *Father and Son*. Finally there were the children of the first Lord Wedgwood, who married the daughter of the judge Lord Bowen: his son the artist and second baron; his fourth daughter, the anthropologist the late Hon. Camilla Wedgwood; and his eldest daughter Helen, who married Mr. Michael Pease, the geneticist and son of E. H. R. Pease, the secretary and chronicler of the Fabian Society and grandfather of Mrs. Andrew Huxley.

The Peases lead us into the Quaker country and E. H. R. Pease is an interesting example of the way in which the Society of Friends breeds that kind of non-conformity which is the life of an intelligentsia. The senior branch of the family produced members of parliament, business men and bankers; the cadet branch to which he belonged was for the most part content to live quietly on its patrimony. But comfortable mid-Victorian philanthropy, or even the activity of his uncle Albert Fry, prime founder of Bristol University College, was not enough to satisfy this young man who, earning £400 a year on the Stock Exchange, which was more than he spent, with a small capital of his own and handsome prospects, suddenly decided to become a cabinet maker, and study the theory of Socialism. He ended by becoming secretary to the Fabian Society and to

Sidney Webb, at £100 a year. Among these Quaker families the inter-marriages are so frequent that the scent is hard to follow. E. H. R. Pease's mother, for instance, was Susan Fry, sister of the judge Sir Edward Fry who married Mariabella Hodgkin, sister of Thomas Hodgkin, whose wife was Lucy Anna Fox, sister-in-law of Sir Joseph Pease, the grandson of the man who built the first railway between Stockton and Darlington and who was first cousin to the grandfather of E. H. R. Pease. Here the fox is running like a hare. Among these families perhaps the best to draw is the Hodgkins, where we will find a straight-necked one.

Thomas Hodgkin was a successful banker with a taste for archaeology and history, and he had the good sense to resign from his bank to write a history of early Britain. But his fame rests on one of the most splendid pieces of historical description in the English language, *Italy and Her Invaders*. Three of his ancestors were Fellows of the Royal Society: Hodgkin of 'Hodgkin's disease', Luke Howard the friend of Constable and meteorologist who first classified clouds, and Isaac Fletcher the astronomer. Thomas's elder sister was the mother of Roger Fry, and of Margery Fry, principal of Somerville; his younger sister married the architect, Alfred Waterhouse, whose daughter was the wife of Robert Bridges, the Poet Laureate. Thomas Hodgkin's second son, the Anglo-Saxon historian, became Provost of Queen's, Oxford. Among his grandsons are the Bishop of St. Albans, who married his cousin, the sister of Mr. Charles Bosanquet, Rector of King's College, Newcastle and kinsman of the philosopher, Bernard Bosanquet; and the physiologist, Mr. Alan Hodgkin, Fellow of Trinity and professor of the Royal Society, who married the eldest daughter of the American researcher on cancer, Dr. Peyton Rous, who is a foreign member of the Royal Society and an Honorary Fellow of Trinity Hall.

And now the chase has led to Oxford—to another famous sisterhood, the daughters of A. L. Smith, Master of Balliol. Professor Alan Hodgkin's mother married in her widowhood the eldest son of the Master. He had been a Fellow of All Souls and of Magdalen and became Rector of Edinburgh Academy. Her brother-in-law by her first marriage, Robert Hodgkin, Provost of Queen's, was also her brother-in-law by her second marriage as he was the husband of the third daughter of the Master. Smith's eldest daughter married Sir Harold Hartley, F.R.S., Fellow of Balliol and chairman of British European Airways. The second daughter, Molly, married first a Barrington-Ward, who was a Fellow of All Souls, and brother of the editor of *The Times*; and second Sir Frederick Hamilton, who made his fortune in South Africa. The fourth daughter, Miriam, married Sir Reader Bullard, the ambassador who was the son of a wharf foreman. The sixth daughter, Rosalind, was the wife first of Murray Wrong, Fellow of Magdalen and son of the historian of Canada, and, second, of Sir Henry Clay, Warden of Nuffield. The youngest daughter, Barbara, married the brain surgeon, Sir Hugh Cairns. The youngest son of the Master, Mr. Hubert Smith, is the chief agent of the National Trust.

The grandchildren of A. L. Smith include: Mr. Thomas Hodgkin, Fellow of Balliol, who married Dorothy Crowfoot, F.R.S., tutor of Somerville; Mr. Edward Hodgkin, foreign leader writer on *The Times*; Mr. Julian Bullard, Fellow of All Souls and diplomat; Mr. Oliver Wrong, of the department of medicine at Manchester; Mr. John Cairns, biologist; and Mr. Anthony Smith, author and *Manchester Guardian* correspondent. One granddaughter has married an official in the International Monetary Fund, another an official in Transport House and another Dr. Murdoch Mitchison, Fellow of Trinity and lecturer in zoology at Edinburgh. Dr. Mitchison comes of a long line of scientists and his mother is the novelist Mrs. Naomi Mitchison, who descends from the Haldanes.

The Haldane-Burdon Sanderson marriage is of peculiar interest. The Haldanes can be traced back to Bishop Burnet and they number among them many lawyers, physicians, sailors, such as Duncan of Camperdown, and soldiers such as Abercomby of Aboukir.[15] James Haldane's father and uncle gave up their naval careers to spread evangelicalism in Scotland and for similar reasons Robert Burdon, after a brilliant Oxford career, threw up his post as secretary of presentations disgusted at the way in which church patronage was conducted. His uncles were the great maritime lawyer, Lord Stowell, and the die-hard Tory Lord Chancellor, Lord Eldon. Some members of Eldon's nepotic succession could certainly not be accused of Toryism; and a

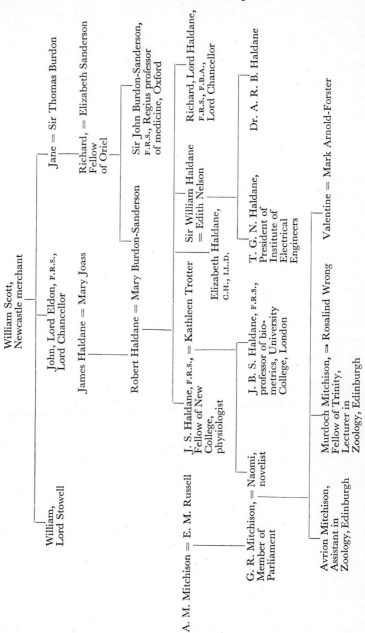

later successor to the woolsack, Lord Haldane, was not only a brilliant Secretary for War and an Hegelian philosopher but Lord Chancellor in the first Labour administration, while his niece is married to a Labour M.P., Mr. G. R. Mitchison.

Dr. Murdoch Mitchison's sister is married to Mr. Mark Arnold-Forster. His grandfather was the Rt. Hon. Hugh Arnold-Forster, P.C., M.P., the second son of William Delafield Arnold, and had been adopted by his uncle, the Minister of Education in Gladstone's first administration, who came of Quaker abolitionist stock. Hugh Arnold-Forster married Mary Lucy Story-Maskelyne. Her sister was the wife of the scientist, Sir Arthur Rücker, principal of London University, and her father was professor of mineralogy at Oxford where he was a prime mover in establishing the study of the natural sciences. Her great-grandfather, Nevil Maskelyne, was a Fellow of Trinity, Astronomer Royal and author of the Nautical Almanac. Nevil's sister was the mother-in-law of Henry Strachey and sister-in-law of Robert Clive. Mary Story-Maskelyne's father, brother-in-law, maternal grandfather, paternal grandfather, paternal great-grandfather, uncle and uncle's father were all Fellows of the Royal Society.

The Peases who led us to the Hodgkins will also lead us to the Butlers, another Cambridge family of public servants and scholars, in that the only daughter of Joseph Beaumont Pease married Sir Cyril Butler. The Butlers descend from Weeden Butler, the friend of Burke, through his son, George Butler, Senior Wrangler, Fellow of Sidney Sussex and headmaster of Harrow. The following are notable among his children and descendants.

1. George Butler, Fellow of Exeter, principal of Liverpool Collegiate Institution, *m.* Josephine Grey who worked in the cause of women's rights.
    2. A. S. Butler, professor of natural philosophy, St. Andrews, *m.* Edith Bolton.
        3. Arthur S. G. Butler, architect and author.
    2. George Grey Butler, Wrangler, permanent examiner to the Civil Service.
    2. Charles Butler, relief worker.

1. Spencer Perceval Butler, double first in classics and mathematics, barrister and public servant, *m.* Mary Kendall.
     2. Sir Cyril Butler, public servant and a founder of the Contemporary Art Society.
     2. Sir Spencer Harcourt Butler, Governor of Burma.
     2. Sir Montagu Butler, Governor of Central Provinces, India, Master of Pembroke, *m.* Ann Gertrude Smith, daughter of George Adam Smith, Indian correspondent of *The Times*, who was great-nephew of the Rector of the Royal High School, Edinburgh in Sir Walter Scott's day.
          3. R. A. Butler, Fellow of Corpus, Chancellor of the Exchequer, *m.* Sydney, daughter of Samuel Courtauld, industrialist and connoisseur.
     2. Arthur Francis Norman-Butler, Wrangler, Inspector of Schools, *m.* Sibella Norman.
          3. Edward Norman-Butler *m.* Belinda Ritchie, granddaughter of Sir Richmond Ritchie and Anne Thackeray, whose father was W. M. Thackeray; also granddaughter of Charles Booth.
          3. Susan *m.* Sir George Abell, Viceregal secretary in India, director of the Bank of England.
     2. Ralph Butler, Fellow of Corpus Christi.
     2. Sir G. G. G. Butler, M.P., Fellow of Corpus Christi, university burgess.
     2. Isabel *m.* Sir Henry Erle Richards, Fellow of All Souls and Chichele professor of international law, Oxford; legal member of the Viceregal council.
          3. Audrey Richards, anthropologist and director of Makerere College, Uganda.
          3. Enid *m.* Geoffrey Faber, Fellow of All Souls, publisher and author.
               4. Tom Faber, Fellow of Trinity and then of Corpus Christi, Cambridge.
          3. Katherine *m.* Eric Beckett, Fellow of All Souls, legal adviser to the Foreign Office.
               4. Philip Beckett, lecturer in geology, Oxford.
     2. Margaret *m.* Alan Macpherson, solicitor, uncle of R. E. Macpherson, Fellow of King's, whose aunt was a Fellow of Girton, and whose second cousin, Mr. George Rylands, is a Fellow of King's.
          Mr. Alan Macpherson's great-grandfather was Principal of Aberdeen University, his grandfather sub-Principal

and professor of oriental languages and his cousin, H. M.
Innes, Fellow of Trinity. One of his aunts married the
13th Sir John Peter Grant and hence became a niece of
Lady Strachey, the wife of General Sir Richard Strachey,
F.R.S.; another aunt married a brother of Maria Edgeworth.

1. Arthur Gray Butler, Fellow of Oriel, first headmaster of
Haileybury, *m.* Harriet, niece of Maria Edgeworth.
>   2. Harold Edgeworth Butler, professor of Latin, London,
>   *m.* Margaret, daughter of A. F. Pollard, Fellow of All
>   Souls, professor of history, London.
>>   3. David Butler, Fellow of Nuffield.
>>   3. Christina *m.* Howard Colvin, Fellow of St. John's,
>>   Oxford.
>>   3. Honora *m.* Norman Addison, master at Eton.

1. Louisa *m.* Sir Francis Galton, cousin of Charles Darwin by
Erasmus Darwin's second wife.
1. Henry Montagu Butler, Senior Classic, headmaster of Harrow,
Master of Trinity, *m.*
(i) Georgina Elliot.
>   2. Agnes *m.* E. W. Howson, Fellow of King's, master at
>   Harrow.
>   2. Edward Butler, master at Harrow.
>   2. Arthur Hugh Butler, Librarian of the House of Lords.
>   2. Maud *m.* Bernard Morley Fletcher.

(ii) Agnata Frances Ramsay, daughter of Sir J. H. Ramsay,
F.B.A., whose brother was Professor of humanity, Glasgow.
She was placed alone in the first division of the first-class,
Classical Tripos, 1887.
>   2. James Ramsay Montagu Butler, Fellow of Trinity,
>   Regius Professor of modern history.
>   2. Gordon Butler, obtained a first-class in classics and history;
>   died in the first World War.
>   2. Sir Nevile Montagu Butler, ambassador to the Nether-
>   lands.

Three connexions in this list of achievement are of particular
interest. The first is the link through Mr. Geoffrey Faber to his
great-uncle F. W. Faber of the Oxford Movement, which,
unlike the Clapham Sect, has produced few notable descendants. The second is the relationship of the Master of Pembroke
to the present Master of Corpus. Lady Butler was an Adam
Smith and sister of Janetta, wife of the philosopher Professor

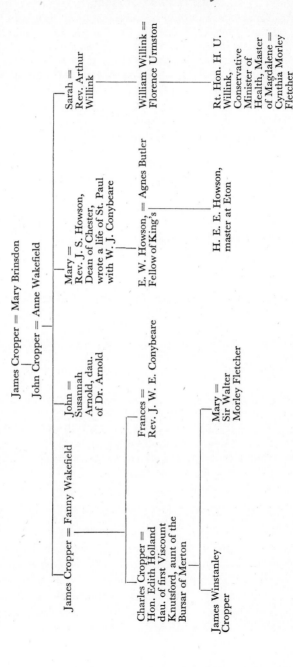

James Cropper = Mary Brinsdon
John Cropper = Anne Wakefield

James Cropper = Fanny Wakefield

John =
Susannah
Arnold, dau.
of Dr. Arnold

Mary =
Rev. J. S. Howson,
Dean of Chester,
wrote a life of St. Paul
with W. J. Conybeare

Sarah =
Rev. Arthur
Willink

Charles Cropper =
Hon. Edith Holland
dau. of first Viscount
Knutsford, aunt of the
Bursar of Merton

Frances =
Rev. J. W. E. Conybeare

E. W. Howson, = Agnes Butler
Fellow of King's

William Willink =
Florence Urmston

Mary =
Sir Walter
Morley Fletcher

H. E. E. Howson,
master at Eton

Rt. Hon. H. U.
Willink,
Conservative
Minister of
Health, Master
of Magdalene =
Cynthia Morley
Fletcher

James Winstanley
Cropper

W. R. Sorley, Fellow of Trinity and then of King's, and mother of Charles Sorley the poet. She was also the sister of the Very Rev. Sir George Adam Smith, the Old Testament scholar, who married a daughter of Sir George Buchanan, F.R.S. One of Lady Adam Smith's sisters was the first woman to be elected a Fellow of University College, London, another the first woman to be elected a member of the British Physiological Society. One of Sir George Adam Smith's daughters married Ian Clarke, a master at Stowe who was related to the Geddes connexion and to Lord Bryce; another is Miss Janet Adam Smith, literary editor of the *New Statesman*, otherwise Mrs. Michael Roberts, widow of the poet and critic; and another married Sir George Thomson, F.R.S., and Master of Corpus whose son-in-law was a Fellow of St John's. The Master of Corpus is the son of the great physicist, J. J. Thomson, O.M., Master of Trinity; and Lady Butler was his wife's aunt.

The third connexion also relates the heads of Cambridge colleges. Bernard Morley Fletcher, the husband of Maud Butler, was the brother of Sir Walter Morley Fletcher, F.R.S., and Fellow of Trinity, and their niece is married to the Right Hon. H. U. Willink, Master of Magdalene. And this brings in another family, the Croppers, in that Sir Walter married Mary Cropper. The Master of Magdalene's grandmother was a Cropper, and the mother of E. W. Howson who married Agnes Butler was also a Cropper. One of the Croppers married a daughter of Zachary Macaulay and on her death the widow of her brother, H. M. Macaulay; another married a son of Lord Brougham, a third a daughter of Dr. Arnold, and a fourth J. W. E. Conybeare, so that Lady Morley Fletcher and Miss Rose Macaulay both share an uncle. Nor are these links with Clapham surprising because the family descends from James Cropper, a quaker who was prominent in the anti-slavery movement; and through the Croppers and Butlers the ties between Trinity, Corpus and Pembroke are certainly strong.

Though this fox would run much further we had better hack back to the Babingtons where there is a gap in the hedge for us to jump into the Stephen country. One of Thomas Babington's sons, Matthew, had a daughter Rose Mary who married the

Rev. Charles John Elliott. His mother was a great-great-granddaughter of Isaac Newton's mother and his father was the son of an adherent of the Clapham Sect who married the Rector of Clapham's sister. The two tables below show the connexions between the Elliotts and Venns and hence between them and the Stephens.

Thus the present President of Queens' and Provost of Eton are cousins, and Dr. Venn represents the ninth generation of this notable clerical and academic family to graduate from Oxford or Cambridge.[16]

James Stephen, Master in Chancery and member of the Clapham Sect, bred a generation of academic lawyers and writers.[17] His second son was 'Stephen on Pleading', whose son and grandson edited successive editions of his *New Commentaries*. The Master in Chancery's fourth son was the author, Sir George Stephen, and his second daughter the mother of Edward Dicey, editor of the *Observer*, and of A. V. Dicey, professor of law at Oxford and author of *Law and Public Opinion in England*. His third son, Sir James Stephen, was the *Edinburgh* reviewer and colonial under-secretary who drafted the bill to free the slaves in the British Colonies. From his union with Jane Venn came two distinguished sons. The elder was Sir J. Fitzjames Stephen, High Court judge, *Saturday* reviewer and author of a powerful attack on Mill's liberalism entitled *Liberty, Equality, Fraternity*. He had the following children:

Katharine Stephen, principal of Newnham.
Sir Herbert Stephen, clerk of assizes and legal author.
J. K. Stephen, Fellow of King's, parodist and author of *Lapsus Calami*.
Sir Harry Lushington Stephen, Indian judge, *m.* Barbara Nightingale.

Barbara Nightingale was a great-granddaughter of William Smith, M.P.; her great-aunt was Florence Nightingale's mother; her aunt married the poet A. H. Clough; Clough's sister was the first principal of Newnham; and his daughter was also head of that college.

The second of Sir James Stephen's sons who won distinction was Sir Leslie Stephen, Fellow of Trinity Hall, critic, historian,

Rev. Henry Venn, Rector of Yelling

Sarah Ann Sherman (i) = Charles Elliott = (ii) Eling

J. S. Elliott = Harriet Warner

Rev. Edward Elliott, author of works on prophesy

Edward Elliott, author

Rev. H. Elliott, Fellow of Trinity

Sir Charles Elliott, Chairman of Toynbee Hall Lt.-Gov. of Bengal

Rose Mary Babington = Rev. C. J. Elliott, grand-dau. of Thomas | Canon of Christ Church B. and great-niece of | and member of O.T. Henry Thornton's wife | Revision Committee

C. H. B. Elliott, school inspector

Ernest Elliott, schoolmaster

Evelyn Elliott, schoolmaster

Mary = Rev. B. Popham = (i) Louisa

Margaret Popham, HM. of Cheltenham Ladies' College

Rev. H. V. Elliott

= (ii) Alice Gaussen

Claude Elliott, Fellow of Jesus, HM. and later Provost of Eton

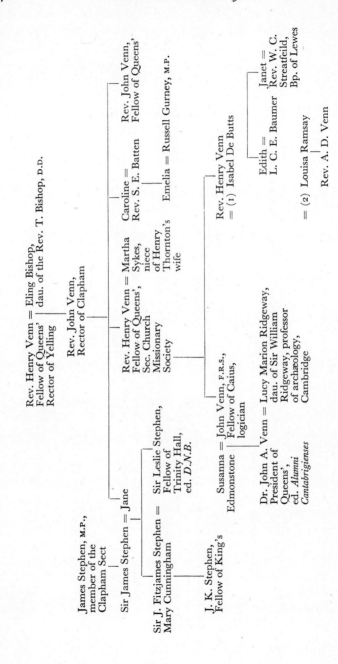

editor of the *D.N.B.* and as much a touchstone to this academic class as Sidgwick. He married first a daughter of Thackeray and, second, Julia, the widow of the publisher Herbert Duckworth. Julia was a daughter of one of the beautiful Pattle sisters. She was thus a niece of Mrs. Cameron, the photographer, and of Mrs. Fisher, wife of the Prince of Wales's tutor and mother of H. A. L. Fisher, Warden of New College and president of the Board of Education under Lloyd George. One of Fisher's nephews is Professor Adam Curle of Exeter University. Fisher's sister married first, F. W. Maitland, the constitutional historian, and, second, Sir Francis Darwin; her daughter by her first marriage married Gerald Shove, Fellow of King's and economist. Nor does this exhaust Mrs. Leslie Stephen's relations. Her sister married Henry Halford Vaughan, professor of history at Oxford, who retired to write a *magnum opus* which he was believed to have destroyed in scholarly despair. But the Vaughans must wait and we must pursue the children of Sir Leslie.

Mrs. Vanessa Bell, wife of Mr. Clive Bell, and Virginia Woolf, wife of Mr. Leonard Woolf, require no introduction. Adrian Stephen as a young man took part in the *Dreadnought* hoax in which he and a party of his friends *en travestie* were welcomed with royal honours on board a battleship. He and his wife were both psycho-analysts. She was Karin Costelloe, stepdaughter of Mr. Bernard Berenson, niece of Logan Pearsall Smith and of his sister Alys, the first wife of Bertrand Russell. She was also a sister of Mrs. Ray Strachey. Adrian Stephen's elder daughter married the chemist, Dr. Richard Millington Synge, Nobel Prizeman and kinsman of the Irish playwright. Mrs. Bell's son, Mr. Quentin Bell, lectures in the fine arts at Newcastle and is the son-in-law of Mr. A. H. Popham, Keeper of prints and drawings in the British Museum, who married a daughter of the Fabian Lord Olivier. Mrs. Bell's daughter is the second wife of Mr. David Garnett. Mr. Garnett's grandfather was Keeper of the printed books in the British Museum, his father an editor and tireless counsellor of young authors, and his mother, Constance Garnett, by her translations virtually introduced Russian literature to England. His eldest son married the offspring of the union between Professsor Bruce Dickins and the daughter of Professor Sir Herbert Grierson, F.B.A.

We can still move dry-shod through Mrs. Ray Strachey, the chronicler of women's emancipation, to another family, famous for their brains since the days of the friendship of a Strachey with John Locke. The history of the Stracheys has recently been traced by Mr. C. R. Sanders and is so well known that a list of the notable members of the family would be superfluous. Apart from Lord Strachie who was a student of Christ Church and Miss Pernel Strachey, principal of Newnham, they have made their reputations as orientalists, or administrators and scientists in India, or in the London literary world. The wife of the editor of the *Spectator*, Mrs. St. Loe Strachey, wrote: 'The Stracheys are most strongly the children of their fathers, not of their mothers. "It does not matter whom they marry", said one of St. Loe's aunts to me when I was quite young, "the type continues and has been much the same for three hundred years." '[18] Still, they had mothers: and some of their marriages are interesting. St. Loe Strachey's mother was a daughter of John Addington Symonds, and he himself married the granddaughter of the economist Nassau Senior. His own daughter married the architect Mr. Clough Williams Ellis. Miss Julia Strachey is the wife of Mr. Lawrence Gowing, the painter and professor of fine art at Newcastle, and her aunt married the son of Sir Alexander Rendel, whose sister, as we have seen, married into the Wedgwood family; and Wilson Harris, last university burgess for Cambridge and editor of the *Spectator*, was also connected to the Rendels. Sir Charles Strachey married a sister of the literary critic, Sir Walter Raleigh, and his sister Winifred married an Indian administrator, Sir Hugh Barnes. The daughter of this marriage, Mrs. St. John Hutchinson, had two children. The elder married Lord Rothschild and, on the dissolution of that marriage, became the wife of the novelist, Mr. Rex Warner; the younger married the actress, Miss Peggy Ashcroft.

Sir Hugh Barnes married again and by his second marriage produced a pro-consul of a new cultural medium. Sir George Barnes was the first director of the B.B.C.'s Third Programme and is now director of television. His wife comes of impeccable academic stock.

Thus if we recollect that Mr. E. M. Forster is a great-grandson of Henry Thornton and that Mr. Duncan Grant is a first